Video Techniques

Video
Techniques

Gordon White

CGIA, CEng, MIERE

Newnes Technical Books

Newnes Technical Books

is an imprint of the Butterworth Group
which has principal offices in
London, Sydney, Toronto, Wellington, Durban and Boston

First published 1982

©Butterworth & Co. (Publishers) Ltd, 1982

British Library Cataloguing in Publication Data

White, Gordon
    Video techniques
    1. Videotape recorders and recording
    621.388   TK6655.V5

    ISBN 0-408-00506-8

Typeset by Butterworths Litho Preparation Department
Printed and bound in England by The Camelot Press Ltd., Southampton

Preface

The nineteenth century heralded a transformation to the world as the Industrial Revolution, commencing in Britain, rapidly changed the character of towns, the environment of the countryside and the social life of the people in an irreversible manner. While the nineteenth century will be remembered for the 'Industrial Revolution', the twentieth century must, surely, be remembered for the 'Communications Revolution'.

Whether it is air travel, radio and television, telephony, telex, computers, satellites or intercontinental rockets, the ability to communicate rapidly, either locally or in any part of the world, has transformed our lives to a greater extent than most of the events in the previous two million years man has spent evolving his way of life.

We have seen only the start in the twentieth century and if the world survives the next 200 years the possible advances in all forms of communication may well make the artificial boundaries of countries, established solely for contemporary political reasons, obsolete.

Once technology has started it is impossible to stop as long as there is competition in the world. While vast amounts of money are being spent on defence and education and the desire of all the nations is to progress technically such a halt is improbable.

Video Techniques aims at describing only one aspect of this communication revolution although possibly it is the most familiar, useful and influential in everyday life to the majority of people.

Until a short time ago television was used only as a form of entertainment and although this is still the primary function the use now made of it in industry, education, medicine, security, satellites, surveying and other new uses constantly being found, make it an indispensable tool to many professions.

Equipment in the last ten years has improved in all fields to give a performance and reliability which at one time could only have been optimistically hoped for. Considerable praise should be given to the designers, development engineers and the component manufacturers in many countries who have achieved the present situation.

Video Techniques does not describe circuitry or individual pieces of equipment, unless it is to illustrate a principle, as these rapidly change. The book describes the principles of television and shows how the equipment is designed and functions in the complete system and, with present day technology, its capability and limitations. These principles generally remain the same irrespective of the model, which usually involves only modifications to the performance or operation.

G.W.

Acknowledgement

The author wishes to thank the following companies for their assistance in the preparation of this book by their provision of information and illustrations.

Ampex
Amperex
ATV
Barco
F. W. O. Bauch
BBC
Bell and Howell
Bosch
British Aerospace
British Telecom
C. W. Cameron
Decca
Dolby Laboratories
Eidophor
Electrocraft
Electrohome
EMI
Gallenkamp
Grundig
Hitachi
IBA
IVC
Jerrold International
JVC
Link Electronics
Link House Magazines

Marconi
Memorex
Michael Cox Electronics
Micro Consultants
Mitsubishi Electric UK
Mullard
3M
NEC
Paltex
Philips
Photoscan
Quantel
Rainbow Video
Rank Cintel
Rank Video
RCA
Rediffusion
Sony Broadcast
Sony UK
Telecine
Teleng
Telespec
Thomson CSF
VEL
Walmore Electronics

and the many engineers who have given their time to lecture at the Royal Television Society and IERE/IEE conferences and provide information on the latest developments.

The cover photograph shows a CCTV studio (courtesy Howden Management Services).

Contents

Broadcasting
Video disc for the home
Digital recording
Advantages of video tape
Magnetic process
Modulation systems
F.M. signal
Design of a practical VTR
Helical scan recording formats
Layout of a video recorder
Dolby noise reduction system
Profesional helical scan recorders
Video cassette recorders
Video tape manufacture

Broadcast video disc
Domestic video disc systems

Video tape editing
Duplication of pre-recorded tapes
Anti-copying systems

Designing a closed circuit television studio
Telecine: Multiplexer; Flying spot; Digital telecine
Control room equipment: Sync pulse generators;
    Genlock; Assignment systems; Distribution
    amplifiers; Synchronisers; Time base correctors;
    Vision mixing and effects; Captioning; Chroma
    key; Digital effects
Outside broadcast vehicles

British Telecom TV distribution network
Satellites for broadcasting
Master antenna television and community antenna
    television
Fibre optics
Outside broadcast microwave links

Chapter 1

The Television Waveform

The television signal

A television system must provide the means to translate an optical image of any scene into an electrical signal and from the electrical signal to reconstitute a visible image. The method of transmitting the electrical signals from the generator to the receiver depends upon the nature of the electrical signal to be transmitted. Early

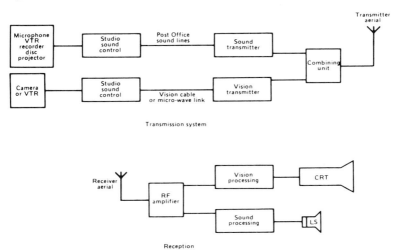

Figure 1.1. In the transmission and reception of television the audio and video are separate signals and only combine to form a single signal in the combining unit of the transmitter. At the receiver the signals are again separated after amplification

inventors concentrated on the generation and reception of the signals but an intermediate signal distribution network is essential for any system to be a success. Improvements in transmission lines and transmitters, no less than improvements in generation and

1

reception equipment, have made present day high definition television possible.

Fortunately for the early experimenters, the bandwidths required for their early 30-line systems was only about 13 kHz which the medium-wave transmitters and specially treated telephone lines, then existing for sound transmission, could handle. Today, bandwidths exceeding 5 MHz are required.

Any practical broadcast system must include an audio signal. Two separate channels, which usually only combine in a television aerial, and are again separated in the television receiver, are required (Figure 1.1).

Details in a picture

If a photograph is examined under a microscope it will be seen that the picture is made up of fine grains of silver distributed in various densities to represent the light and shade in the original picture. The silver grains are the picture elements and constitute the basic structure of the image. The finer the grain, the smaller the detail that can be observed at a normal viewing distance. Ideally it should be possible to examine the picture closely without the individual grains becoming visible.

Moving pictures

A 'moving picture' is produced in the camera by creating a series of stationary pictures each differing very slightly from the preceding and following pictures. In the cinema, the illusion of movement is obtained by displaying a series of stationary pictures and cutting off the light while the film is moved to the next picture. If this is done at a sufficiently fast speed, the eye does not notice the dark periods but sees only a continuous succession of stationary pictures, creating the impression of motion. Because the eye does not respond as quickly to the intervals of darkness as to the high illumination of the pictures, the scenes are 'seen' as smooth continuous motion.

The still pictures (frames) must be presented at a sufficiently high rate to avoid flicker on the screen, requiring a speed of not less than 15 to 20 frames per second. The picture rate in the cinema is 24 frames per second, but due to the high illumination levels used, flicker would still be apparent, so each frame is projected twice for equal lengths of time, which has the apparent effect of doubling the projection rate to 48.

The same problem relating to the flicker and picture elements must be taken into consideration when designing a television system.

Picture transmission in an electrical system

A transmitter and receiver system is a single communication channel which can handle only one piece of information at any time. Where a signal is progressive, as in sound, this is not a disadvantage as each electrical signal representing the sound is handled sequentially. However, a picture is not a sequential signal as all elements in the scene are presented simultaneously to the camera. Simultaneous transmission of all the elements is obviously impractical and a means had to be provided to make the video

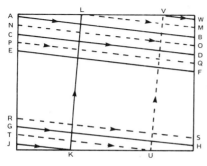

Figure 1.2. The picture is scanned a line at a time and at the end of each line a new line is started at the left-hand side until the bottom of the picture is reached. In the first downward movement the odd lines are scanned after which the beam returns to scan the even lines

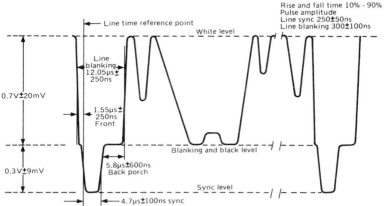

Figure 1.3. A typical line waveform of a TV signal. At the end of each line is a synchronising pulse. The amplitude of the analogue video waveform corresponds to the picture brightness at any particular moment. All levels and waveform timings must be precise in a modern TV system. Timings shown are for UK 625-line system

signal into a sequential signal, so that the information relating to each individual element should not be lost.

A system of scanning was devised whereby the picture is scanned in a similar manner to the way in which one reads a book. The picture is scanned one line at a time and at the end of each line a new line is started at the left hand side until the bottom of the picture is reached, when a new picture is started (Figure 1.2).

The electrical signal produced is an analogue signal (Figure 1.3) whose amplitude at any moment is proportional to the brightness of the picture falling on the particular picture element being scanned. The picture element is produced by a number of materials which vary their electrical properties depending upon the light falling upon them.

It is obviously essential however, that the signal generating equipment and the reception equipment remain synchronised, otherwise the displayed signal would be meaningless. Therefore, the television waveform is provided with both line and field synchronisation signals so the the scanning of the receiver screen is exactly synchronised with the scanning of the camera tube.

The early inventors of television

In 1884 Nipkow described his scanning method in a German patent. His system consisted of a large disc with a series of small holes arranged to form a spiral near the edge. The first hole scanned one line of the picture formed by a lens and the holes were so arranged that, as the first hole left the picture, the second hole began scanning the second line (Figure 1.4). This procedure

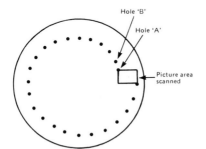

Figure 1.4. Nipkow disc for early TV scanning systems. As hole 'A' leaves the scanned area, hole 'B' begins to scan the next line. The series of holes form a spiral

continued until the disc had turned one revolution when the first hole began to scan the first line again. Behind the disc, a lens focused the light passing through the holes on to a selenium photocell which converted the light into an electrical signal.

At the receiver a similar disc was held in synchronism with the transmitter by synchronous motors powered from the same electricity supply. At the receiver light passed through a polarising Nicol prism, a block of flint glass and then an analysing Nicol prism, and was viewed through the receiver disc. The flint glass was held in a magnetic field to which was fed the transmitter signal causing rotation of the glass and therefore a variation in the intensity of the light to the viewer due to the varying plane of polarisation.

Between 1929 and 1935 the Baird company and the BBC operated a 30-line television system based on this principle. The light source at the receiver was a neon lamp whose brightness could be directly modulated by the transmitter signal current. The system was further modified by illuminating the scene with light passed through the Nipkow disc, the signal being picked up on large potassium photocells. These were later replaced with caesium photocells.

Initially, the performers had to keep still to ensure that they fitted into the patch of illumination cast by the spot light scanner. Mirror drums soon replaced the discs and more sensitive photoelectric cells allowed larger scenes to be covered. Baird continued with a 60, 90, 120 and eventually 180-line system in the form of film scanners. However, the television system we know today was being invented by others.

Vladimir K. Zworykin, who like Nipkow, was a Russian, went to America in 1919 and at Westinghouse worked on the production of camera tubes first suggested by Campbell-Swinton in 1908.

In 1931 EMI were working on mechanical television systems but under Isaac Shoenberg they were by 1934 making pictures produced by the Emitron tube. From then on, EMI abandoned mechanical scanning in favour of electronic scanning.

In November, 1936 the BBC operated both the EMI and the Baird systems simultaneously, allowing both companies the chance to prove which system should be adopted. Due to the inflexibility and limited potential of the Baird system the EMI system was adopted (in January 1937). From February 8, 1937, the BBC transmitted only the EMI 405-line system which forms the scanning basis for current television systems, although the number of lines and frames rate are different in different parts of the world.

Interlacing

The picture rate in television, as in the cinema, must be sufficiently high to avoid flicker. Choice of picture repetition rate is invariably controlled by the mains frequency of the electricity supply, since the timebases of both the picture generating equipment and the receiver use the mains frequency for synchronisation. 50 Hz or 100 Hz interference causes objectionable brightness modulation. By synchronising with the mains frequency, any residual hum will be stationary and this is accepted more readily by the eye.

However, in colour transmission the field scanning frequency is related to subcarrier and line frequency and is crystal locked. Once the picture rate has been determined, the number of lines governs the number of picture elements and therefore the definition obtainable from the system.

Since the whole picture is not generated simultaneously in television as it is in the cinema, the technique of double projection to reduce the actual picture frequency rate and still avoid flicker is not possible.

Instead, a reduction in picture repetition rate, and hence system bandwidth requirements, is made by scanning a complete picture at half the mains frequency but using two vertical traverses for each completed picture. In the first traverse (scan), the odd numbered lines are scanned after which the beam returns to scan the even numbered lines. Each traverse is known as a field and it requires two fields to produce a complete picture (a frame) (Figure 1.2). This procedure produces the effect of scanning the picture at a 50 Hz rate as the discrepancy between two lines is too small for the eye to distinguish at normal viewing distances.

In all modern TV systems, an odd number of scanning lines is used instead of an even number to simplify interlacing. Using an even number of lines, a different blanking would be required for the two fields as the last line of one field (end of frame) would have to return to line 1 of the next frame while the last line of this field would have to return to line 2 of the next.

Similarly each field consists of an odd half line so that each field is exactly the same and line and field scans are regular. The line systems for colour today are 525 lines at a picture repetition rate of 30 per second and 625 lines with a picture repetition of 25 per second. Additional monochrome systems operate with 405 and 819 lines at a picture repetition rate of 25 per second. (Both will become obsolete standards.)

Bandwidth requirements

It is essential in video engineering to know the bandwidth requirements of any particular signal in order to assess the performance of modulating systems, transmission lines and amplifiers. However, bandwidth on its own is only part of the requirements of a good system. Phase distortion and group delay distortions are of equal importance. 'K' rating testing has been in use for many years and this allows simple practical tests by semi-technical staff to be carried out and the measurements of pulses obtained can be directly related to imperfections in the observed pictures (see Chapter 8). The general requirements, however, of any video amplifier or transmission system are that adequate bandwidth be available for satisfactory definition to be transmitted and the amplitude and phase of each of the component frequencies must remain the same from the input to the output of the system. When a large bandwidth signal is passed through a system of restricted bandwidth, the transitions in the picture will tend to show edge ringing at a frequency corresponding to the cut-off frequency of the system. The severity with which this occurs depends on the energy in the signal at the frequencies being cut off and the electrical characteristics of the system. This is why distortion is experienced when transferring a broadcast signal to a restricted bandwidth recorder. Everything, of course, depends upon picture content.

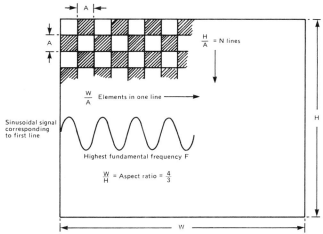

Figure 1.5. Diagram showing a signal of maximum rate of variation. Each black and white square corresponds to one cycle

Let us assume, for approximate calculations of the bandwidth required, that a signal with a maximum rate of variation is used, that is, a variation from black to white of each successive element in the picture where an element is considered to be a square with the thickness of a scanning line.

Looking at Figure 1.5.

The number of elements = $\dfrac{W}{A}$
in one line

The number of lines   = $\dfrac{H}{A}$

Therefore the number of elements in the picture equals

$$\frac{W}{A} \times \frac{H}{A}$$

If P is the picture frequency, the number of elements transmitted per second is

$$\frac{W}{A} \times \frac{H}{A} \times P$$

If each transition from white to black is one cycle, then the frequency is equal to half the number of elements

$$F \;=\; \frac{1}{2} \times \frac{W}{A} \times \frac{H}{A} \times P$$

but as $\dfrac{H}{A}$ is the number of lines (L)

and $\dfrac{W}{H}$ is the aspect ratio (R)

where $R \;=\; \dfrac{\text{Width of picture } (W)}{\text{Height of picture } (H)} \;=\; \dfrac{4}{3}$

then the frequency required

$$F = \frac{1}{2} \times \frac{W}{A} \times \frac{H}{A} \times P = \frac{1}{2} \times \frac{W}{A} \times \frac{A}{H} \times \left(\frac{H}{A}\right)^2 \times P =$$

$$= \frac{1}{2} \times \frac{W}{H} \times \left(\frac{H}{A}\right)^2 \times P = \frac{1}{2} \; L^2 \, RP \text{ Hertz.}$$

This formula indicates how the bandwidth requirements increase considerably with the number of lines. In practice the formula is modified due to line and frame blanking times and spot (scanning aperture) size and shape. From experiments it has been found that the resolution averages 70% of the theoretically calculated results.
    A modified formula would be $F_{max} = 0.35 L^2 \, RP$.

Characteristics of television waveforms

For transmission purposes the composite video signal (Figure 1.3) is restricted to 1 V of which 0.3 V is synchronising signals and 0.7 V is the actual analogue video waveform. At the end of each line a blanking period is provided known as the front porch. As an electrical signal in a restricted bandwidth system is unable to fall instantaneously to zero, this period allows lines which end in peak white sufficient time for the voltage to fall to zero before the sync pulse starts. If this were not provided, the leading edge of the sync pulse would be disturbed and cause instability in the picture. A further period of black is provided after the sync period (back

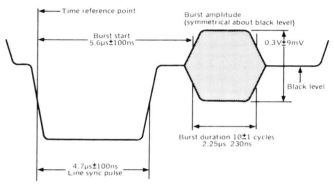

Figure 1.6. In the PAL colour system the colour burst signal is placed on the back porch of the line waveform

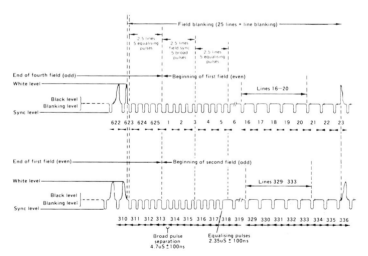

Figure 1.7. At the end of each field, field pulses are provided for field synchronisation. In the 625-line PAL system, equalising pulses are placed before and after the field pulses. Note: Lines 16–20 may contain identification or test signals. Initially lines 17 (330) and 18 (331) are being used for teletext

porch). This is the only time in a television waveform when the video level is known and consequently it is often used in equipment as the period for black level clamping circuits to operate. In colour television, the colour burst is also placed in this part of the waveform for synchronisation of the colour circuits (Figure 1.6). At the end of each field, a series of frame pulses lasting longer than line pulses is inserted to give frame flyback (Figure 1.7). In most systems (405 lines and 819 lines are exceptions), equalising pulses are provided before and after the frame pulses to ensure the frame circuits are stabilised before the commencement of the frame pulses.

As television sets have improved over the years, the need for long periods of frame blanking has been reduced and advantage has been taken of this by using the frame blanking period for other uses such as test signals and teletext services (Chapters 8 and 9).

Colour engineering – variations on a theme

The outstanding achievement of the National Television Systems Committee (NTSC) when establishing the parameters for the original broadcast colour system was to evolve a system which modified the already standard monochrome signal to allow colour to be transmitted but still retain a monochrome transmission. If the engineers had been free to develop a system to transmit only colour television then broadcast engineering may have evolved entirely differently. Not only did the engineers have outstanding success in developing a compatible monochrome and colour television system but the basic system of transmitting the luminance signal (monochrome picture) separately from the chrominance signal (colour) allowed a variety of coding systems to be developed and allow the signals to be modified for the purpose of recording on low-cost video tape recorders. Perhaps the original restrictions placed on the development engineers allowed a basic system to be developed which could not have been bettered even with the hindsight of a further 25 years of operational engineering.

The basic system

The original television system (Figure 1.8) came into service in the United States in December, 1953 after many years of experiments. Considerable credit should be given to RCA for the original pioneering work.

The principle adopted was to obtain three colour signals (red, green, blue) from the scene and from combining portions of these

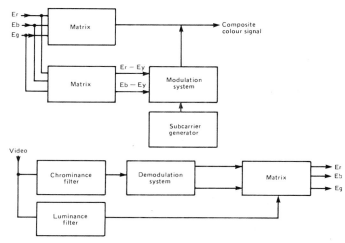

Figure 1.8. Modern colour system

signals to obtain the luminance signal (E_y). The red, green and blue colours are the primary colours for television which is an additive colour system. Various combinations of ratios of the primary colours will produce the remaining colours. Simultaneous transmission of the three primary colours in the ratios of 0.3 R + 0.59 G + 0.11 B will produce white (see Chapter 3). The luminance signal corresponds to the brightness of the picture and is, therefore, the monochrome signal. Two colour difference signals are also obtained, but they contain no brightness informaton as they are obtained by elecronically subtracting the luminance signal from the output of the red and blue amplifiers ($E_r - E_y$ and $E_b - E_y$). Using colour difference signals has advantages over transmitting the colour signals directly:

(1) If the original scene is monochrome the colour signals are zero.
(2) They are true colour signals and contain no luminance or monochrome information.

Obviously, knowing two of the colour difference signals and having the luminance signal available allows the third signal to be obtained electronically. This system is the basis of all colour television irrespective of the final coding method used for transmission.

The colour difference signals have a relatively narrow band and therefore can be used to modulate a subcarrier which is added to

Figure 1.9. Video bandwidth

the luminance signal in the upper part of the video passband (Figure 1.9).

The problem arises, of course, that two separate signals must be modulated onto the subcarrier to carry the colour information. It is the method of modulating the subcarrier which differs in colour systems used today.

NTSC system

The problem of simultaneously carrying two signals on the same carrier (Figure 1.10) was overcome by using the concept of quadrature amplitude modulation. This system uses two carriers of the same frequency separated by a 90° phase relationship (Figure 1.11) each independently modulated with one of the colour

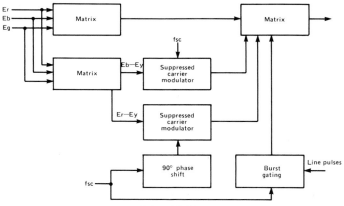

Figure 1.10. Basic coding NTSC and PAL system

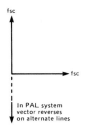

Figure 1.11. Quadrature modulation. The subcarrier is split to form two carriers of the same frequency but spaced by 90°. Each carrier is modulated with a signal derived from a colour difference signal. The two signals can then be separately carried without interference with each other

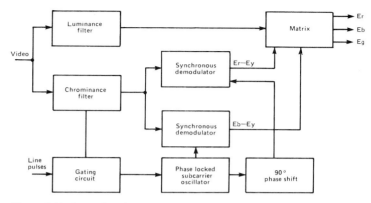

Figure 1.12. Basic decoding NTSC and PAL system (no delay line)

difference signals. The signals can be recovered in the receiver by synchronous demodulators driven from a local reference generator locked to the colour reference burst transmitted with the television signal (Figure 1.12).

Although successful, problems arose in transmission links as any phase distortions encountered caused changes in colours and subcarrier amplitude errors caused the intensity of the colours (saturation errors) to alter. This led to NTSC being known within the industry as 'Never Twice the Same Colour'. However, some of the criticism of the system was caused by the electronics not being to the standard which exists today. Equipment used valves and was consequently subject to drift, while video tape recording was technically inadequate to produce good quality NTSC recordings.

However, when Europe was in a position to contemplate a colour television system the search began for an improved system.

SECAM system (Séquence à Mémoire)

In 1959 Henri de France proposed the basis of the present SECAM system (Figure 1.13) where each colour difference signal is transmitted in turn on alternate lines using frequency modulation of the subcarrier.

In the receiver a one-line delay alternately stores the transmitted colour difference signal so that two colour difference signals are always available even though they are from different scan lines.

This obviously reduces the vertical colour definition but the main object is to prevent crosstalk between the two colour signals when transmitted simultaneously. Crosstalk is due mainly to non-linearities in the system causing differential phase, differential gain and vestigial sideband distortions.

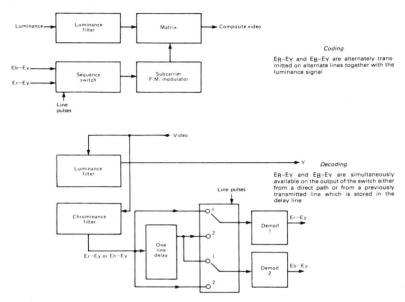

Figure 1.13. SECAM coding and decoding system

However, SECAM coding produced new problems. As the carrier is always present the signal-to-noise ratio of SECAM is worse than either NTSC or PAL. To improve this the subcarrier is increased with deviation and pre-emphasis is used on the chrominance signals as in all FM systems. This allows the undeviated subcarrier to be reduced.

When the luminance signal contains frequencies near the carrier frequency the amplitude of the subcarrier is increased to minimise the interference the frequencies will cause to the chrominance signals.

Even though new difficulties were evident, Europe nearly adopted SECAM due to its better transmission and recording capabilities.

Choosing the colour system for Europe

In 1962 the EBU Ad Hoc Group was formed to choose the European colour television system and by 1963 Walter Bruch of

Telefunken had complicated the choice by proposing the PAL system. Several other systems were also proposed which are now mainly history. The situation was becoming governed by politics as NTSC, PAL and SECAM could all produce excellent pictures and had advantages and disadvantages. NTSC gradually lost support in Europe except from parts of the Post Office, BBC and Holland and after 1965 was not considered as a potential system. By this time France and her associated countries were determined to have SECAM irrespective of everyone else's decision and, by the 1966 CCIR conference in Oslo, it was obvious that Europe would split and initially France, Russia and the Eastern bloc countries would adopt SECAM, while the UK, West Germany, Scandinavia, Holland and Belgium would use PAL. The remaining countries in Europe would decide at a later date which system to adopt.

The situation today

In addition to France, Russia and her satellites SECAM has been adopted by Saudi Arabia, Iran, Iraq, Lebanon, Zaire, Gabon, Ivory Coast, Senegal, Morocco, Tunisia and Egypt. Cuba, Haiti and French Guiana have also adopted the system with the added disadvantage that they use 525 lines and not 625 lines as do the other countries using the system.

NTSC is not only adopted in North America but also in Japan, Korea, Surinam, Dominican Republic, Philippines, Taiwan, Mexico, Costa Rica, Panama and parts of South America. The marketing problems all manufacturers have when designing television equipment is the realisation that the NTSC countries account for possibly 75% of the world market which has the ability to purchase equipment.

The countries adopting PAL later include Australia, New Zealand, New Guinea, Indonesia, Malaya, Singapore, Thailand, United Arab Emirates, Kuwait, Jordan, Italy, Spain, Jugoslavia, Austria, Switzerland, Algeria, Sierra Leone, Nigeria, Tanzania, Zambia, South Africa and Iceland. Brazil also operate a PAL system but on 525 lines.

PAL system (phase alternation line)

This system continued the earlier work on colour phase alternation by Hazeltine and Henri de France. The principles of NTSC were used with the modification that one of the subcarrier vectors reverses in phase on alternate lines (Figures 1.10 – 1.12).

Any phase distortion caused to the transmitted signal still causes a displacement of the vector representing the colour difference signal and in NTSC this causes a wrong colour to be reproduced. In PAL the same displacement of the vector takes place but because one vector is reversing in phase each line, the reproduced colour on two consecutive lines tends to deviate from the true colour in opposite directions. The eye averages between the two extremes and tends to see the true colour. The averaging can obviously be performed more satisfactorily by electronics using a delay line so that both lines are available simultaneously. Delay lines are used in all modern sets.

Unsuccessful systems

Although PAL, NTSC and SECAM were eventually adopted for broadcasting, these were not the only methods investigated. Some of the systems such as FAM (frequency amplitude modulation) were resurrected and used in the early colour recorders for producing accurate colour on the first helical scan recorders.

Four field repetition sequence

It has been shown that the interlaced monochrome signal repeats itself after two fields. In the description of the PAL system it was shown that the corrected R-Y (V) vector reverses every line. Consequently, due to the odd number of picture lines the 'V' signal differs on line 1 of picture 1 from that of line 1 on picture 2. It is found that it repeats exactly every four fields (two pictures).

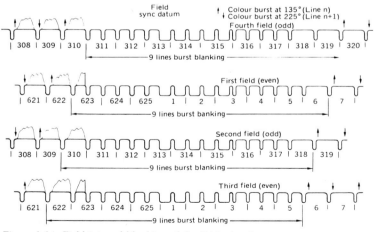

Figure 1.14. Field interval blanking of the PAL signal

As the subcarrier burst is suppressed in PAL during the vertical synchronising pulses and the PAL signal is exhibiting a four field sequence, pairs of fields start and end with the positive or negative phase bursts if a simple field blanking system is used as in NTSC. This can cause difficulty with certain types of reference oscillators and, to avoid this, a modified suppression system known as 'Bruch

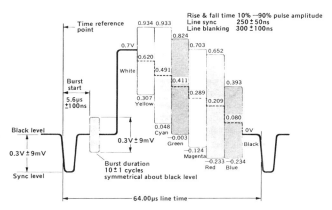

Figure 1.15. The line waveform of a 100% colour bar

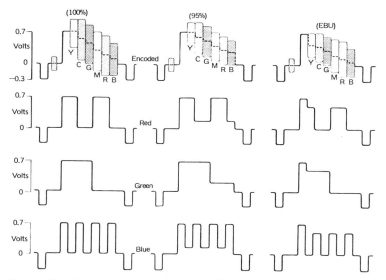

Figure 1.16. The complete line waveforms and luminance contents of three common colour bar waveforms

blanking' has been adopted. Its purpose is to ensure that all fields end and start with the burst in the same phase. To achieve this, a special field blanking sequence is used whereby the blanking is advanced by half a line each field for four fields and then returned to its original starting position (Figure 1.14). Bursts in the wrong phase are suppressed and the new first and last burst in each field are all in the same phase.

Colour bar waveforms

The most common way of testing equipment is by using colour bar waveforms and a 100% colour bar line waveform is shown in detail in Figure 1.15. The common 100%, 95% and EBU colour bar waveforms are shown in comparison in Figure 1.16.

In the 95% and 100% colour bar waveforms the chrominance signal exceeds 1 V and this should be considered when used with a system using a modulator (e.g. video tape recorders and RF distribution systems) as over-deviation of the carrier can easily occur.

Standards conversion

A problem often arises when programmes recorded or transmitted live on one standard are required for transmission in a country using a different standard. This is, of course, the great advantage film still retains, being completely independent of television standards and can be shown using a telecine encoded in any colour system.

However, once a television signal has been generated playing the programme on a different system requires considerable engineering and usually results in degradation.

Conversions are required for two situations:

(1) Where the new system has the same line and field rate but requires coding in a different colour system.
(2) Where the line and field rates are different.

If the programme has been recorded on a video cassette, the solution is simple. Several manufacturers' video cassette recorders can play tapes of different standards but invariably a special monitor has to be used as the replayed signal is non-standard (see Chapter 4).

Transcoding of a colour system to the same line standard (e.g. European PAL to SECAM) requires equipment which initially decodes the original colour signal and remodulates the luminance signal with the chrominance signal encoded in the new system.

Problems arise transcoding SECAM to PAL as the line frequency tolerance of SECAM is excessive and it is impossible to obtain the correctly related PAL subcarrier frequency. On the output, a choice is given of a crystal controlled subcarrier for transmission or an output whose line frequency is locked to the subcarrier for video tape recording purposes.

In order to change the line and frame standards as well as the colour standard, optical and electronic equipment has been developed. In the optical system, the video is separated into its chrominance and luminance parts and displayed on separate cathode ray tubes after the chrominance has been remodulated with the separated colour subcarrier. The CRTs are scanned by cameras (at the new standard rate) and the output is a standard converted signal. SECAM cannot be directly converted in such a manner and must first be transcoded into PAL.

The best standard conversion results have been demonstrated using DICE. Designed by the IBA, this is an entirely electronic system in which all the processing is done digitally. The problems are considerable for the main conversions which must take place are:

	525/60	625/50
Field frequency	60 Hz	50 Hz
Lines	525	625
Field blanking lines	21	25
Line period	63.55	64
Active line period	52.6	52
Colour coding	NTSC	PAL or SECAM

Conclusion

The television waveform and method of generation have decided the design of all television equipment. Its transmission in analogue form without distortion is essential for good pictures in present day systems and will remain so until digital television becomes standard. Only when this occurs will the signals be capable of being regenerated as a new signal at each transmission point and this will obviously start with the next generation of transmission equipment.

For the broadcaster, scientists and development engineers, the introduction of colour television has been an exciting period where politics, far from frustrating the engineers, has created ingenuity which today allows three colour systems with different line and frame standards to be passed around the world, converted and displayed at a higher standard than many monochrome pictures were being transmitted 25 years ago.

Whether it will ever be resolved who has the best system is of little consequence as countries are now committed and the viewers have their sets.

However, whether this situation will affect, in the distant future, possibly the next great engineering step in broadcasting when, if politics ever allow, satellite reception becomes possible and permits the choice of programmes from other countries remains to be seen.

Chapter 2

Television Camera Tubes

History and materials

Camera tubes, together with the picture display tube, control the quality of the television system to a greater extent than any other single part of the system.

The history and technical improvement in television have to a considerable degree been controlled by the progress made in picture generation equipment. In addition to engineering quality, the production methods possible with any particular size and sensitivity of camera tube and its necessary lighting requirements determine the type of programmes which can be produced.

It was Nipkow who first realised that successful transmission of a picture could take place only after the original scene had been dissected into discrete elements and then reassembled after transmission so that the eye saw the complete visual image.

However, it was a suggestion by Campbell Swinton which led to the first practical camera tube, the iconoscope, invented by Zworykin in 1932; the predecessor of the different types of camera tube subsequently invented and which continued to improve the television standard. The iconoscope was followed by the image iconoscope, orthicon, image orthicon, vidicon and the variety of photoconductive targets used today.

The first photoelectric substance to be discovered was selenium (1873) when it was found that its resistance changed in value according to the intensity of light falling upon it. Substances in this group are called 'photoconductive'.

Other substances produce an effect known as 'photovoltaic', since a potential is produced depending on the amount of light falling on it. These substances are not used in television but in such items as exposure meters.

A third effect is 'photoemission' where electrons are emitted by certain substances when subjected to electromagnetic radiation. Light provokes some metals into photoemission while other metals require ultra-violet radiation or x-rays. For a suitable photoemissive substance the atoms in the emissive layer should part easily with electrons. The most suitable substances are the alkali metals with only one electron in their outer shell. Efficiency is increased if an alkali metal is coated with a layer of electropositive material such as antimony-caesium or silver-oxygen-caesium. Antimony-caesium has a spectral response which approaches that of the average human eye and is therefore preferred for television applications.

Silver-oxygen-caesium initially had a response which was low in green and high in infra-red. This created unnatural contrasts and required special make-up, and was later improved.

Until the production of the 'plumbicon' camera tube photoemissive tubes were primarily used in broadcasting while photoconductive tubes were used in industrial television (vidicon).

The improvements in photoconductive tubes and their considerably reduced size compared with photoemissive tubes have ensured universal use in modern colour cameras. Prior to colour television the image orthicon had been the standard for all high quality television broadcasting.

High and low velocity beam tubes

Television tubes can be classified into two groups: 'high velocity beam tubes' and 'low velocity beam tubes'.

The iconoscope was a high velocity tube while the orthicon, invented by Iams and Roase of RCA in 1939, and the vidicon and its derivatives are low velocity tubes.

In any tube a beam of electrons emitted from the gun travels towards the 'target', which, if it is not connected to a constant potential, acquires a potential, the value depending on the initial potential and the gain or loss of electrons from the target surface. Some electrons are emitted by the target (secondary emission) and two potential levels exist at which the secondary emission and received electron ratio is unity. Below the first potential the number of electrons striking the target is greater than the number released and the target potential falls until equilibrium results and the potential is sufficiently low to reduce the velocity of the incident primary electrons to zero. As the target potential is now slightly less than the tube cathode the state is known as 'cathode potential stabilisation' and is used in all low velocity camera tubes. If the initial target potential is above the second potential for unity secondary emission its stabilisation potential depends upon the final anode potential. In high velocity tubes 'anode potential stabilisation' is used and this occurs when equilibrium is reached and the number of secondary electrons reaching the final anode from the target is equal to the number of primary electrons received from the beam by the target. At this point the target potential is slightly higher than the final anode potential.

The iconoscope

The iconoscope developed by RCA was identical except in construction detail to the Emitron independently developed by EMI in Britain. The principle of operation is shown in Figure 2.1.

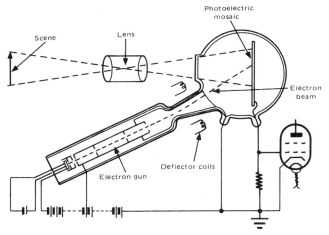

Figure 2.1. The iconoscope, the first practical camera tube used in television

The tube consisted of a spherical bulb with a long neck and a polished flat glass window. The target was a clear sheet of mica, 0.025 mm thick and about 12.5 × 10 cm in area, with a photoelectric mosaic, made from silver oxide or antimony caesium, coated on the front surface; on the reverse was a coating of platinum to which was attached the external connection. The electron gun fired a beam of electrons onto the target. The angle of the beam made considerable geometric (keystone) correction necessary but this was easier to do electrically than to provide mechanical correction to the optical system. The 'keystone' distortion was corrected by amplitude modulating the line waveform with the field frequency so that the angular amplitude of line scan decreased as the beam travelled towards the top of the mosaic, resulting in a rectangular scan. The accelerating gun potential was approximately 1500 volts. The complete tube was mounted in a light-tight housing except for the light entry via the window.

It was found that although the mosaic was scanned every $\frac{1}{25}$ s, moving images were not blurred and gave the appearance of very short time exposures. This is because electrons liberated by secondary emission at the target fall back onto the mosaic and modify the charge pattern.

When the line is scanned the potential of the spot scanned changes quickly by about 4½ V from a negative state to a positive state due to secondary emission electrons leaving the mosaic as it is bombarded by the beam.

The effect of the potential across the scanning area is to pull the photoelectrons from the area to be scanned to the area which has just been scanned, and the effect is appreciable for 10 to 20 lines ahead of the scanning beam. This is the time available to build up the charge pattern and accounts for the apparent short time exposure of the tube.

A white image, however, falling on the mosaic will cause more photoelectrons to be emitted and this area becomes more positive than the dark regions. When scanned, these areas produce a smaller potential excursion than a dark area. The difference in potential between the dark and white areas is about 0.2 V, which is sufficient to produce the required signal. The signal is inverted but this is reversed in later circuitry.

During the line and frame flyback there were no neighbouring areas to absorb the electrons caused by secondary emission so these electrons were spread over a larger area and more than average were lost to the wall. This created a picture which was dark at the top and on the left and light at the bottom and on the right. The shading errors had to be counteracted with 'tilt' and 'bend' waveforms and continuously monitored and adjusted by an engineer.

The iconoscope was followed by the 'Super-Emitron' in Britain, first used by the BBC in 1937, and the 'image-iconoscope' in the USA. These tubes were similar and improved in that the photocathode and the mosaic were separated. The photocathode was a uniform surface so far greater efficiency of conversion of light to signal current could be obtained. As the mosaic was now not photosensitive a variety of surfaces with high secondary emission could be used and a signal improvement of about 20 was obtained over the 'iconoscope'.

Smaller iconoscopes were produced later, less than half the size of the original Super-Emitron. These were 'Midget Super Emitron' and the 'Photicon'.

Low velocity camera tubes

The disadvantages of the high-velocity tubes were:
(1) Spurious shading signals caused by secondary electrons falling back onto the mosaic due to the weak electric field between the target and the final anode.
(2) Limited sensitivity due to the electrons emitted from the mosaic not being collected by the final anode, again caused by the weak electric field.
(3) No definite signal corresponding to black.

These major disadvantages are eliminated by 'cathode potential stabilisation'.

However, problems of focus arise with low velocity beams as small electric fields have greater effect. Beam spreading, due to repulsion between electrons, can also occur at low velocities and so the wall anode is extended to the region of the target to keep the electrons at high velocity until close to the target.

A further problem is caused by the fact that the beam electrons reaching the edges of the picture arrive at a different velocity to those in the centre unless they arrive perpendicularly to the target. Different velocities cause a rise in potential at the edges and stabilisation breaks down.

The solution adopted was to use 'orthogonal scanning'. Under the influence of the long focus coil and the transverse deflection plates the electron beam follows a series of cycloids as shown in Figure 2.2. It must be arranged that the electrons leave the electric field after an integral number of cycloids when the transverse component of velocity is zero.

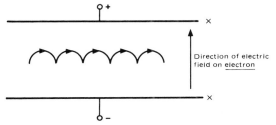

Figure 2.2. Orthogonal scanning. The beam follows a path which is a series of cycloids. (A cycloid is a point on the circumference of a circle rolled along a straight line.) This method is used in 'low velocity' tubes

Orthicon and image orthicon

The 'orthicon' is shown in Figure 2.3. The target is a sheet of transparent dielectric such as mica, and on the scanned side is a transparent photoelectric mosaic through which the scene is transmitted. On the window side is the signal plate which is connected to the amplifier.

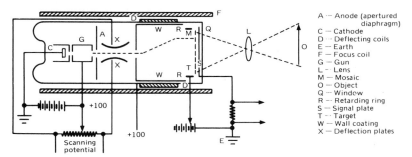

Figure 2.3. *Construction of an orthicon tube*

A — Anode (apertured diaphragm)
C — Cathode
D — Deflecting coils
E — Earth
F — Focus coil
G — Gun
L — Lens
M — Mosaic
O — Object
Q — Window
R — Retarding ring
S — Signal plate
T — Target
W — Wall coating
X — Deflection plates

A retarding ring is placed near the target and adjusted to a potential close to that of the cathode. This decelerates the scanning electrons and ensures the mosaic stabilises at approximately cathode potential. The electrons, after passing through the combined effects of the focus and scanning fields, approach the mosaic at right angles and parallel to their original direction.

The optical scene causes a charge pattern on the mosaic which is slightly positive to the cathode depending upon the light and shade within the scene. All the electrons liberated are drawn away from the mosaic by the same field which decelerates the beam and as the scanning beam passes over each element in the mosaic it is discharged and causes a capacitive current to flow in the signal output. Shading is prevented due to very few secondary electrons being produced by the low velocity of the scanning beam and any which are produced are quickly pulled away from the mosaic surface by the electric field.

A natural black level is established as no photoelectrons are released where there is no light.

The 'image orthicon' is shown in Figure 2.4. The scene is formed on the transparent photocathode by the camera lens. Electrons are released dependent upon the brightness of the different parts of the scene, and accelerated by a difference in potential of about 300–600 V between the target mesh and the photocathode. These photoelectrons are focused onto the target so that a replica of the image occurs. However, as the photoelectrons hit the target secondary electrons are emitted and collected by the 'target mesh'. A positive charge pattern is therefore built up on the target which is scanned by the low velocity beam from the gun on the reverse side. Where there is a positive charge on the target, electrons are removed from the beam sufficient to bring the target element back to cathode potential. Where no positive charge exists the beam is returned to the area of the gun and the electron multiplier. The return beam is, therefore, amplitude modulated.

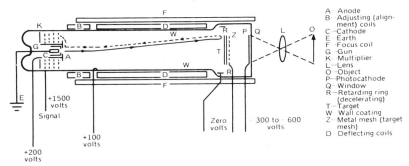

A — Anode
B — Adjusting (alignment) coils
C — Cathode
E — Earth
F — Focus coil
G — Gun
K — Multiplier
L — Lens
O — Object
P — Photocathode
Q — Window
R — Retarding ring (decelerating)
T — Target
W — Wall coating
Z — Metal mesh (target mesh)
D — Deflecting coils

Figure 2.4. Construction of an image orthicon tube

The multiplier consists of five separate electrodes each with a successively higher potential and capable of secondary emission. The returning beam hits the first electrode of the multiplier and produces secondary emission. This is amplified by the second electrode and repeated for the other electrodes in the multiplier. The overall sensitivity due to the gain of such an amplifier and improvements due to the image section of the tube is between 100 and 1000 times greater than that of the orthicon, depending upon whether it is a high or low intensity picture.

Modern tubes

Vidicon

RCA introduced the antimony trisulphide vidicon in 1950 and at that stage the picture did not compare with those from the photoemissive tubes.

The vidicon (Figure 2.5) is a photoconductive type and much smaller than photoemissive tubes. The common range of sizes is 13, 17, 25 and 38 mm while the face size of image orthicons is 76 and 114 mm. When colour cameras were introduced and the standard complement became three tubes there was considerable advantage in adapting the smaller tubes. Over the last 25 years many variations of photoconductive tubes have been produced, using different materials and successful variations include the lead oxide vidicon (plumbicon), saticon, newvicon, silicon diode vidicon and chalnicon.

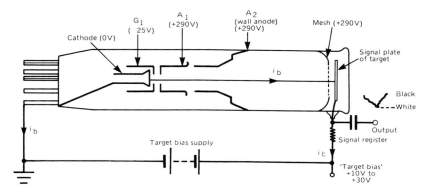

Figure 2.5. Construction of a vidicon tube. Beam electrons not used to discharge the target are returned to the anode

The vidicon target has an extremely thin layer of photoconductive material which is an insulator in darkness but becomes slightly conductive when exposed to illumination. Each element in the target is separate and behaves like a leaky capacitor. The target signal plate has a fixed potential set by the 'target bias' control while the other plate has a positive potential dependent upon illumination. The potential rise is due to the uniform electrostatic field between the target and a fine mesh situated close to the photoconductive surface and connected to the wall anode. The mesh also ensures, together with the axial magnetic field, that orthogonal scanning is obtained.

The beam scans the target and sufficient electrons are provided from the beam to return each element to cathode potential. The electrons not removed from the beam return down the tube and are collected by the first anode. The electrons taken by the target produce a current in the signal resistor creating a negative picture signal at the output of the tube.

In photoconductive tubes the energy for the current is provided by the target bias supply and the illumination acts as a means of controlling the current. With adequate illumination the efficiency of the vidicon can be high but at low illumination there is a time lag due to the resistance through the target. As the illumination decreases and the target voltage is lowered fewer electrons can land and the charging current falls. On moving scenes this causes smearing and the picture becomes unacceptable. In such cases a much higher light level is required, consequently the full sensitivity of the tube cannot be utilised. In order to improve the lag characteristic it is necessary to make the target capacitance as small as possible. This ensures that the target surface potential is increased for any given photocurrent. The larger the tube the greater the problem and this fault cannot be entirely eliminated. A method of light bias is used by some manufacturers where a uniform background illumination increases the dark current in the target and prevents it reaching a negative value relative to the cathode (Figure 2.6).

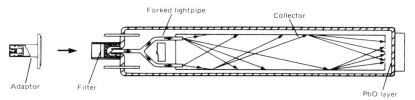

Figure 2.6. Light bias in the plumbicon tube

Another cause of lag in the vidicon is due to impurities or defects in the photoconductor, which apparently charges carriers and releases them after the light has been removed, producing a delayed signal. This is the main cause of lag in antimony trisulphide vidicons and prevents its use in broadcasting except in areas of high illumination, such as telecine and captions. The vidicon has advantages, however, for many uses as it is a relatively cheap tube with good resolution and unity contrast range (gamma). As the signal is controlled by the target bias it also allows automatic sensitivity controls to be easily constructed.

Plumbicon and lead oxide tubes

In 1962 Philips introduced the plumbicon using lead oxide, the first successful photoconductive material to be found after antimony trisulphide although experiments had been made with the compounds of zinc, cadmium, lead, antimony and arsenic.

The main advantage of the lead oxide tube over the antimony trisulphide target is that the chemistry of the target results in a low and uniform dark current, usually less than 1 nanoamp, which is not affected by the target voltage setting. The material used for the target is extremely pure so that the charge carriers are not trapped.

The target can be made thicker than for most other target materials, resulting in a tube of good sensitivity and improved lag characteristics. The spectral response is limited in the deep red but improvements have been made by treating the target with hydrogen sulphide. The lead oxide tube has now become a standard tube for broadcast colour cameras and high grade monochrome cameras.

Silicon diode vidicon

The silicon diode vidicon provides a sensitivity ten times that of the normal vidicon and is capable of withstanding extreme illumination without apparent damage. The principle of operation is the same as for other photoconductive tubes except that the target has to be prepared as it contains a large number of discrete diodes, numbering at least 500 000. Bell Laboratories patented a process in 1958 whereby the diodes are etched into n-type phosphorus doped silicon which is oxidised and diffused with boron.

The main disadvantages compared to the lead oxide tube are the lag caused by the high target capacitance and higher dark current. It can also suffer blemishes due to production problems. However, it is used in the security industry and other areas where high sensitivity is required.

Japanese tubes

The tubes currently marketed by Japanese companies are the Chalnicon (Toshiba, 1972), Saticon (Hitachi, 1973) (Figure 2.7) and Newvicon (Matsushita, 1974) (Figure 2.8). The targets consist of several layers of different materials and they are known collectively as heterogeneous vidicons.

The newvicon is the most sensitive, being 20 times that of a vidicon and twice as sensitive as a silicon vidicon. Its target is made of zinc selenide and zinc cadmium telluride.

The chalnicon has good resolution but a lag higher than that of a lead oxide tube although its sensitivity is higher. Its target, which due to the good light absorbent characteristic can be made thin, consists of a film of cadmium selenide and a layer of arsenic sulphide on the scanned side, creating a junction with a low dark current.

The saticon target is made from selenium, arsenic and tellurium. The photoconductive characteristics are based on the amorphous selenium which tends to crystallise at temperatures above 50°C. The arsenic is used to dope the selenium and prevent this while the tellurium is used to extend the red sensitivity of the tube. Using bias illumination the tube has good resolution, low dark current and a spectral response similar to extended red plumbicons.

Diode gun plumbicon

Although the principle of this tube has been known for several years the manufacturing problems have only recently been mastered; it was demonstrated at NAB in 1979 and is widely used in

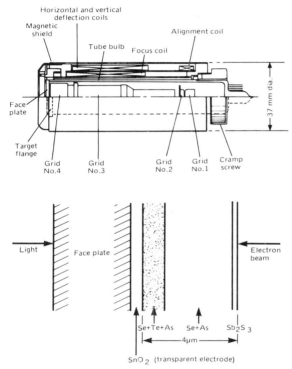

Figure 2.7. Structure (top) of the Saticon tube and its yoke assembly, and (bottom) schematic representation of the target structure. The gradation in tellurium concentration is shown by the distribution of the dots

the latest cameras. The tube is produced by Philips-Ampex and provides a considerable improvement in picture resolution without increase in lag or picture noise characteristics.

The conventional tube has a negative voltage on the control grid and the resulting beam has variable diameter and variable velocity. The diode gun has a positive voltage on the control grid and the result is a precisely focused and uniform velocity beam.

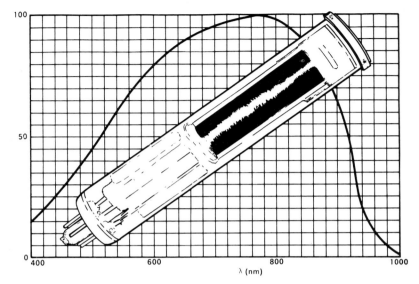

Figure 2.8. The newvicon tube and its spectral response

Conclusion

The time required to develop a new tube is considerable and research and development are expensive.

The current tubes, especially for broadcasting, will be with us for a long time but on the horizon are charge-coupled devices bringing a new theory and technology to picture generation. Due to their complexity, the cost will doubtless be higher than conventional tubes, but as digital techniques increase the technology of charge-coupled devices, involving matrixes of diodes from which the signal is transferred into memories for readout and processing, becomes part of the changeover. Cameras may then be extremely small as the CCD is amongst the smallest of elements.

Until then, however, the equipment buyer and systems engineer has available a range of tubes which will satisfy most needs.

Chapter 3

Television Cameras

Types and uses

In broadcasting television cameras fall into approximately the following categories:
  (1) In permanent studios where the camera is used
    (a) Permanently on one set;
    (b) Where several sets are used in a production;
    (c) For presentation purposes and announcers.

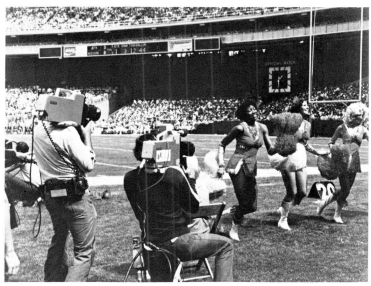

Figure 3.1. For outside broadcasts a combination of portable and static cameras are often used. These are fed back to the scanner (mobile control room) where they are mixed into the programme

(2) In outside broadcast situations for sport or special occasions (Figure 3.1).
(3) For news gathering or documentaries (Figure 3.2).
(4) For obtaining pictures from film.

Figure 3.2. ENG portable television cameras and recorders used to replace normal filming. Sony BVP300 camera and BVP100 VTR being used on location by Channel Television

In all these situations, the camera can be either monochrome or colour. Each situation has its own special requirements and a camera suitable in one situation may be unable to operate in another, due to the facilities available or the physical conditions.

In broadcasting studios the highest quality is required, but less restrictions are placed on the designer as all facilities are available such as pulses, lighting systems, dollies, hoists and professional staff. The restrictions on weight, size and optics are less, and so the amount of electronics can be increased as can the size of the cameraman's viewfinder (Figure 3.3).

Figure 3.3. RCA TK47 automatics extend to the camera set-up procedure where microprocessor-controlled systems provide computer-aided semi-automatic set-up of the camera. Optionally, the camera can be equipped for totally automatic set-up and pre-operational check at the touch of a button

For economic reasons a cheaper camera may be suitable in less demanding situations such as in presentation and announcer's studios, where the picture content and lighting is fixed. Normally, these cameras are remotely controlled.

In CCTV, budgets usually determine the price and a compromise between cost and performance must be made. In situations such as security, sensitivity, automatic operation and reasonable size may be critical factors. Observation in industry may require small size, high sensitivity, and the ability to function in hostile environments.

For news gathering and documentaries, portability and the ability to match the pictures to those of the studio cameras may be important, especially if inserts into studio produced programmes are made. However, a lowering of picture quality for topical subjects and news can be tolerated provided the subject is of interest to the public. These cameras usually have restricted optics and are capable of being operated from a battery.

Thus there is available a wide range of cameras with different performances and prices to fill all the different requirements. It is,therefore, pointless choosing a camera without knowing the use for which it is intended.

Standard cameras can be also modified to operate in telecines and advantage can be taken of the facts that the object is at a fixed focus and there is plenty of light. Correction is usually included for poor quality colour printing and for the colour characteristics of the dyes used in colour films. Automatic light correction is also possible by adjusting a variable neutral density filter in front of the camera to keep the projected light constant. This is especially useful when the film has a variable density. More than one source can be projected into a telecine camera by using a multiplexer, where mirrors can be remotely operated to direct the required light source to the camera. Alternatively a 'flying spot telecine' can be used, which operates by a different principle.

Component parts of a camera

The colour signal is formed by combining the outputs from three tubes which separately produce voltages from the red, green and blue components of the picture. In essence, the three-tube colour camera has three separate monochrome chains all accurately aligned, one for each colour. An explanation of the principles of a colour camera will, therefore, cover also a monochrome camera.

Each camera consists of:
(1) Common optical system;
(2) In colour cameras, a method of separating the primary colours;
(3) Camera tube – In colour cameras three or four matched tubes are required, although four tube cameras are now rare.
(4) Head preamplifiers – These high gain, low noise amplifiers must be as close to the tube as possible.
(5) Gamma correction.

(6) Scanning and, in colour cameras, convergence circuits.
(7) Power supplies, including all the voltages required by the tube.
(8) Blanking and clamping circuits.
(9) Sync addition.
(10) In some cameras a colour coder is included to produce a composite waveform for PAL, SECAM or NTSC systems, otherwise RGB outputs are provided and a separate external coder is used.
(11) Viewfinder display, usually a small monochrome TV, for the cameraman.

A camera can either be externally driven by pulses fed from a central sync pulse generator (SPG) or, as found mainly on cheaper cameras, can generate its own pulses locked to the mains power supply. The final video output must in cheap cameras resemble and in broadcasting accurately reproduce the TV system waveforms.

It is essential in a multi-camera studio where mixing and special effects are used that all cameras are fed from a central sync pulse generator, and that at the mixer all sources appear at a particular part of the waveform simultaneously. To do this artificial delays are placed in the shorter signal leads, so that it appears the delays due to equipment circuitry and cable lengths are the same at the mixer for all signal sources. Sources can then be switched wihout picture disturbance.

A different approach to this problem is where each camera produces its own waveform, which is genlocked (slaved) to the central waveform generator. This ensures that waveforms are synchronised with each other and phase differences at the mixer can be easily compensated at the camera. This avoids the need for distributing all the different pulse waveforms to all the cameras. One signal is sufficient to lock the cameras (this is normally produced from a colour black generator).

A high frequency loss occurs as the cable length is increased, so 'cable compensation' circuits are usually used to provide high frequency boost.

Additional circuits for crispening the picture (high frequency boost), contours out of green (edge effect to images from the green channel), automatic alignment circuits, intercom and signal are provided depending upon the manufacturer and the standard and intended use of the camera (Figures 3.4 and 3.5).

To reduce the camera head size of the more sophisticated cameras, the main video processing and voltage and waveform generation are performed in a separate 'camera control unit' (CCU) joined to the camera head by a multiway cable.

The camera head in such instances contains the viewfinder, camera tubes and scanning coils, optical system, head amplifiers and intercom. Such systems also allow the CCUs of a multi-camera installation to be centrally placed and controlled by a single

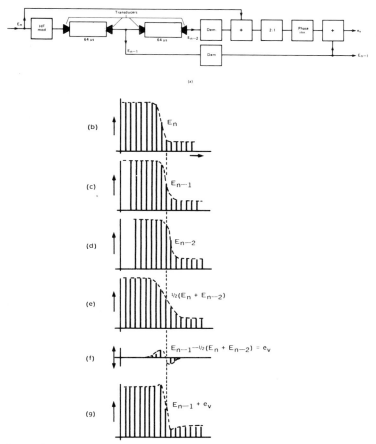

Figure 3.4. Principle of vertical contour enhancement. (a) Simplified circuit diagram; (b, c, d) signal amplitudes of non-delayed (E_n), one-time delayed (E_{n-1}) and twice delayed (E_{n-2}) series of scanning lines at a brightness transition from bright to dark; (e) resulting signal amplitudes after adding series E_n and E_{n-2} and halving the sum; (f) correction signal e_v obtained by subtracting the signal series $\frac{1}{2}(E_n + E_{n-2})$ from E_{n-1}; (g) enhanced amplitudes of the signal series E_{n-1} by adding to it an appropriate amount of correction signal e_v. Compare parts (g) and (c)

engineer who then has the facilities to match the pictures from all the cameras.

Single tube colour cameras are, of course, produced – but as each colour is produced by the same tube using a stripe pattern, it is not possible to balance the outputs of different cameras to produce matched pictures. These cameras should only be used in low budget, single camera installations.

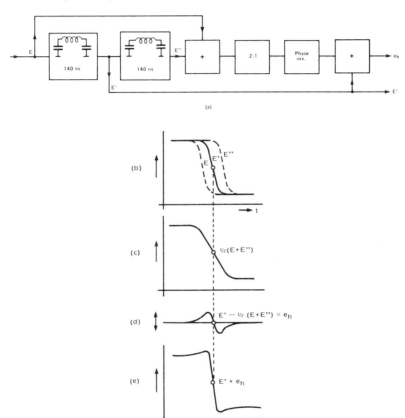

Figure 3.5. Principle of horizontal contour enhancement. (a) Simplified circuit diagram; (b) non-delayed signal E, one-time delayed signal E', and twice delayed signal E", as occurring with a transition from bright to dark; (c) halved sum of signals E and E"; (d) correction signal e_h obtained by subtracting $\frac{1}{2}(E + E'')$ from E'; (e) improved transition of signal E' by adding to it an appropriate amount of corection signal e_h. Compare this accentuated curve with the soft ones of (b). The circuits of Figures 3.4 and 3.5 are combined and the corrector can be inserted in the green channel to provide 'contours from green' (Philips system)

The camera lens

Apart from the pickup tube, the camera lens decides how good the pictures will be. Electronics can usually be perfected to produce the required results without degrading the picture. Many electronic circuits are also used to correct distortions and compensate for inadequacies in the electrical circuits. However, the lens is a complex item which has inherent distortions and its quality is directly related to cost.

Lens aberrations

These are the deficiencies in the image due to the lens, and include:
(1) Spherical aberration
(2) Coma
(3) Astigmatism
(4) Curvature of the field
(5) Distortion of the image
(6) Chromatic aberration

These distortions require considerable mathematics and drawings to describe them, and for those interested they can be found in any reasonably advanced standard physics book. However, a brief description of each follows.

Spherical aberration causes rays equally spaced and parallel to the axis to meet at different focal points. It can be corrected by combining a convex and a concave lens.

Coma is caused by differences in the power of various annular zones of the lens (i.e. from the thick part to the thin part), and occurs when the parallel rays are at an angle to the principal axis. This results in the image produced by the marginal rays having a reduced brightness and an image is produced which has a comet's tail appearance.

Astigmatism produces a line focus instead of a single spot focus and occurs for oblique incident rays only.

Curvature of the field causes the outer edges of the image to move towards the object when using a convex lens. By using a combination of lenses it is possible to correct for curvature. A combination which corrects for curvature and astigmatism without distorting colour is known as an 'anastigmatic lens'.

Distortion of the image is due to the magnification of the lens being dependent upon the direction of the incident rays, and is therefore greater when the object distance is sufficiently small to be of the same order as the focal length. At this point the incident beam has a larger angle than a more distant object. Correction can be made by a suitable combination of lenses with a stop placed between them.

Chromatic aberration is caused by the focal length of a lens being dependent upon its refractive index, which differs for the different wavelengths. The clarity of the image and magnification will, therefore, depend on the colours. Achromatic lenses are produced by cementing together or spacing elements of different dispersive powers and indices.

Zoom lens

On some broadcast monochrome cameras, and almost universally on broadcast and semi-professional colour cameras, the lens used is a zoom lens. This is a multi-element lens corrected, depending upon cost, for all the errors inherent in simple lenses and some modern lenses are capable of zoom ranges up to 30:1.

However, the larger the ratio, the heavier they become and the less light they transmit. This becomes a problem with portable cameras when a high ratio of zoom is required, while the camera also has to be light in weight.

A zoom lens system is shown in Figure 3.6 and only elements 2 and 3 need to be movable. Moving their axial position and spacing varies the magnification and creates the impression of moving towards or away from the object.

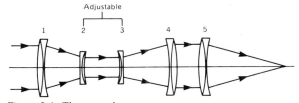

Figure 3.6. The zoom lens

However, with zoom lenses, the perspective remains the same throughout a zoom, creating an unreal situation as the human eye expects the ratio of background and foreground to vary as a camera moves towards it. Therefore, zooming while on air should be avoided unless the effect is especially required.

Separation of colours

The sensitivity of the human eye is greatest in the yellow-green part of the spectrum (555 nm, nanometre = 10^{-9} metre) decreasing towards both the red and blue ends of the spectrum. The limits are 700 nm (red) and 400 nm (blue) beyond which the eye is not sufficiently sensitive (Figure 3.7). As the different colours are seen with different intensities, white light can be produced by mixing 30% red, 59% green and 11% blue. The ratios of 30, 59 and 11 are important. However, for the practical purposes of designing

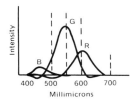

Figure 3.7. White light is obtained from red, green and blue in the ratio 0.59G + 0.3R + 0.11B

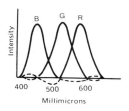

Figure 3.8. To simplify design all channels are amplified to produce equal R, G, B voltages for the white signal. Correction is inserted later to restore the correct ratio

filters, mirrors, amplifiers and control circuits, the ratios are altered within the camera by adjustment of either tube or amplifier to make the output from each tube the same when peak white is transmitted (Figure 3.8). This means that later the original ratio must be reconstructed to obtain the correct colour, although allowances for other non-linearities within the system must also be taken into consideration. The wavelengths of the primary colours used in colour television are approximately green 532 nm, red 615 nm and blue 470 nm.

Dichroic mirrors

Light entering through the lens must be split into its red, green and blue components and directed to the appropriate tube in order to produce the required signals. This must be done with as little light loss as possible and each cut-off defined as sharply as possible. This is achieved by dichroic mirrors, which use the principle of interference to produce the colour filters. The mirrors are very efficient as all the light which is not reflected is transmitted. Colour filters, however, absorb a considerable amount of light.

A dichroic mirror consists of a glass on which is coated an interference layer, partially transparent and with a high refractive index, to a thickness of about ¼ of the wavelength of the light at which separation is to take place. Light entering the layer is partially reflected, but the rest passes to the glass which has a lower refractive index. Reflection, therefore, takes place and the light passes back to the surface. At the desired frequency, due to the layer being ¼ wavelength thick, a 180° phase shift will have taken place at this frequency in the layer on entering and leaving.

A further 180° phase shift takes place on reflection causing 360° total shift between the entering and emerging beam, which means they are in phase. The reflective properties of the beam at this particular frequency are, therefore, far greater than at other frequencies.

A mirror which has a maximum output of 700 nm and a minimum of 350 nm is known as a red reflecting mirror. If the glass is made with a higher refractive index than the layer, the 180° phase shift will not take place at the surface and the maximum output will be at 350 nm, and is a blue reflecting mirror. In practical mirrors, several layers of different refractive indices are used to obtain the desired characteristics.

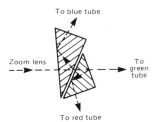

Figure 3.9. The dichroic prism

The dichroic layers are now applied to the mating surfaces of glass prisms. This prevents dirt forming on the sensitive layers and allows a reduction in the distance between the camera tubes and the lens. This simplifies the lens design (Figure 3.9).

Gamma correction

It is essential that linearity is maintained throughout the system from the camera tube to the television screen, in order to achieve correct colours and luminance signals. The problem areas are mainly the camera tubes and the television screen. The mathematical relationship of th input signal to the output signal is known as gamma (γ). If the relationship is linear, the gamma is 1. If the plotted relationship is a parabola then the gamma will depend upon the power ($y = x^2$, $\gamma = 2$).

A colour tube has a gamma of about 2.2 and a vidicon about 0.5 while amplifiers are designed for a gamma of 1 (Figure 3.10). The overall gamma of a system must be calculated taking all the individual gammas into consideration and a reciprocal network is inserted in the camera to produce an overall linear signal. When film is used the linearity of the film reproduced as a TV signal must be taken into consideration and the gamma adjusted accordingly.

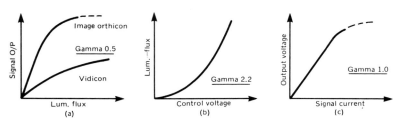

Figure 3.10. The gamma of (a) TV camera tubes; (b) the television colour tube; (c) linear system video amplifiers

Single tube colour camera

To produce a colour picture from a single tube camera, filters and processing circuitry are used. A successful system by JVC employs a new technique called the 'virtual step energy system', comprising a vidicon in front of which is a colour stripe filter having equal pitch vertical stripes of green, cyan and white. In front of this is an optical band erase filter which prevents interference beats when the subject being televised has vertical stripes coinciding with the vertical stripes of the filter. This would create spurious colour signals to occur along the edges of the subject (Figure 3.11).

When light hits the target the output of the tube consists of a signal modified by the filter (Figure 3.13). The average value of the signal passed through a low pass filter represents the luminance (Y) of the signal. The signal which is passed through a bandpass filter comprises high frequency colour signals. These can be processed to obtain colour difference signals which, with the luminance signal, are applied to an encoder to produce the composite PAL video signal (Figure 3.11).

Figure 3.12 shows that white light passing through the filter produces an output from the vidicon which is stepped as shown. At the green stripe, red and blue are obstructed. At the cyan stripe, red is obstructed while the white stripe will pass red, green and blue. It can be seen that the average value of this stepped waveform corresponds to the average luminance component.

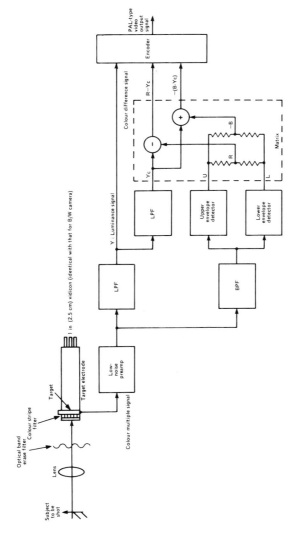

Figure 3.11. Block diagram showing the principle of the JVC single-tube colour video camera

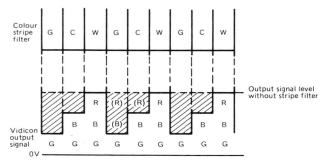

Figure 3.12. Vidicon output signal (white light) of the JVC virtual step energy system. Cross hatched areas represent no output of a particular colour

The bandpass filter is followed by two envelope detectors which detect the upper and lower parts of the stepped waveform. The upper detector (U) corresponds to the energy lost due to the filter,

$$U \quad \frac{1}{3} \times (2R + B)$$

The lower detector (L) corresponds to the energy passed,

$$L = -\frac{1}{3}(2B + R).$$

From these formulas the values of the red and blue with respect to U and L can be derived.

Red $= 2U + L$
Blue $= -(2L + U)$

These values are fed to a matrix from where the colour difference signals can be derived.

Such technology has enabled production of cameras of low cost but relatively high performance, and enabled video to compete with amateur movie film and be used where cost would have prevented the use of a colour camera.

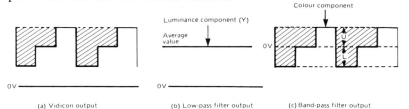

Figure 3.13. Low pass and bandpass output waveforms of the JVC virtual step energy system. Cross hatching as for Figure 3.12

Conclusion

The camera is the workhorse of television. It is the most mobile piece of equipment in the TV system and its design must make it both robust and practical. The new generation of portable cameras has continued the evolution of TV and given entry to places which previously only allowed the film cameraman. Progress in the near future will mainly be concentrated on reducing weight and power requirements. However, we still look to the designers tubes and lenses for any major improvements.

Figure 3.14. A TV camera used in a different environment – on the Space Shuttle. This is one of the cameras used to guide the astronants in handling payloads and in deploying and retrieving satellites. It is enclosed in an insulating layer of gold foil and weighs 7.27kg (16lb). The system also transmits signals back to earth so that TV audiences can see space activities in colour (courtesy RCA Astro-Electronics)

Chapter 4

Video Recording

Although only a practical reality for the broadcaster since 1956 the impact of video tape recording on broadcasting, education and other fields has been far greater than its short history would normally justify. In this time there has been a transition from large bulky equipment, which required a good engineer to control it continuously but still produced characteristic VTR errors, to the modern relatively cheap machine which can be operated by anyone and can record and play colour signals in any standard with a quality the average viewer cannot fault. In the broadcast field multiple generation copies can be made on machines and still produce broadcast quality recordings.

There has always been a need for a reliable method of storing picture information which could be reproduced immediately the recording was made and before artists and studio staff dispersed. Prior to videotape recording studios produced recordings on film with telerecording systems. This was usually a film camera which filmed the screen of a picture monitor. The quality of the recordings obtained was normally not of a standard which would be acceptable today. There were also delays in film processing and if problems arose there was little chance of repeating the programme.

Broadcasters in America also had a problem, with the requirement for delayed transmissions due to several time zones across America. It was necessary to store programmes initially transmitted on the East coast and delay their transmission to a more suitable time in other areas.

There was, therefore, an initial market for such equipment and although many were working on the problem, the solution which made the equipment practical and set the present broadcast standard was discovered by a small team of engineers at Ampex in

48

Redwood City, California. It is generally accepted that the major contributions to this project were made by Charles Ginsberg, Charles Anderson, Ray Dolby, Fred Pfost and Alex Maxey. Their achievements have been recognised in the many awards given by the broadcasting organisations and professional institutes.

The early pioneers

Like all major technical advances, original ideas usually have to await the invention of other processes, materials, components or equipment before they can be fully implemented. This has applied in the case of video recording, where today's equipment is the result of improvements in video tape and oxides, head materials and construction, integrated circuits and mechanical manufacturing processes.

The first successful magnetic recording equipment was developed in 1900, when Valdemar Poulson patented his 'Telegraphone' in the USA. He had previously produced a magnetic wire recorder in Europe, but its output was very low and noisy.

By 1906, Poulson and Penderson had discovered that premagnetising the wire of their 'Telegraphone' created a greater output, but the signal still had a poor signal-to-noise ratio. In 1927 Carlson and Carpenter discovered that by using an alternating current as the bias for the tape the results were superior.

In Germany in 1928 Dr. Pfleumer patented a plastic tape coated with a powdered magnetic material, and in 1935 this was improved by using iron oxide as the magnetic material. In the same year the first magnetic tape recorder was introduced in Europe, using a paper or plastic base coated with iron oxide. Progress continued throughout World War II, especially in Germany, and audio systems were developed which gave results comparable to that obtained with disc and film.

High frequency recording

The overriding problem of recording video is the bandwidth that needs to be recorded in order to reproduce a picture. The frequency response is determined by the number of lines in the television system and the picture repetition ratio. This can range from 3 MHz in a 405-line system with a picture repetition of 25 pictures a second, to 5 MHz for 625 lines and 10 MHz for 819 lines. Compare this to audio recording where the bandwidth requirements range from 8 kHz to 20 kHz, depending upon the quality required, and understandable voice reproduction is possible with 2 to 3 kHz. The relationship between the tape to head velocity, the frequency of the signal and the resulting wavelength of the signal recorded on the tape will be discussed later, but these parameters affect the head design whose output is controlled by the materials used and the mechanical precision. It is also of paramount importance that intimate contact is kept between the head and tape otherwise serious losses occur. The problems therefore associated with the physics of video recording had to be learned and solved and the practicality of any solution depended on both electronic and mechanical engineering skills.

Writing speed and frequency response

The major problem to be solved in the development of the video recorder was how to provide a high writing speed to record the very high frequencies involved.

The relationship of tape speed and frequency response is governed by the formula

$$\lambda = \frac{v}{f}$$

where λ is the recorded wavelength of the signal, f is the frequency of the signal to be recorded and v is the tape velocity.

In order to recover a signal from tape, it is essential that the gap in the replay head must be narrower than one wavelength of recorded signal. When the signal wavelength is equal to the gap width of the head the output is zero as the two opposite halves of the recorded wavelength will appear simultaneously in the gap and their effects will therefore cancel.

There is obviously a physical limit to the minimum size of the gap and if video frequencies up to 5 MHz are to be recorded some method must be found of obtaining a high head to tape velocity which is mechanically controllable to very precise requirements and also uses a reasonable amount of tape for at least one hour of recording.

In audio recording the tape is moved past a static head at speeds ranging from 4.8 cm/s (1⅞ in/s) to 38 cm/s (15 in/s), depending upon the highest frequencies to be recorded. In video, speeds of 3800 cm/s (1500 in/s) are required and obviously the mechanical problems and the amount of tape used make this an impractical system without considerable modification.

The problem was finally solved by adopting a rotating head while the tape moved longitudinally at a conventional speed. This immediately solved the problem caused by the volume of tape required for the recording of a normal TV programme in a high speed longitudinal recorder.

Transverse scanning

Several scanning methods were investigated before Ampex developed a practical system. The method, which when first demonstrated in 1956, finally revolutionalised the television broadcasting industry, was to rotate four heads across the tape while it was firmly held in a vacuum guide. The penetration of the tape by the heads was controlled by the position of the guide relevant to the drum.

The advantages of the system were the very high writing speeds, good timebase stability (due to the tracks being almost at right angles to the tape movement), the ability to record wideband signals and the possibility to design into the system the maximum operational flexibility. The disadvantages were the necessity to switch between four heads, segmenting of the images into discrete portions which result in certain geometric distortions, and the need to equalise four separate channels which must all be exactly matched. These problems were overcome by additional electronics, each correcting for specific errors. After nearly 25 years, these disadvantages will gradually cause the decline of the format as new machines become available. However, due to the vast amount of pre-recorded tapes and the expected life of these machines, they will survive for many years. In today's studios, where complex editing of programmes takes place, the broadcast VTR is possibly the most complex piece of equipment used and the results obtained make it almost impossible for anyone except experienced engineers to know which programme is live and which is recorded.

The need for compatibility between recorders ensured that the broadcast standard committees quickly standardised the format. The success of Ampex caused other manufacturers to seek licensing arrangements to make similar machines.

The standard tape was 5 cm (2 in) wide and, with a head rotating at 250 rev/s (25 pictures/s) and longitudinal tape speeds sufficient to give good quality sound and adequate track spacing (38 cm/s, 15 in/s), it was possible to record a one hour programme on 4800 ft (1500 m) of tape. This is easily handled and stored. The writing speed is sufficient to record the full 5 MHz bandwidth required for the colour television waveform.

Helical scan recording

If VTRs were to be used by industry, education and the home user, a simpler, less sophisticated system had to be used. A helical scan format and a multiplicity of standards hit the market in the 1960s and many manufacturers had two or more standards in operation, none of which were compatible with another. Timebase stability and frequency response were usually of secondary importance to cost.

In a helical system the tape is wrapped around the head drum in one of several possible ways and the tape moves longitudinally (Figure 4.1). Because the tracks are more parallel to the direction of tape travel, inherent timebase errors are greater than in

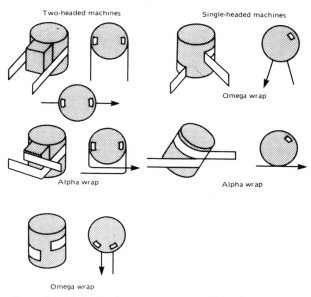

Two-headed machines   Single-headed machines

Omega wrap

Alpha wrap   Alpha wrap

Omega wrap

Figure 4.1. Methods of wrapping tape round heads

transverse scanning. One head, however, can be made to record one complete field, so no segmentation of the image occurs and one channel only need be provided and equalised. Systems using two heads provide continuous signal without the break in continuity experienced in one head systems when the head momentarily leaves the tape. The cost and quality of the helical scan recorder varies considerably from semi-broadcast machines capable of 5 MHz reproduction to domestic models.

When colour became a priority the restricted bandwidth and timebase errors made direct recording and recovery of a colour signal impossible so a number of systems were adopted where the colour signal was split into separate luminance (monochrome picture) and chrominance (colour components) signals. The luminance was recorded while the chrominance was remodulated onto a separate subcarrier and recorded within the bandwidth capability of the recorder. The recovered colour signal then had to receive timebase correction before remodulating on its correct subcarrier frequency, so that a normal TV set would recognise it as a colour signal.

The helical scan system was not widely accepted at first due to the continuous proliferation of formats, equipment and general reliability. Video equipment still required experienced staff and correct operating environments. Simplicity, cost, and sufficient machines of one type to give some degree of compatibility did not start until the 1970s when video cassette recorders became available. Video cassette recorders are helical-scan machines with the tape enclosed in a protective cassette which allows machines to automatically lace themselves. This overcame the main user problems and, with the advent of integrated circuits, the quality and reliability was sufficient to create enough confidence to produce substantial sales in education and industry. Duplicating centres to copy films and TV programmes were built in Europe, Japan and the USA and the new areas of use, such as video cassettes on ships and corporate communication networks, were created. Today, the market is the general public with a new and cheaper range of video cassette recorders capable of being programmed to record 2, 3, 4 and 8 hours of continuous TV programmes enabling viewing at a time convenient to the viewer.

EVR and SelectaVision

Due to initial difficulties with helical scan recording, systems not using tape evolved. The only one to really make any impact was EVR (Electronic Video Recording), a replay only system, developed by CBS Laboratories in America. The system could produce a colour picture on a normal TV from a cartridge 1.2 cm (½ in) thick and 17.8 cm (7 in) diameter. This gave 30 minutes of colour or 60 minutes of monochrome programmes. A film 0.344 in (8.75 mm) wide was used and two frames of a picture were placed side by side. The audio track was a magnetic stripe down the side of the film. In a colour system the two frames were associated, one containing the luminance signal and the other a coded chrominance signal. In monochrome both pictures were luminance signals and were played separately by reversing the projector after 30 minutes.

Reproduction was by flying spot scanning methods similar to those used in telecine systems (Chapter 2). The output signal was modulated onto an RF carrier similar to domestic VTRs to enable reception on a normal receiver.

The design philosophy for the entire system was that the complications necessary for the system should take place in the recording system and the equipment necessary for playback should be as simple as possible.

Special recording systems were set up in different parts of the world for transferring programmes to EVR cartridges.

However, a replay only system depends upon large duplication orders and these were not required at that time. Even today in many VTR duplicating centres the average most customers require is, with the exception of large orders for copies of popular films for the VHS and Betamax cassette market, less than 10 copies. Failing large orders, sufficient programmes of interest must be available to encourage large sales. This is the same problem faced by video disc systems. Unfortunately the sale of audio records cannot be equated with the sale of video programmes. One can listen to a piece of music many times and still enjoy it, but to watch a film or TV programme several times becomes a chore. EVR gradually declined, until today only a few programmes can be bought in Japan for educational purposes.

Holograms

Another system, produced by RCA, used phased holograms and it was the first equipment to use a laser in equipment designed primarily for the consumer market. Its main advantage was supposed to be the simplicity of the replay unit and the cheapness of the replay medium, which was clear polyvinyl chloride, the same material as used for wrapping food. The process produces patterns on the medium instead of distinct images, and these are unaffected by scratches and dust. Holograms are capable of producing three-dimensional images, but they can only be produced by coherent light, for which lasers are the only practical source.

A recording is made by splitting the light from a laser so that one beam passes through the film being recorded to the recording medium, while the other beam is passed directly to the recording medium where it interferes with the other beam in a complex pattern.

This film, after processing, forms the master from which copies are made. In replay the film is viewed with a low power laser and the images are reconstructed. Perhaps a hologram system will reappear when three-dimensional systems become a necessity.

Broadcasting

As machines improved editing became possible. Systems evolved from physically cutting the tape until today small computers do the work electronically.

In 1958 NTSC colour was possible, but with many imperfections due to the modulator frequencies used in the VTR. These frequencies were increased and by 1963 high-band systems were in operation and PAL and SECAM were being recorded. Because some TV stations needed to show many short VTR recordings, especially for commercial purposes, the cartridge recorder was introduced and the prototype was first shown in 1969. Each cartridge contained three minutes of programmes and these could be programmed to play continuously, if required.

Today, the broadcaster is using more broadcast standard helical scan recorders as new formats and standards evolve for these extremely sophisticated machines, which have advantages in size, capital cost, running costs and performance (p. 74).

The greatest impact on television sport was made by the video disc. Several systems had been tried to achieve slow or stop motion, but the most successful was that produced by Ampex and first used in Europe at the Grenoble Winter Olympics. The recorder can record 30 seconds of programme on four sides of two discs. Each disc has a head and each head records or plays back in sequence. Each head records one complete TV frame on a single continuous track and, while one head is recording, the other heads are moving to a new track or becoming ready to record their frame of information.

Stop motion is achieved by continuously replaying the same frame. Slow motion is achieved by repeating each frame several times before moving to the next frame (Chap. 5).

Video disc for the home

The introduction of video discs for the home user has been a long-running saga in video. Systems have been promised but their introduction was always delayed.

Telefunken produced a mechanical system which is now recognised to be a failure. Most of the large video manufacturers have either produced systems or are backing a proposed system and limited marketing has taken place. These systems are explained in Chapter 5. However, the consumer cannot record programmes and their introduction relies on sufficient recorded programmes being available at a cost the consumer finds attractive.

It may be that when these systems finally come to the market their real use is finally resricted to more sophisticated areas of systems engineering, although the manufacturer's intention is for use in the home. The problem is that the video recorder, using re-usable media, already has the lead and gives the owner freedom to record his own programmes.

Digital recording

At present only experimental recorders are available but the technical possibilities are increasing at a considerable rate. Multiple generation copies are possible without degradation and Sony have demonstrated two television programmes being simultaneously recorded on the same tape. Technical standards have to be eventually approved and the facilities which are normal on an analogue recorder have to be developed, but no insurmountable problem is envisaged. Recording densities on tape are continually increasing and greater densities than are being demonstrated at present are both practical and will possibly be employed (Chap. 10).

Conclusion

Once the major problems of achieving wideband recording had been solved, the associated problems could be understood and engineering solutions found. Systems could then be devised and new uses found. However, it was the breakthrough resulting in the VR1000 which set the pattern for the last 25 years and created a new industry.

Advantages of video tape

It is not by chance that video tape enjoys such a success for there are inherent qualities in magnetic recording tape which favour it as a medium. These are:
  (1) The ability of a magnetised tape to maintain its magnetism until required means it has almost permanent stability.
  (2) It is the only medium which can be erased and re-used continuously.
  (3) The resolution of signals obtainable from magnetic tape is extremely high and can be obtained with an exceptionally good signal-to-noise ratio.
  (4) Magnetic tape has a low inherent distortion characteristic, so that if overload occurs it happens gradually.

(5) It has a very wide dynamic range.

(6) It permits accurate and linear recording over a range from full modulation to less than one per cent of full modulation.

Above all, however,

(7) It allows replay immediately after recording without any intermediate processing.

These characteristics are difficult to find in any other medium.

Magnetic process

Only a small group of materials of all the known elements exhibit the phenomenon known as magnetism. In the periodic table of the elements these appear adjacent to iron and each has an incomplete third shell in its atomic structure. The other elements are chromium, manganese, cobalt and nickel. The theory of magnetism can be found in most advanced physics textbooks. However, in a simplified explanation, each atom can be assumed to be internally magnetised to saturation but due to random orientation the material does not appear to be magnetised. If a magnetising force is applied to the material, the individual magnets align themselves and when the force is removed the atoms remain aligned and the material exhibits magnetism. If a force of opposite polarity is applied the magnetic field is reversed.

Magnetisation curve

When the magnetising force is increased it causes an increase in magnetism until saturation point is reached. If the magnetising force is reduced the material retains a certain level of magnetism,

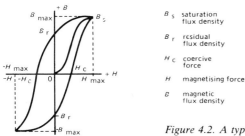

B_s saturation flux density

B_r residual flux density

H_c coercive force

H magnetising force

B magnetic flux density

Figure 4.2. A typical hysteresis curve

depending upon the remanence of the material. When the force is reduced to zero the remanent magnetism represents the peak magnetism that the material can retain. This is known as the retentivity of the material. If the force is reduced further through zero in a negative direction another saturation point is reached and increasing the force again to zero describes a hysteresis loop. The area of this loop is an important characteristic (Figure 4.2). The coercive force is the force required to reduce the magnetism of the saturated condition of the material to zero. The higher this force, the higher the value of signal that can be recorded.

Tape specifications are still often quoted in the old units of oersteds. Ferric oxide tapes range from 20 000–28 000 A/m (250 to 350 oersteds), while high energy tapes have values from 32 000 A/m (400 oersteds) to over 80 000 A/m (1000 oersteds). Advantage of increased signals obtained from high energy tape is used in cheaper recorders to simplify the signal system electronics.

To erase the recorded signal completely, the magnetic material is placed in a gradually diminishing a.c. field, which makes successive hysteresis loops smaller until finally no magnetisation remains.

Recording and reproduction

The current in the coils of the recording head varies with the signal waveform. As the tape passes the poles of the head, the area in front of the gap becomes permanently magnetised. If the writing

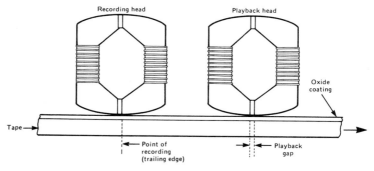

Figure 4.3. Magnetisation of the tape by the recording head

speed is sufficiently high the magnetic pattern on the tape has a direction and magnitude representing the magnetising effect at the instant the area of tape leaves the gap. The field is concentrated around the edges of the gap so the trailing edge will be the most effective when recording (Figure 4.3). When the magnetised tape passes the playback head the field is distorted by the presence of the high permeability core. The flux travels along the paths of least reluctance in the core and links the coil windings, where the flux changes induce voltages dependent upon their rate of change. The output is, therefore, frequency dependent and doubling the frequency will double the output. In a practical system losses occur due to the dimensions of the head gap. At high frequencies the output will fall to zero as the recorded wavelength approaches the width of the gap and at low frequencies when the wavelength is long compared to the gap (Figure 4.4).

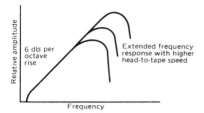

Figure 4.4. Example of response curve for a playback head

Video heads

Video head design must be a compromise, as it is used for both recording and replay, which can have conflicting requirements. In replay the gap must always intercept less than one complete wavelength of the highest frequency. However, too small a gap will give low output, as flux will not be forced through the coils. The head must also have a resonance above which its output is of no use. To keep this resonance outside the desired high bandwidth means the head must have a low inductance. This can be achieved

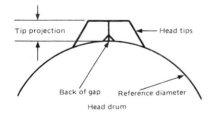

Figure 4.5. The tip projection is the distance that the video heads extend from the face of the drum

only by using coils of few turns which produces a low output. The depth of the gap can be reduced, but this would shorten head life as the heads are worn by the tape (Figure 4.5). As the output from the head is halved (6 dB) for each octave drop (halving the frequency) the low frequency characteristic of the head is determined by the acceptable noise figure of the system.

Head to tape contact

Intimate head to tape contact is of paramount importance in video recording. The serious loss which can occur can be judged by the empirical formula 55D/λ dB loss, where *D* is the effective spacing between the tape coating and the head, and λ is the recorded wavelength measured in the same unit as the effective spacing.

In video recorders, the head physically distorts the tape to ensure that contact is kept, and this places considerable requirements on the mechanical properties of video tape, which must be able to withstand the friction and physical distortion without

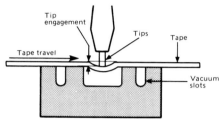

Cross section of vacuum block (quad machine)

Figure 4.6. Tip engagement or penetration is the negative clearance between the head tips and the tape in the guide

permanent damage and retain its oxide (Figure 4.6). Variations in the head to tape contact greatly affect the signal to noise performance of the recorder and visible dropouts occur when contact between oxide and head is momentarily lost. A build-up of tape oxide on the head produces the same effect and causes a loss of picture due to head clogging. Improvements in heads is an essential part of video recording development. High efficiency ferrite core material with low wear characteristics has contributed considerably to the development of video cassette recorders, some of which initially used chromium dioxide high energy tape, which is considerably more abrasive than the normal ferric-oxide tape. Replacement heads form a considerable part of the running costs of video recorders.

Modulation systems

A further major problem had to be solved before a practical system could be constructed. This was the actual form of the recorded signals. Doubling of any frequency causes the output to rise by 6 dB. At low frequencies, therefore, the signal obtained from tape is small and noise becomes the controlling factor. Tape can be satisfactorily used over ten octaves, which produces a ratio of 60 dB output difference between the highest and lowest recorded signals, above which it is difficult to separate the low frequencies from the noise of the system. A video signal, however, occupies approximately 18 octaves, assuming the lowest frequency is 25 Hz and the highest 5 MHz, which means that a direct recording system is impossible and a method must be found to reduce the octave range to be recorded.

The solution is to modulate the video signal onto a carrier and due to inherent safeguards against noise, the most suitable form is frequency modulation. If a 6 MHz carrier is modulated with 5 MHz the upper and lower sidebands will range from 1 MHz to 11 MHz. The octave range is now reduced to 4 and easily handled. However, although this produced a practical solution a new set of problems have been created.

F.M. signal

To achieve a frequency modulated signal the carrier frequency must be varied between certain limits. This is known as the deviation of the system and it depends upon the amplitude of the modulating signal (Figure 4.7). The rate at which the carrier

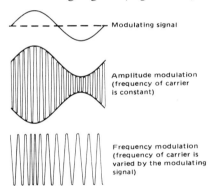

Modulating signal

Amplitude modulation
(frequency of carrier
is constant)

Frequency modulation
(frequency of carrier is
varied by the modulating
signal)

Figure 4.7. Comparison of AM and FM signals

frequency is varied is dependent upon the frequency of the modulating signal. The modulated carrier contains sidebands which are equal to plus and minus the modulating frequency, second order sidebands which are ± 2 times the modulating frequency ($\pm 2f$) and so on for higher orders. ($\pm 3f$, $\pm 4f$ etc.). The importance of the individual sidebands is determined by the power in the particular sideband. Normally, a frequency modulated signal requires a much greater bandwidth to transmit the same information as an amplitude modulated signal, but with the advantage that the amplitude is constant and can be limited. As most interference signals are predominantly amplitude modulated, these can be minimised by limiter circuits in the processing system.

An amplitude modulated signal carries its information in a bandwidth which is twice the modulating frequency (double sideband working). An f.m. modulated system can also carry all its essential information in the same bandwidth if the 'modulating index' is less than 0.5.

$$\text{Modulating index} = \frac{\text{Deviation of frequency from carrier frequency, } f_c}{\text{Modulating frequency, } f_m}$$

$$= \frac{\triangle f_c}{f_m}$$

Negative frequencies and folded sidebands

The bandwidth of the f.m. signal is infinite, although the power in the sidebands is dependent upon the factors previously mentioned. In a broadcast f.m. system the carrier is of such a high frequency compared to the modulating frequencies that by the time the lower sidebands reach zero frequency their power is negligible. However, in a VTR system the carrier frequency that can be used is restricted by the practical design of the head and the tape characteristics and is relatively low. Consequently, the power in the lower sideband, which can reach zero frequency, can be the limiting factor in the recorder's performance. The problem arises because the sidebands do not cease to exist when zero frequency is reached – instead they are folded back into the signal system and appear as interfering signals (Figure 4.8). In colour recording especially this is a problem as the video signal contains a considerable amount of energy in the higher modulating frequencies due to the presence of the colour subcarrier. Obviously, the higher we can make the carrier frequency, the higher will be the order of sideband which causes the interference and the lower will be its power.

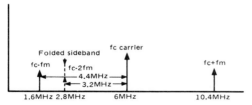

Figure 4.8. With a carrier of 6 MHz and a colour subcarrier of 4.4 MHz modulating the signal, an interfering signal appears 3.2 MHz from the carrier due to the folded sideband. As the carrier frequency is increased, the interfering signal moves away from the carrier at twice the rate (colour subcarrier frequency to first decimal place only in order to simplify explanation)

Second harmonic sidebands

If second harmonics are produced they will become modulated
and produce sidebands (Figure 4.9). The lower order sidebands
will produce signals within the required frequency spectrum which
will ultimately be filtered and demodulated as interference in the
video signal, appearing as moiré patterns on the picture. The level
of interference will depend upon the amount of second harmonic
carrier generated by the distorting network. It is essential, therefore, that the design of modulators and associated circuitry does
not produce second harmonics.

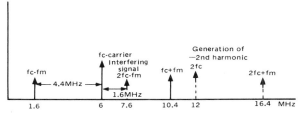

*Figure 4.9. Lower sideband of the second harmonic produces an interfering signal
1.6 MHz from carrier with 6 MHz carrier frequency and 4.4 MHz modulating signal*

In a similar manner, lower sidebands of the carrier's third
harmonic are also created from limiting the carrier frequency
followed by filtering.

Pre-emphasis

In order to improve the signal-to-noise ratio in an f.m. system, it is
normal to boost the high frequency signal with a pre-emphasis
network and to use an equal amount of de-emphasis on replay.
Normally the higher frequencies contain only a small portion of
the total energy, but are a large part of the bandwidth. However,
with a colour signal the subcarrier is amongst the higher frequencies (4.43 or 3.58 MHz) and contains a large amount of energy,

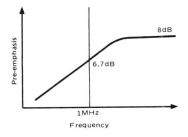

*Figure 4.10. Pre-emphasis response on a
broadcast VTR*

limiting the pre-emphasis that can be used. In addition, the eye is also most sensitive to frequencies around 1 MHz and pre-emphasis should be given to the most visible parts of the frequency range (Figure 4.10). Pre-emphasis is given to the video signal, in preference to the r.f. signal, due to the difficulties of designing r.f. pre- and de-emphasis networks and because it is easier to specify accurately the video networks.

Choice of carrier frequency

As the carrier frequency is raised both interfering signals move away from the carrier at twice the rate at which the carrier frequency is raised. By using a higher frequency carrier a greater deviation can be used before interfering signals become objectionable, but this results in a lower recovery efficiency of the signal from the tape. A low deviation creates a poor signal-to-noise ratio, although too high a deviation of the low frequencies can cause differential gain and differential phase problems.

Whether a recorder can operate with high carrier frequencies depends on the quality of the recorder. Modern broadcast recorders tend to operate with frequencies known as 'high band' (Table 4.1), as opposed to 'low band', which was the standard in the first recorders. The latest broadcast recorders have the facility to operate in an even higher range known as 'super high band'. In general, the lower the price of the recorder the lower the carrier frequency, thus improving the efficiency of the recovery of r.f. signals from the tape. Further modification is made to the signal by restricting the bandwidth of the video signal, which, of course, reduces the interfering sidebands. It does, however, also make recording of a composite colour video signal impossible, even if the mechanical stability of the recorder allowed it, and consequently the colour video signal is modified before recording on less costly VTRs.

Design of a practical VTR

The preceding sections have covered the general principles which allow a video signal to be recorded and replayed. The characeristics which determine the usability of a video recorder for any specific purpose are (1) the frequency response of the signal system, (2) the degree of timebase stability and (3) the operational flexibility of the complete recorder (electronic editing, multiple speeds, animation, switchable standards, etc.). As each of these three parameters increase so does the cost and versatility of the machine.

Table 4.1. Television recording frequency standards (Quad)

Modulated frequencies	525/30 *Low band mono*	525/30 *Low band colour*	*Highband mono colour*	625/25 *Low band*	625/25 *High band*	405/25 *Low band*	625/50 *Super Hi-band*
Tip of sync (nominal), MHz	4.28	5.5	7.06	5.0	7.16	4.28	11.00
Carrier frequency (blanking), MHz	5.0	5.79	7.9	5.54	7.8	5.0	11.35
Peak white, MHz	6.8	6.5	10.0	6.8	9.3	6.8	12.2 Pilot 2.65

Large bandwidths require high writing speeds and suitable f.m. carriers. Differential gain and phase have to be minimised and heads and tapes must be efficient at the higher carrier frequencies. Timebase stability for broadcast colour recording requires several correctors acting on different errors and a final stability under 5 ns can be achieved.

Transverse scanning

For this format four heads are mounted 90° apart on the edge of a head wheel and rotated transversely across the width of a 5 cm (2 in) tape.

The head drum rotates at 240 or 250 rev/s (depending upon whether it is a 60 Hz or a 50 Hz picture rate) and simultaneously the tape travels longitudinally at 38 cm/s (15 in/s) (it can be reduced to 19 cm/s (7½ in/s) with different heads and reduced performance). The tape is held in a vacuum guide and tip penetration is adjusted by moving the guide closer to or further from the head. The specification for the tape format is critical to ensure interchangeability between machines and is laid down by the broadcast standards committees (Figure 4.11). Between each video track is a

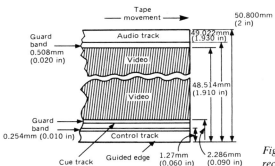

Figure 4.11. Quadruplex recording format

guard band to prevent crosstalk between tracks. The audio is recorded along the top edge with a conventional static audio head, which at 38 cm/s (15 in/s) will record good quality sound.

Along the bottom of the tape a separate control track is recorded. This is used for synchronising the position and speed of the heads and tape motion in record and replay modes. The recorded pulses are derived in the record mode from a tachometer generator attached to the head drum. This track is again recorded by a conventional static head. An edit pulse is also added to the control track signal which identifies the physical position on the tape of the vertical synchronising pulses initiating the television picture. On the original recorders this pulse was at picture rate (25 Hz or 30 Hz) but, because the basic information sequence in the PAL 625-line colour standard repeats itself over four television fields, this pulse is now recorded at 12.5 Hz in order to identify an exact field in the PAL waveform (Figure 1.14).

A further conventional track, known as the cue track, is laid down and on this editing time codes or verbal instructions can be recorded.

Because the video heads lay down tracks which are almost perpendicular to tape travel, conventional wow and flutter induced into the video signal is greatly reduced. However, much of the electronics of a professional recorder is to correct for the various timing errors inherent with the system. The advantage of the transverse system is the very high writing speeds achieved with reasonably good timebase stability, allowing wideband signals to be recorded and a system to be designed with the maximum operational flexibility.

The main disadvantages are caused by the segmenting of the video images into discrete portions (which results in some geometric distortion of the picture). The system requires switching between four heads which must be matched and considerable equalising problems must be overcome to ensure that the picture is not composed of differing bands of signals of varying quality.

Helical scan recording

Around 1960 the first VTRs for other than professional broadcasting were marketed. Timebase stability and writing speeds were of secondary importance to price, and the format universally adopted was 'helical scan'. With this system the tape is wrapped around the head drum in one of several possible ways (Figure 4.1). Again, the tape is transported longitudinally from reel to reel and as it passes the head drum a rotating head lays down one complete field at an angle dependent upon the diameter of the drum and the velocity of the tape. One or more heads are used and compatibility between machines is only possible with machines having exactly the same specification. The audio and control tracks are recorded by static heads in the same way as in an audio recorder, although the control track signal is generally not as complex as in the transverse recorder (Figure 4.12).

The mechanical wow and flutter is considerably higher than the transverse method since the track is at a smaller angle to the edges of the tape. Electronics to correct timebase stability are omitted on helical scan machines due to cost, but 'timebase correctors' (TBC) can be added (generally at several times the cost of the VTR) to stabilise the picture on replay. If the machines are played directly into a receiver it is essential that the time constant of the line oscillator is short enough to prevent jitter. Very often a special input position is provided which automatically switches to the correct time constant.

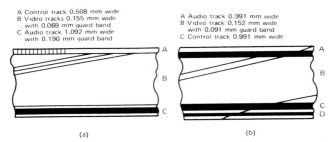

A Control track 0.508 mm wide
B Video tracks 0.155 mm wide
with 0.069 mm guard band
C Audio track 1.092 mm wide
with 0.190 mm guard band

A Audio track 0.991 mm wide
B Video track 0.152 mm wide
with 0.091 mm guard band
C Control track 0.991 mm wide

(a)   (b)

Figure 4.12. Helical scan recording formats: (a) typical; (b) IVC

Tape tension is critical if the heads in replay are to follow the recorded tracks correctly. In any design of machine the head must always leave the tape if only for a short time, during which, if the machine has only a single head, there is a complete loss of video information. This period is generally positioned at the bottom of the picture so that the vertical scan on the TV can be extended, eliminating from the viewer the band of noise caused by loss of signal. With two or more headed machines it can be arranged that at some period of time both heads record the same signal simultaneously and an instantaneous switch can be made.

Because a complete frame is laid down on a single track without segmentation it is possible with helical scan recorders to achieve 'stop motion' by stopping the tape. However, because the track position takes into account the tape movement the head will cross the guard band and play across two tracks. The guard band is seen as a band of noise on the picture. The problem has been partially eliminated in the latest cassette recorders as described later (this does not apply to helical scan machines using segmented formats).

The new generation of cassette recorders has evolved from early reel-to-reel recorders, the usefulness of which was often limited, due to the damage resulting from incorrect handling of the tape when threading and storing the tape. By placing the tape in a case to protect it and by making the VTR capable of automatically threading the tape, the recorder was able to operate in harsher environments and became capable of being used more generally by non-technical people.

The format of the long play VTRs recently introduced (VHS, Betamax, Grundig SVR, Philips 1700) has increased the packing density on the tape by omitting the guard band between the tracks. This can obviously create problems due to crosstalk and this will be covered in detail later.

As writing speed decreases the ability to record large bandwidths sufficiently to cover the full 5 MHz spectrum of the video signal diminishes. Although the luminance signal can be reduced, with a resulting loss of definition, it becomes necessary to separate the chrominance signal modulated on the subcarrier in the top part of the spectrum (4.43 MHz or 3.58 MHz depending upon number of lines) and reprocess this in a different part of the frequency spectrum.

Layout of the video recorder

A block diagram of a typical quadruplex recorder is shown in Figure 4.12. The design of a high quality machine must produce flat amplitude response, linear phase characteristic, minimum noise and spurious components, and extremely good timebase stability.

Magnetic shielding is extensively used as stray fields will modify the record characteristics and cause second harmonics to be generated. The modulator is balanced throughout in order to cancel out even harmonics and a linearity of better than 1% is required in order to avoid differential gain problems. The video heads are inductive and, as such, have a response which falls by 6 dB/octave. The record equalisers must, therefore, modify the drive from the modulator so that the group delay and amplitude versus frequency response of the current in the record head exactly matches the response of the voltage from the modulator to compensate.

Replay system

The typical video replay system is shown in Figure 4.13. In order to obtain a good signal to noise and the minimum number of dropouts very close contact must be kept between tape and heads. This is automatically adjusted by the guide servo. Head switching is electronically controlled by 250 Hz and 500 Hz switching signals which switch pairs of heads alternately. The switching is timed to occur on the front porch so that the following sync is related to the

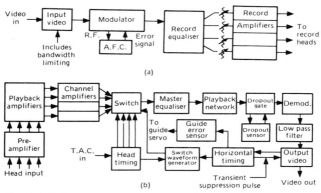

(a)

(b)

Transient
suppression pulse   Video out

Figure 4.13. Typical quadruplex (a) record system and (b) playback system

video signal and the waveform correctors therefore apply the right
amount of correction. The master equalisers following the switches ensure that the signal has a completely flat response and a
playback network is inserted to eliminate the upper sideband to
improve the noise figure for the system. The signal is then limited
and demodulated and care is taken in the design to obtain
cancellation of distortion and the best linearity. The output is
passed through a low pass filter and finally de-emphasised, un-
balanced and amplified to produce the final video output.

Dropout compensators

A normal undamaged video tape usually becomes unusable when
the dropout count becomes objectionable. Dropouts are invariably caused by dust, dirt or missing oxide. The degree of severity
of any dropout is subjective and invariably depends on the picture
content, appearing worst when highly saturated colours are replayed. A partial solution is the one line delay (Figure 4.14). In this

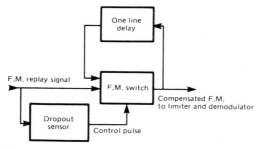

Figure 4.14. One-line delay drop-out compensator

system the FM signal is sampled to ensure that it does not fall below a predetermined level. This controls an FM switch fed with both the direct FM signal and the output from a one line delay, which is obviously the signal from the previous line. If the FM decreases the FM switch operates and inserts the portion of the waveform which is in the delay line until the input FM signal level is restored. As the content of the picture varies only minimally between two lines, the signal can be inserted without distraction and considerably improves the picture. In colour recording the problem is compounded and the inserted signal must have the correct colour phase, otherwise the colour will be wrong.

Servo system

The servo systems components form a considerable part of any recorder and control the capstan and drum motor, although in cheaper helical scan recorders capstan control is not used. In broadcasting the principal function is to maintain the synchronisation of the replayed signal with other video sources sufficiently to allow switching between them without interruption of the picture.

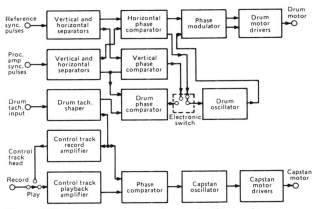

Figure 4.15. Basic servo system of a quadruplex machine

This is accomplished by locking the reproduced picture to the same sync reference to which the other sources are locked and holding the errors in the reproduced picture to very narrow limits (Figure 4.15).

In record mode the recorder is locked to the incoming video signal and a direct relationship is maintained between video scanning by the heads and the longitudinal speed of the tape. This must be exactly reproduced in replay and to obtain this the control track is added in record mode. On replay the recovered pulses from the control track are initially compared with a reference derived from the station vertical synchronising pulses and the resulting error is used to position the tape longitudinally by use of the capstan motor. By using the output from the head drum

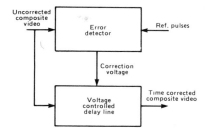

Figure 4.16. Waveform correction made by comparing reproduced and station line sync (Ampex-Amtec)

tachometer, the head drum is simultaneously synchronised to the vertical signal. Once the recorded video begins to be reproduced, the recovered vertical syncs are compared in phase and the output of the comparator drives the head drum to achieve final frame synchronisation. When vertical synchronisation is achieved the sequence is continued until the recovered horizontal pulses and station horizontal pulses are synchronised. Final capstan control is obtained by comparison of the control track and drum motor tachometer. This type of servo will correct to within ±0.1 ms, which is insufficient for colour recording. Further correction is required and variable voltage controlled delay lines are used where comparison is made between the timing of the line pulses from the reference generator and the reproduced line pulses

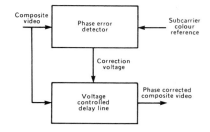

Figure 4.17. Colour correction, comparing reproduced burst and reference subcarrier (Ampex-Colortec)

(Figure 4.16). The delay is continuously varied to remove the timing errors. In the second corrector comparison is made between the subcarrier of the reference generator and the reproduced subcarrier (Figure 4.17). With both correctors the time base variations can be under 5 ns.

In later broadcast machines (AVR1 onwards) (Figure 4.18) digital techniques are used, but the principles are the same. The

Figure 4.18. Ampex AVR1 broadcast quad machine

description given is only one example of the possibilities and is given solely to show the principles of servo control.

In helical scan recorders, the capstan is often driven directly from the mains frequency and no relationship exists between the head drum and the capstan motor. In studio work these machines have limited applications, especially where editing is required.

Further correction is required in professional broadcasting machines, due to velocity errors. These errors occur between the

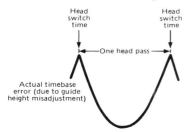

Figure 4.19. Parabolic waveform caused by velocity error

pulses measured in the variable voltage delay line correctors and are caused by incorrect guide height, incorrect video head tip projection or dynamic unbalance of the video head (Figure 4.19). These errors show themselves as hue or saturation errors throughout the line. Each rotation of the head, in a broadcast quad machine, covers 64 lines and the velocity error for each line is stored in a capacitor memory in the correction equipment. From the measured errors a correction ramp is produced in conjunction with the delay line correctors and the appropriate correction waveform is added to each line.

Helical scan system layout

The simplified block diagram of a helical scan system is shown in Figure 4.20. The special circuitry to reprocess the colour signal is not shown, as this will be examined later. The same engineering

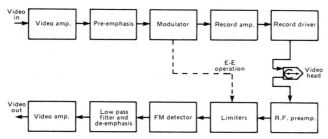

Figure 4.20. Typical record/play chain in helical VTRs

requirements are needed in this type of recorder as in a quadruplex machine, but obviously cost determines the degree of sophistication. Economies can be made by restricting the bandwidth recorded, which directly affects the writing speed, video filtering, spectrum noise and the generated distorting signals. However, with the same attention to the electronics as in quadruplex and timebase correction applied, the helical scan recorder can be made superior to the quadruplex machine used today. The designs for the next generaton of broadcasting machines will concentrate on this standard.

Dolby noise reduction system

As the VTR improved in video performance it has been necessary to raise the quality of the audio side, leading to some manufacturers incorporating the Dolby A noise reduction system into the profesional VTR and the Dolby B system into domestic video recorders. The systems are widely used throughout the audio recording industry to reduce background noise. The quality of the audio track on both quadruplex and helical machines is inferior to professional audio recorders, due to compromises which have to be made with the video. Consequently the audio suffers with a narrow track width, thin oxide coating, orientation of the oxide particles optimised for transverse video recording and spurious signals due to the control and video tracks.

Dolby B was developed for non-professional applications and although simpler and less expensive its principle of operation is the same as Dolby A.

Audio recorded on a tape varies both in loudness and pitch. Noise and hiss from the tape, however, tend to be constant and determines the lowest level of sound which can be recorded before the signal-to-noise ratio becomes unsatisfactory for high quality reproduction. The Dolby system overcomes the problem by increasing the volume of the lowest level sound be be recorded on the tape and reducing this to the original level on replay. In the process, however, the noise signal is also reduced in the areas of minimum sound so that a higher signal-to-noise ratio results.

Dolby A circuitry consists of a differential network which splits the sound into four frequency bands, each of which is limited and added in the record processor to the original signal. In the playback mode the same circuit is used but the output of the differential network is subtracted to produce the original audio specrum (Figure 4.21). The frequency bands used are band 1, 80 Hz low pass; band 2, 80 Hz to 3 kHz; band 3, 3 kHz high pass; and band 4, 9 kHz high pass. System B uses from about 500 Hz to the upper limit of audibility for economy.

Conclusion

The performance of a VTR needs minute attention to every engineering detail. It has evolved over the last 25 years to become the most sophisticated equipment used in broadcasting, but it also retains a reputation for reliability.

It was said by one of the early pioneers that once the scanning system and head switching has been conceived the rest was only competent engineering. When one looks at a broadcast recorder today and realises the precision that goes into the domestic recorder at such a low production cost, we must conclude that we have some of the most competent engineers in industry working in the VTR field.

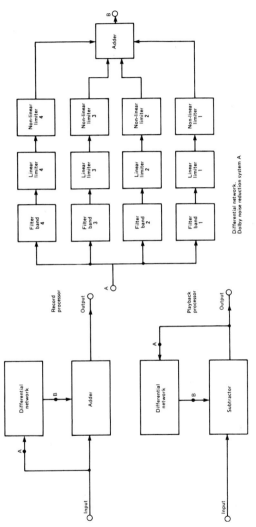

Figure 4.21. Basic block diagram of Dolby noise reduction system. The differential network is the same for both recording and playback; the filters and compressors work under identical conditions, both statically and dynamically, in the two modes

Professional helical scan recorders

Although the quadruplex 2 inch format has been standardised for the broadcasting industry there have been several attempts to produce a broadcast quality helical scan recorder to take advantage of its size, simple design, cost and to overcome segmentation of the picture waveform.

Quadruplex 2 and the IVC 9000 are examples of new designs and formats (Figure 4.22). The results were good but since they

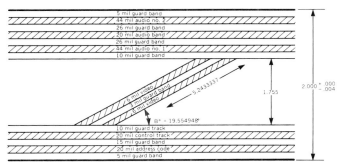

Figure 4.22. Two-inch IVC9000 recording format – designed to provide a broadcast quality helical scan recorder before the introduction of the one-inch B and C formats

still used 2 inch tape there was insufficient progress to convince the broadcaster that any of the new formats should be adopted.

It was not until 1970 that the EBU produced a first specification for a 1 inch professional recorder. The 1 inch previously, such as the Ampex 7900 and the IVC 900, could not match the quality of a 2 inch quadruplex machine.

Philips with Bosch attempted to design a recorder to the EBU specification for 1 inch tape and using a single head field scanner to produce a non-segmented picture. The machine was known as the

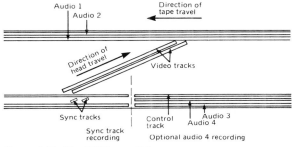

Figure 4.23. The EBU type C format

BCR but due to instability it was abandoned in favour of a two-headed segmented machine known as the BCN, first shown in 1975.

In 1976 both Sony and Ampex modified their earlier non-segmented formats with the result that three different systems were competing for recognition. The problem was simplified in 1977 when the SMPTE formed two working groups to try and produce specifications for two formats, the first for segmented machines, known as 'Format B', and the second for non-segmented machines, known as 'Format C'.

Towards the end of 1978 the EBU proposed a format for non-segmented machines and the new Sony and Ampex 1 inch machines became compatible when the format (Figure 4.23) was adopted.

This then left Bosch with BCN equipment using format B and Sony and Ampex with format C equipment marketing BVH and VPR ranges respectively (Figure 4.24). As these machines have the same recording bandwidths as quadruplex machines, both formats allow recording of the composite colour signal.

Design considerations

There is obviously an advantage in producing a single frame of picture by one head from a single track. This eliminates the problems associated with head switching and banding within the picture, simplifies editing and allows such effects as slow motion and stop motion.

However, the penalty for such a format is the long track at a small angle and the need to wrap the tape around the relatively large scanner. The speed of the scanner is then restricted to the field frequency which, for European systems, is 50 Hz, 17% slower than for 60 Hz systems, thus causing a reduction in writing speed compared to that for USA. A long track inevitably leads to instability which must be corrected. The tension of the tape around the input and exit guides and scanner increases enormously with an omega wrap and a large scanner, and these factors can seriously affect compatibility between machines.

In the Sony C format the track is 400 mm (16 inches) long and is wrapped over an angle of 343°. Two heads are used for recording the video. The first head records all the active picture and the second 'sync' head records the blanking period when the main video head is not in contact with the tape. In PAL and SECAM this occurs in lines 1–15 and 313–328. However, four additional heads are used on the head drum (Figure 4.25), two for confidence

Figure 4.24. The BVH-1100PS type C format Videocorder from Sony broadcast, which features confidence video replay, built-in electronic editing and dynamic tracking for broadcast quality slow and stop motion replay

replay of both picture and sync information and the fifth and sixth are flying erase heads for precise erasure of picture and syncs when editing (see Chapter 6).

Three audio tracks are part of the format but recording of the syncs is optional and a fourth sound track, if required, can be provided in the space. The syncs are then reconstituted in the waveform processing equipment.

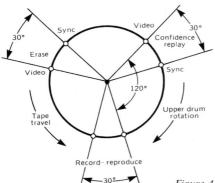

Figure 4.25. BVH-1100PS head configuration

The BCN type B format reduces mechanical and compatibility problems by reducing the size of the scanner and the degree of wrap of the tape around the scanner. The drum diameter is 500 mm producing a track length of 80 mm at an angle of 14°. The wrap angle is 190°. The penalty is a segmented picture which is possibly prone to banding, difficult monitoring and slow and stop motion is only possible with a field store (Figure 4.26).

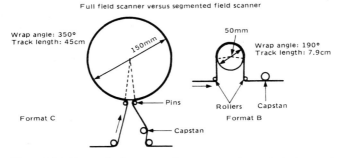

Figure 4.26. Format B allows a smaller scanner to be used which provides better tape handling characteristics

The design makes it easier to ensure compatibility under different ambient conditions as the track is shorter, the scanner has less mass and should react quicker to servo changes and be less affected by mechanical shock. The smaller contact area between the scanner and the tape also means that tape tension is far lower. Rollers can be used instead of pins on the tape guides for entry and exit points to the head drum and this considerably reduces the friction on the tape.

The video writing speed can also be adapted to different requirements as the track is no longer governed by the TV frame speed.

Recorder facilities

The obvious advantage of full frame single track recording (Format C) is the possibility of stop and slow motion directly from the tape. In the BCN format a field store is used to provide this facility. Although far more expensive, one field store can be shared between several machines and used as required. The advantage of such a system is that no time restriction is placed on a still frame when taken from the store but when taken directly from tape a time limit must be imposed otherwise the tape will be physically damaged. Normally such playbacks from tape are performed with reduced tape tension which can affect the picture, especially in the higher frequencies where the colour is recorded.

However, the principal operational advantage of a non-segmented 'C' format is that editing can be performed quickly and accurately. Because a complete picture is obtained with each revolution of the head drum, still frame and pictures with fast forward and reverse make positioning of an edit far simpler. Stable colour pictures are possible with up to ten times normal play speeds and monochrome pictures are viewable with up to 50 times the normal speed.

The BCN B format system provides editing facilities which interface with computer control systems and other SMPTE controlled systems.

Dynamic tracking

A feature of both the Ampex and Sony machines is an additional system to provide accurate tracking at various tape speeds. At tape speeds other than normal, the playback head can be physically moved under the accurate control of a servo system to exactly follow the video track whose angle, in relation to the head, changes with varying tape motion. In the Ampex system this is known as AST (automatic scan tracking). The head movement is produced by a piezo-electric effect and variations in the off-tape signal produce the servo signals to move the head.

Conclusion

Although limited to two formats at present (with strong commercial competition between Ampex and Sony for C format machines) the lack of a single standard perhaps restricts the acceptance of such equipment at present as the alternative to quadruplex. However, several other companies have indicated that they will produce format C machines in the future.

Although there are theoretical advantages to both formats the quality of engineering leaves little to choose between the final results. All the recorders should be regarded as a system where editing, effects and timebase correction are an integral part if full advantage is to be taken of the particular formats.

Obviously such machines or similar ones will eventually replace quads due to size, lack of compressed air requirements, cost, facilities and quality.

Video cassette recorders

Although the helical scan video recorder made its introduction in the 1960s, the multiplicity of standards, questionable reliability and the difficulty of handling tape by relatively unskilled people prevented any manufacturer dominating the industry and creating a standard.

The fortunes of the manufacturers rose and fell as each new model came onto the market. While monochrome was the standard Ampex had success in education and industry with their 7000 series but with the introduction of colour IVC, for a period, had a lead in the semi-professional field. Philips, Sony and other manufacturers also periodically gained successes. However, all this activity had no effect on the domestic consumer.

It was not until the 1970s that Philips and Sony started to set a new standard and open up new markets with the introduction of the video cassette recorder.

Philips aimed at both education and the domestic market but Sony concentrated on the semi-professional field. The result was a much cheaper recorder from Philips but with problems due to it being used in unsuitable environments, while the Sony U-matic began, for the first time, to set a standard for the semi-professional market. With improvements in later years but with the basic format, the U-matic series, now licensed to other manufacturers, has broken into professional broadcasting for ENG (Electronic News Gathering) equipment.

Philips, however, have continued to redesign, producing a series of recorders capable of different playing times but incompatible with each other.

As the domestic market seemed penetrable, a new range of recorders capable of extended playing time of 3 hours or more became available from Philips, Grundig, Sony and JVC.

There seems little doubt that although Philips have had some success the real battle at present is between the Sony Betamax system and the JVC VHS system. In different parts of the world the relative successes have been different. In Europe, however, the VHS system appears to have the lead.

The manufacturers, each trying to design equipment for the same market at a similar price, obviously had the same problems to overcome and it is not surprising, therefore, that the solutions should be similar. We will, therefore, concentrate on the U-matic and VHS as examples of this type of equipment.

The problems

There is no inherent problem in putting video tape into cassettes and this avoids the great enemies of video tape – dirt and unskilled handling. However, once tape is in the cassette the recorder must be equipped with an automatic loading mechanism and examples of these are shown in Figure 4.27. The cassette itself is fairly complex and has to be made with precision if new problems are not to be introduced. The requirement, therefore, of the automatic threading mechanism for the cassette obviously increases the cost of manufacture of the machine and tape over reel-to-reel machines. A reduction in cost can only be achieved by large sales which were never obtained for previous machines. Now over a million video recorders are being produced in Japan alone every year.

The colour carrier in the PAL system is at 4.43 MHz and on low bandwidth recorders this cannot be recorded directly. The stability of the machines is also insufficient for the colour carrier to be

Sony U-matic

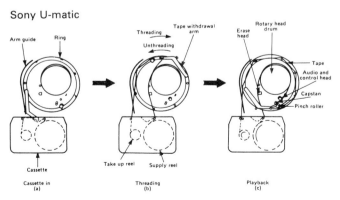

Figure 4.27. Automatic tape threading systems

Philips VCC

Philips

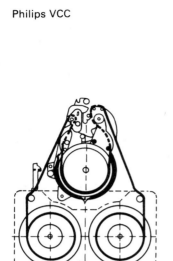

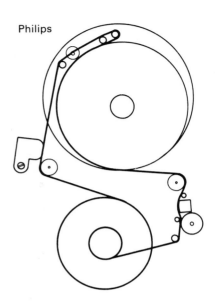

VHS

Betamax U-matic

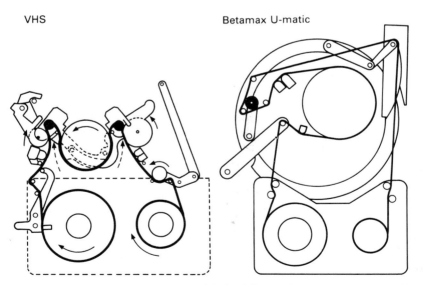

The tape from the cassette passes around the head drum and stationary audio, control tracks and erase heads and then re-enters the cassette

recorded and replayed without a method of timebase correction to produce an accurate colour subcarrier on the output.

As the demand for long-play in domestic machines has been solved without an increase in the bulk of tape used, the guard band between tracks has disappeared. This has been a major advance in making a domestic machine.

The U-matic machine

It is interesting to look at the specification of the U-matic which has made it such a success.

Playing time with standard tape	1 hour
Tape speed	3¾ in/s (9.53 cm/s)
Video recording system	Rotary two-headed helical scan
Luminance	FM recording
Colour signal	Converted subcarrier direct recording
Playback on PAL machines	CCIR PAL and modified NTSC colour signal
Horizontal resolution	Monochrome: more than 300 lines
	Colour: more than 240 lines
Signal to noise	Better than 40 dB
Audio	Two tracks
Frequency response	50 Hz–12 kHz
Signal to noise	Better than 42 dB
Tape used in 1 hour	342 metres 1.9 cm wide (¾ inch)

The tape format is shown in Figure 4.29.

Apart from its acceptable specification for the semi-professional market its reliability and ease of operation opened new markets to video tape recording. Large companies such as Ford and IBM began to use the system for dealer organisation and company communication. Television programmes were recorded and distributed to ships at sea, and in America, Europe and Japan the video duplicating companies came into existence to make many copies of films and TV programmes.

Video processing

Although both the early Philips VCR and the U-matic systems record and replay relatively low bandwidths the subjective results

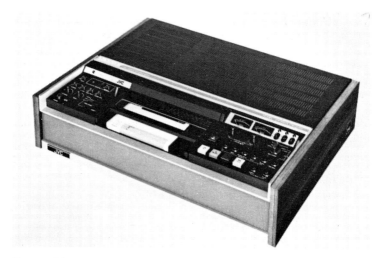

Figure 4.28. JVC CR-8300E U-matic recorder

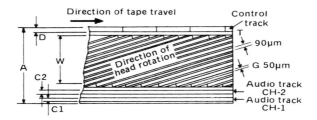

	Tape speed	9.53 cm/s
(A)	Tape width	19.00 mm
(W)	Video tracks	14.8 mm
(T)	Width of video track	0.090 mm
(G)	Width of guard band	0.050 mm
(D)	Control track	0.6 mm
(C_1)	Audio track CH-1	0.8 mm
(C_2)	Audio track CH-2	0.8 mm

Figure 4.29. U-matic VCR video tape pattern

are very acceptable for the market in which they are used. Less than 2 MHz, including 500 kHz of chrominance, are used and this should be compared with the 5.5 MHz required in a broadcast TV system. Both cassette systems separate the luminance and the chrominance from the television signal before recording. The luminance is used to frequency modulate an RF carrier and the chrominance signal is used to separately modulate a lower frequency carrier which then amplitude modulates the FM signal (Figure 4.30).

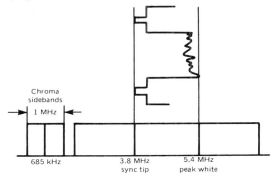

Figure 4.30. U-matic frequency range of signal. The chrominance signal modulates a 685 kHz carrier which amplitude modulates the FM signal carrying the luminance

In replay the signals are recovered from tape and separated. The signals have timebase variations due to the wow and flutter inherent in the system and, in order to drive a colour monitor with the replay signal, the chrominance must be processed to produce an accurate 4.43 MHz modulated chrominance signal. The luminance signal, however, is not corrected and further distortion is inherent in such systems due to any timing errors which may occur between the luminance and chrominance signals.

Colour signal processing

The principle of colour recovery systems used in cassette recorders is similar and Figure 4.31 shows the method used in the Sony U-matic.

A subcarrier of 685 kHz is used for recording PAL signals and 688 kHz is used for NTSC. In record mode this carrier is modulated by a chrominance bandwidth of 500 kHz which in turn then amplitude modulates the FM signal.

In playback the PAL chrominance signals centred on 685 kHz are subject to frequency and phase errors introduced by the timebase variations in the video recorder. In order to eliminate these errors the system beats the 685 kHz against a 5.12 MHz signal which has exactly the same frequency and phase errors. This produces a constant difference frequency of 4.43 MHz, the PAL subcarrier frequency.

In Figure 4.31 the burst from the colour output goes to a phase comparator detector for comparison with the local oscillator. The burst contains the frequency and phase errors and the output of the detector is a d.c. error signal used to drive a 685 kHz voltage controlled variable frequency oscillator. The 685 kHz signal is

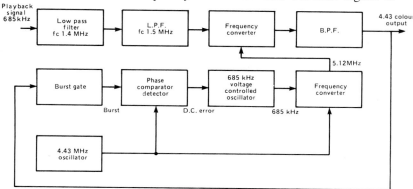

Figure 4.31. Simplified schematic of colour replay system – U-matic

converted to 5.12 MHz and, now subject to the same frequency and phase errors as the incoming chrominance signals, is used to frequency convert the recorded 685 kHz chrominance signals to a stable 4.43 MHz modulated carrier. This is then matrixed with the luminance to provide a composite PAL encoded signal for the monitor.

When the first recorders were delivered in Europe the permissible mains frequency variation was extremely critical if colour lock was to be maintained. A tolerance of only ¼ Hz was permissible after which it was not possible to maintain colour. Subsequent modifications have allowed the tolerance to stretch to ±1 Hz before losing colour lock. However, as a line period in replay alters with mains frequency it is only at the nominal frequency that the luminance to chrominance delay is at a minimum when displayed on a PAL receiver. In order that complete compatibility is achieved it is essential that the mains frequency while recording and replaying is as close to the nominal frequency as possible.

The Sony U-matic is marketed as a dual standard (NTSC and PAL) player. However, it should be realised that this feature is only possible if the display monitor is capable of replaying the non-standard NTSC signal that is produced (Sony and Barco produce monitors). This is because the European player provides a colour subcarrier of 4.43 MHz irrespective of whether the signal is NTSC or PAL. A normal NTSC monitor will not work as it requires a conventional NTSC signal with a 3.58 MHz colour subcarrier.

Servo systems

The servo systems used are relatively unsophisticated. The tape speed is fixed and is controlled by a synchronous motor. The head-drum rotation is controlled by a braking-type servo where the current is controlled to release or apply the brake.

When playback in the U-matic system is selected and the track for field 1 of the prerecorded tape is in position for playback on the head-drum assembly, a control track pulse is read at the control track head. This is compared in time with the pulse generated by the head-drum tachometer. If the head-drum speed is too high the head pulse is too early and the circuitry comparing the two pulses increases the braking current. If the pulse is too late the braking current is reduced.

Later models, as a requirement for editing, also have capstan servos in addition to head-drum servos.

Media

Advantage has been taken when designing these low cost recorders of the advances made in the development of high energy video tape having a coercivity of approximately 40 000–48 000 A/m (500–600 oersteds)compared to 24 000 A/m (300 oersteds) for a conventional gamma ferric oxide tape. This gives greater output and improved signal-to-noise, provided the tape has been recorded with sufficient drive.

Audio

The audio and control tracks are recorded by conventional static heads and a good frequency response of 50 Hz to 12 kHz is obtainable with a signal-to-noise ratio of better than 42 dB.

The VHS home video tape recorder

The innovations in home video recorders to obtain a long playing time on a small cassette have created some of the most fundamental changes in video recording practice for many years. The quality of picture produced on replay must be almost equal to that of a normal television picture if it is to be acceptable to the public. For mass marketing the majority of the recorders must also be capable of being adapted for NTSC, PAL and SECAM systems. The NTSC system first appeared in 1977 and the European versions in 1978.

VHS design

The fundamental change in the home recorder, adopted also by Sony in the Betamax and Philips in their later recorders (N1700 onwards), is the elimination of the guardband (Figure 4.32).

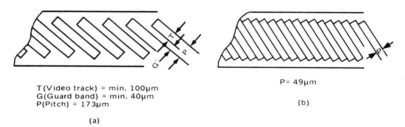

T(Video track) = min. 100µm
G(Guard band) = min. 40µm
P(Pitch) = 173µm

(a)

P= 49µm

(b)

Figure 4.32. (a) Conventional video tape pattern (EIAJ-1 standard); (b) VHS standard video pattern

Normally if there is no guardband then crosstalk is produced from adjacent tracks when tracking errors occur during playback. When guardbands are present in other recording formats noise increases with mistracking as the head loses the signal. To eliminate crosstalk a new head arrangement was produced.

Azimuth recording system

The azimuth, which is the angle that the gap in the head makes to the tape surface, is slanted differently for the two heads, one head +6° and the other −6° from the perpendicular (Figure 4.33). As this effectively increases the gap size, if a head plays the signal from tracks recorded by the other head, crosstalk at high frequencies over 1 MHz is eliminated (see Video Heads). The crosstalk, therefore, of frequency modulated luminance signals in the range 3.8 (sync) to 4.8 MHz (peak white) range is completely eliminated.

However, this can still leave problems at the lower frequencies where the chrominance signals have been recorded after separation from the luminance signal. The chrominance is recorded at a frequency of 627 kHz and the comparative losses in the recorded frequencies when played back by a head whose azimuth is 12° different is shown in Figure 4.34. As crosstalk at these low frequencies cannot be completely eliminated by this method, a further system is adopted known as 'phase-shift colour recording'.

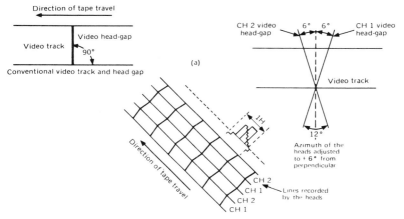

Figure 4.33. VHS azimuth recording system

Phase shift colour recording system

Channel 1 head records the chrominance signal normally but channel 2 chrominance signal is phase delayed 90° every line (1H). The pattern of the adjacent vectors is shown in Figure 4.35.

When CH2 is replayed with the CH2 head it is reproduced with its phase advanced by 90° on every line (i.e. line B1+90°. B2+180°, B3+270°, B4°360°) together with any crosstalk components from CH1 adjacent tracks, which are recorded normally. On replay the phase of the CH2 signal is first returned to its original form which also changes the phase of the crosstalk components. The signal is then added by using a 2−H delay line to the

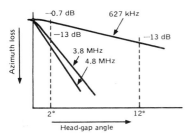

Figure 4.34. Characteristics of the azimuth loss

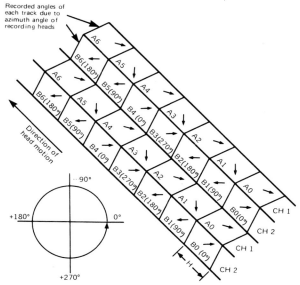

Recorded angles of each track due to azimuth angle of recording heads

Figure 4.35. Arrows indicate the signal phases of the colour signal produced by the VHS phase-shift colour recording system on each line for a PAL signal. Channel 1 chrominance signal is recorded normally. Channel 2 chrominance signal is phase-rotated 90° on every line in the record mode; on replay the phase of Channel 2 is returned to normal but in the process any crosstalk components are also changed in phase. When the signal is added to the previous 1 H signal the crosstalk components will cancel

preceding signal of two lines before. As the required signal components are essentially the same the output signal will be almost doubled. However, because of the phasing difference, the crosstalk components cancel and colour crosstalk is eliminated (Figure 4.36).

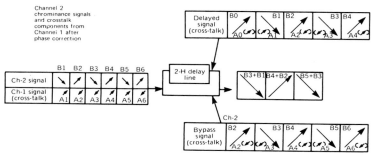

Figure 4.36. JVC phase-shift colour recording system to prevent chrominance crosstalk between tracks

SECAM recording

When recording SECAM the FM colour signals are converted to around 1 MHz by a divide by 4 count down circuit. During playback the original signal is recovered by a quadrupler circuit. There is no problem with crosstalk with this system as the crosstalk decreases by 15dB and, as the interference signal is FM, interference with the required signal is improbable.

VHS tape format

To obtain a small lightweight recorder the rotary head-drum is made smaller. However this also reduces the tape to head velocity, reducing the top frequencies which can be recorded while signal to noise and resolution are also adversely affected. To compensate, JVC developed new head technology and finally reduced the head gap to only 0.3 mm. As the head gap directly controls the top frequencies which can be replayed at any particular writing speed, such a head allows the conventional head drum diameter to be reduced by half.

The tape used for this machine has a coercivity of 48 000 A/m (600 oersted) and the tape format is shown in Figure 4.37.

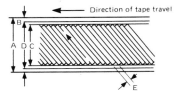

		Tape speed	2.3–2.9 cm/s
A	Tape width		12.65 mm
B	Audio track		1.0 mm
C	Video tracks		10.6 mm
D	Control track		0.75 mm
E	Width of video track		0.049 mm

Figure 4.37. VHS video tape pattern

Pre-emphasis and double limiter

Due to the tape speed of 2.3 to 3.9 cm/s the video track width has been reduced to 49 μm to provide 180 minutes of recording. Reducing the track width reduces the signal-to-noise ratio and to compensate for this the signal is pre-emphasised. A compromise has to be achieved however, between the signal-to-noise improvement with greater pre-emphasis and sharp transients causing overmodulation in the FM system, which causes an increase in the lower sideband amplitude. This generates AM components in demodulation which produce a negative conversion picture and the signal-to-noise ratio is reduced in these areas (Figure 4.38).

If only the centre part of such a signal is passed through the limiter those signals with a low carrier will be attenuated and important sidebands lost, producing a picture with extremely low resolution. To compensate for the low carrier and restore the ratio between the carrier and sidebands a 'double limiter' is provided. This is shown in Figure 4.38. The playback FM containing the low carrier is filtered so that the high frequencies pass through a first limiter but the LF component does not. When the level of the carrier has been restored it is again mixed with the LF component. The signal-to-noise ratio can therefore be improved with considerable pre-emphasis without deterioration of resolution.

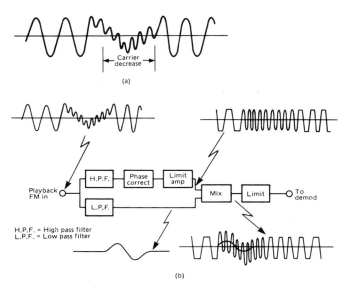

Figure 4.38. (a) Pre-emphasis causes overmodulation in FM system when sharp transients occur in the video. This results in increase in lower sideband and AM components are produced. (b) Double demodulator ensures the carrier is correctly reproduced and sideband components are not lost which would result in extremely low resolution picture

Parallel loading system

Unlike the U-matic, where the tape is pulled around the head when loading, the VHS employs a simple mechanism known as a parallel or 'M' (because of the tape path) loading system. Two loading arms, one for take-up and one for the supply, take the tape from the cassette and place it around the head 180°. This creates a simple mechanism with a loading time of about two seconds.

VHS variable speed

An innovation on some of the later VHS models is variable speed. In record the heads lay down a track whose angle depends upon tape speed and the diameter of the drum. In replay, if the tape speed remains the same the heads will follow the recorded tracks correctly, whereas if the tape speed is varied or stopped the heads no longer follow the individual tracks but cross one or more tracks.

In the U-matic the tape was tilted to offset this error and this solution was possible due to the guardbands and greater mechanical tolerances of the U-matic specification. The narrower tracks and lack of guardbands does not allow this in the VHS recorder; instead the heads have a height which is greater than the track width of 49 μm, since as the height increases so does the track width. In record a track wider than 49 μm is produced but the adjacent track written by the next head will over-write part of the previously written track. In replay, although the heads reproduce signals from adjacent tracks the offset azimuth method of recording eliminates the undesired signal (Figure 4.39).

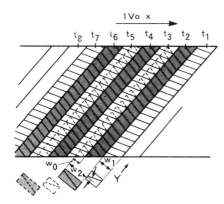

Figure 4.39

In addition head B is made wider than head A. In stop motion the tracking angle alters but sufficient signal is picked up by heads A and B to reproduce the frozen frame. Head B is made larger, as otherwise the head would scan insufficient of the stationary track (Figure 4.40), when the recovered signal would be too weak and only crosstalk would be reproduced.

When slow motion is selected the tape stops and the same procedure as for stop motion is followed. A tracking servo must, therefore, be included which precisely moves the tape to the next pair of tracks (Figure 4.41).

In record a control track is laid down. This is produced from the recorded vertical syncs, and defines the odd and even tracks. In playback this track is compared in phase with the signal from the drum tachometer and the servo ensures that the heads read the correct tracks.

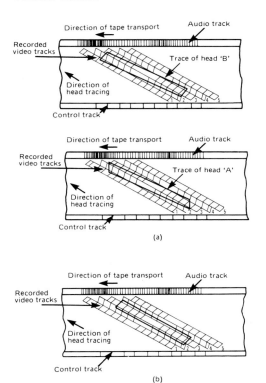

Figure 4.40. (a) Portions of track read when the machine is in stop motion; (b) when the machine returns to normal speed head B scans its own track completely but also reads information from adjacent tracks. The slant azimuth of the heads will cancel out the crosstalk

In stop and slow motion the capstan motor is controlled from a monostable whose time constant determines the length of time the heads read particular tracks. At the end of a timing period the tape is advanced to the next point where a control track pulse is sensed. This operates a flip-flop and stops the tape until the flip-flop is again changed by the monostable.

In fast motion the tape runs at double speed and head A reads track 1 and head B reads track 4 instead of track 2. The greater track angle produced, however, can still be read due to the greater height of head B (Figure 4.41).

In slow and fast modes a crystal controlled oscillator is used to replace the normal control track signal as it no longer relates to the vertical sync frequency.

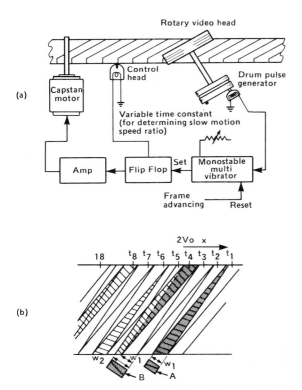

Figure 4.41. (a) Operation of the slow and stop motion stepping servo; (b) tracks read at twice normal speed

In stop and slow motion there is a reduction in the number of lines produced in each frame. This would create vertical instability on a picture monitor if reproduced directly, so to correct this a pulse is inserted near the switching point which compensates the odd or even fields.

Audio compensation

When the recorder is played at twice the normal replay speed the audio pitch will obviously rise. To compensate for this the frequency spectrum is divided by two by the use of memory systems.

A 1024 memory is divided into two 512 stages into which the audio is loaded and read out at a clock rate of 50 kHz. Each stage delays the audio by 10 µs and the outputs are alternately switched through a low pass filter at 20 µs intervals, thus reducing the frequency spectrum by an octave.

Philips VCRs

Philips have, in recent years, produced a range of video recorders including the N1500/1/2 and N1700.

The latest model to be marketed in the 1980s is the VCC (Video Compact Cassette), developed jointly with Grundig, and known as the V2000. The VCC is intended to be a standard for the future and has benefits which can be exploited in later models. The novelty of the new cassette is that it is inverted in a similar way to an audio cassette. The recording is made on only half the tape

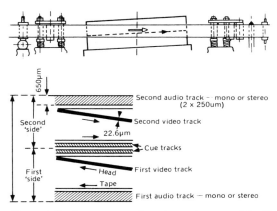

Figure 4.42. Arrangement of tracks on the tape of the Philips VCC system

width of 1.27 cm (½ in) in each direction (Figure 4.42). Slant azimuth recording is used and there are no guard bands. The packing density on such tapes is six times the VCR-LP system and, to achieve this, very narrow tracks of 22.5 µm are used, necessitating such advanced techniques as dynamic tracking, as used in the latest professional helical scan recorders.

A standard using this technique produces still pictures and fast and slow motion pictures free of bands of noise.

The cassette, similar in size to the VHS, is capable of recording four hours on each track giving a total of 8 hours on each cassette (see table).

Comparative table of cassette recorders

	VCC	VHS	VCR-LP	BETA	U-Matic
Tape width mm	12.5	12.5	12.5	12.5	19
Tape speed cm/s	2.44	2.339	6.56	1.873	9.5
Maximum duration	8 hr	3 hr	2¼ hr	3¼ hr	1½ hr
Writing speed m/s	5.08	4.86	8.1	5.83	8.54
Drum diameter (mm)	65	62	106	74.5	110

Dynamic track following (DTF)

The dynamic tracking developed by Philips operates in both record and playback modes and has the advantage that the need for the conventional control track is eliminated. The video heads are mounted on small plates of piezoelectric material attached to the upper section of the head drum (Figure 4.43).

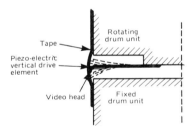

Figure 4.43. In the Philips VCC system the head is mounted on a piezo-electric element

During recording DTF signals are laid down on the track at frequencies below the colour chrominance subcarrier (625 kHz) (Figure 4.44). The frequencies differ between four adjacent tracks and follow a sequence of f_1, 102 kHz; f_2, 117 kHz, f_4, 164 kHz, f_3, 149 kHz. Frequencies f_1 and f_4 are recorded by one head and f_2 and f_3 by the second head. The heads are shown in Figure 4.45 as H_1 and H_2.

When playing back a recorded signal the head scans the recorded tracks and recovers both the video signal and the DTF signal. A crosstalk component of the DTF signal is also recovered producing a difference frequency depending upon which adjacent signal is being picked up. If head 2 is playing back a track with a

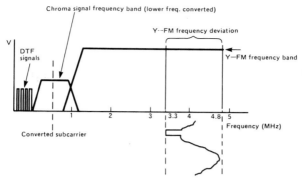

Figure 4.44. Philips VCC recording system

DTF signal of 102 kHz (f_1) its adjacent tracks will contain 117 kHz (f_2) or 149 kHz (f_3) which will produce difference frequencies of 15 kHz and 47 kHz respectively with f_1. The relative amplitudes of the two difference frequencies is compared and the highest indicates in which direction the head is tending to move. A correction voltage can then be obtained which, applied to the piezoelectric plate, will pull the head back into alignment with the track.

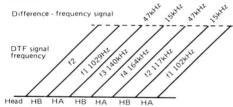

Figure 4.45. The sequence of the dynamic track following signals. Read from the right this is f1, f2, f4, f3

Between fields, one video head is not in contact with the tape and during this period the piezoelectric plate is restored to the position it had at the commencement of the previous track, ensuring that when the head makes contact with the tape it is in its correct starting position.

If, during playback, both heads show equal deviation in one direction the effect is corrected by moving the tape to restore correct alignment.

To minimise any drum diameter variation which would affect the mechanical handling of the tape, the drum is heated and kept at a constant temperature, thus reducing head wear and minimising frictional losses due to tape sticking.

Recording

When recording, the tracks are laid down without any guardband between them. However, as the heads can move there is no fixed position for them and therefore dynamic control is necessary during recording in addition to playback. This is performed by one of the heads being fixed while the other is placed in a control loop. During the period of the field flyback, recorded at the beginning of each track, an additional 223 kHz reference signal is recorded for a one and a half line period (96μs). Due to the alignment of these periods on the tape (Figure 4.46) the following 96μs is adjacent to the previous track and the crosstalk signal can be read to produce any required control signal to reposition the head.

Similarly to other systems using no guardbands between tracks, a slant azimuth technique is used and in the Philips system the heads are angled at + 15° and − 15° with respect to each other. FM recording is used with a colour under system as previously described.

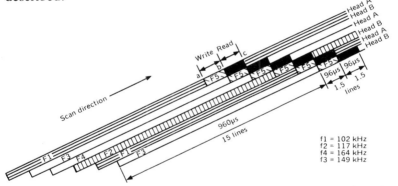

f1 = 102 kHz
f2 = 117 kHz
f4 = 164 kHz
f3 = 149 kHz

Figure 4.46. In record a read and write sequence is performed to provide dynamic control to the head and correctly align the track

Servo system

The tape speed is a constant 2.44 cm/s with the capstan connected directly to the capstan motor spindle, on which is mounted a 216 pole tachometer. The motor speed is 116.4 rev/min and control is achieved by comparing the phase of the tacho signal with that of a crystal controlled oscillator of 419.376 Hz.

The head drum is directly driven by a motor connected to a 125 pole tachometer. The head drum speed is 1500 rev/min and a phototransistor connected to the head drum produces a pulse every revolution (25 per second). During recording these

25 Hz pulses are compared to a reference signal derived from the field frequency of the recorded signal and during playback the reference is a crystal oscillator. The scanning units are complete and factory adjusted for ease of exchange in the field.

The Philips machine is different in many ways to any machine previously produced and provided that field experience shows it to be a reliable machine, its future looks bright, given sufficient facilities to satisfy public demand.

Video cassette manufacturers and marketing companies

Marketing and licensing agreements have been made as follows:

Philips VCR-LP	Philips Grundig	
Grundig SVR	Grundig ITT	
Philips VCC	Philips Grundig	
		US only
JVC VHS	JVC Akai	RCA Magnavox (US Philips subsidiary)
	Matsushita (National Panasonic) Mitsubishi Hitachi Sharp Nordmende (West Germany) Thomson-Brandt (France) Ferguson-Thorn (UK)	General Electric Quasar Sylvania MCA Curtis Mathis Admiral
Sony Betamax	Sony Toshiba Sanyo NEC (Nippon Electric Co.) Aiwa	Zenith Sears

Conclusion

Although there are still major companies competing with systems which are not compatible and with the video disc seemingly ready to make its many times postponed entrance, we are approaching some resemblance of a standard for home and semi-professional video recorders.

Standards are normally set in either of two ways. Either a knowledgeable and powerful committee is set up involving the buyers and manufacturers as occurs in broadcasting or, where no such organisation exists, one manufacturer sells in such quantities that it becomes a standard due to the volume in the field. At this stage smaller companies begin to make accessories and software which consolidates the standard.

In the semi-professional field the U-matic has been successful and there are many makers of compatible machines. In home video recording Philips, Sony and JVC are in competition with the remaining companies backing one or other system.

The problem, however, of a standard set solely by commercial agreement is that new systems can be introduced and affect the situation very quickly if the consuming public is attracted by the product.

We have still to see in the market the BASF and Toshiba systems using static heads, should any of them be fully developed, the impact of video discs and the effect of holographic systems. What may not be possible at the moment can become reality in a very short time. However, only a major breakthrough will make the committed major companies change course with what appear to be very good systems.

Video tape

Although all manufacturers try to keep secret their research and development the most successful seem to be video tape manufacturers. This applies even to their normal coating, production and testing methods. Rarely is anyone allowed to observe the mixing and coating facilities even if one is part of the organisation. There is, therefore, still some element of mystery to the manufacture of high quality video tape although the fundamental technology is straightforward. Large quantities fail to pass the quality control and parameters can vary from batch to batch. Manufacture requires the skill of the chemist, mechanical and electrical engineer to produce the precision product on which picture quality ultimately depends.

Specification for video tape

Characteristics that a successful video tape must possess include:
1. High signal retention
2. High signal-to-noise ratio
3. Low clogging characteristics
4. Low dropout rate
5. Low abrasiveness, to improve head life
6. Long tape life
7. Ability to record both very high frequencies and low frequencies
8. Low print-through characteristics
9. Mechanical strength to resist distortion by head penetration, friction and shuttling between reels
10. Stability in environmental changes
11. Antistatic properties
12. For stop motion recorders, an oxide which does not break down.

The most important factor in this connection is the quality of the magnetic particles, which controls the sensitivity, signal output, noise, print-through characteristics, ability to erase the signal and the stability of the video tape.

The oxides used for broadcast tapes and initially used for helical scan recorders are needle shaped (acicular) particles of gamma ferric oxide (γ-Fe_2O_3), having a coercivity in the range 20 000 –28 000 A/m (250–350 oersteds) (Figure 4.47). Particles with

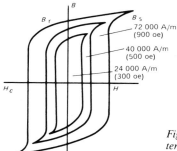

Figure 4.47. Comparison of the B-H hysteresis loop for video tapes of varying coercivity

energy greater than 32 000 A/m (400 oersteds) are now being used, which allowed the introduction of the video cassette machine, giving a relatively high performance for a low price. The high energy particles include chromium dioxide, cobalt doped γ-Fe_2O_3 and cobalt alloy metal particles. However, the chromium dioxide tape is more abrasive and can only be used with ferrite heads, which in turn tend to be brittle and easily damaged. The introduction of cobalt into the oxide allows control of the resultant coercive force but its addition alters the particle size and shape and can make it unstable when heated or flexed. Doping methods have been developed in which the cobalt is treated on the surface of the oxide instead of within the crystal lattice and this had produced considerable improvement. The ability to control the coercivity has allowed the production of tapes with a value greater than 80 000 A/m (1 000 oersteds), although the problems of driving and erasing such a tape then becomes a problem and special settings and heads are required on the recorder. The advantage, however, of a higher signal output with the better signal-to-noise ratio obtained from a reasonably high energy tape is that the writing speed can be reduced, while retaining the same performance, or the bandwidth can be increased over what could be achieved on the same machine with a normal gamma ferric oxide tape.

Smaller and more uniform particles produce less noise and ensure a more even dispersion of the particles in the binder, contributing to more uniform magnetisation throughout the tape. The type of erasure also contributes to the noise factor and an improvement of 10 dB can be obtained from bulk erasure rather than direct current.

Metal particles

Metallic particles can produce a signal-to-noise ratio 10–12 dB higher than standard gamma ferric oxide, thus allowing the same information to be recorded at lower head-to-tape speeds, or more data can be recorded.

At present, due to lack of equipment suitable for such tapes, their use has been restricted to the audio field.

Materials in a video tape – ferric oxides

The gamma ferric oxide used for coating the majority of video tape is made from yellow ferrite ($Fe_2O_3 \cdot H_2O$). When the water is removed this becomes a red non-magnetic oxide Fe_2O_3. Hydrogen or carbon monoxide is heated with the Fe_2O_3 to form Fe_3O_4 which is black ferrous oxide and is magnetic. The final oxide is obtained by heating the material with oxygen which, under very closely controlled conditions, forms acicular crystals of gamma ferric oxide γ-Fe_2O_3 of a controlled shape and size. The method used to achieve the correct particle size, acicularity and distribution is a closely guarded secret by every manufacturer.

Gamma ferric oxide continues to be widely used due to its low cost, chemical stability and the considerable knowledge that has been accumulated about the substance. The iron oxide particles range in length from 40 to 10 μin and have a length-to-width ratio of between 10:1 and 5:1. To obtain a greater signal output and a better signal-to-noise ratio the manufacturer tries to increase the particle packing density on the tape. However, if this is increased by too great an amount for any particular binder system, poor adhesion results leading to a chalky tape that sheds. If the particles are also poorly shaped or fractured the tape will be magnetically unstable and print through problems will be experienced.

Binder system

Whatever the nature of the final magnetic particles that are used they must be secured to the polyester film base. This is achieved by a binder and the characteristics of this considerably affect the mechanical properties of tape. The polyester film itself must be produced to a very close thickness tolerance and free from surface imperfections.

The oxide is suspended in the binder which must be fluid to allow an even dispersion of the particles within the mixture. Clumps of oxide must not be allowed to form otherwise the coated tape will have non-uniformity of signal, dropouts and noise where clumps occur.

When the video head passes across the tape considerable frictional heat is produced and under these conditions the binder must not soften or produce debris to clog the head. It must also have low frictional properties and a low electrical resistance.

The binder comprises several ingrediants which include dispersants to ensure each particle is separated, otherwise the finely particulate material will tend to agglomerate.

The resins used are both thermoplastic and thermosetting polymers. These are the binder materials and must be capable of holding high concentrations of magnetic particles. The early resins used were vinyl resins such as polyvinyl chloride/vinyl acetate, polyvinylidene chloride-acrylonitrile, polyacrylonitrile/butadiene and cellulose nitrate. These formulations are characterised by long polymer chains which are not bound to each other. They therefore flow and soften when heated and are categorised as thermoplastic.

Polyurethanes, due to their toughness and resistance to abrasion, have now become the dominant polymer for magnetic tape. They are blended with other resins such as phenoxy, epoxy, vinyl or polyester to form cross-linked or thermosetting polymers. The cross-linking is achieved by the use of isocyanates.

Lubricants

The binder must also contain a lubricant to reduce tape wear as it passes over guides and heads. Initially silicones fulfilled this function, but later developments have been required due to the requirements of still frame and slow speeds. Lubricants using long chain fatty acids are being investigated and several patents are in the process of being prepared.

Solvents

The polymers must be dissolved in a solvent and their characteristics must allow quick drying for high speed coating without forming skins or impeding the flow of the coating. The solvents must also fix the coating to the base film. The substances commonly used are aliphatic and cyclic ketones and for the newer resins more active solvents such as tetrahydrofuran, dioxane or dimethyl formamide are used.

Stabilisers and fungicides

Certain resins are not stable when ageing and preservatives are added. In the tropics, tapes can be affected by mildew and protection is therefore provided by incorporating fungicides. Plasticisers are also added to make the tape flexible.

Carbon backing

On the back of the tape there is often a thin layer of carbon filled polymeric coating. This must have low frictional properties to ensure stable running on the VTR and it should also be resistant to scratches. The carbon is used to give protection and to reduce the static charge which can build up on the polyester and adversely affect tape movement, as well as attracting dust which will be wound into the oxide layers and cause dropouts.

Manufacturing techniques

The initial preparation requires the mixing of the various ingredients that are used to coat the polyester base. If the resin is either a solid or granular it is dissolved in a solvent. Various additives and the oxide are mixed and once this is homogeneous it is ready for dispersing. The additives mixed with the binder provide flexibility, control head-to-tape frictional properties and include a wetting agent to ensure each particle of oxide is coated with binder material. The mix is agitated with either solid balls or similar objects at a critically controlled speed, depending upon the viscosity of the mixture, to ensure the objects are made to cascade. The time required for dispersion can vary considerably depending upon the physical force used, the properties of constituents in the mixture and the presence or absence of a wetting agent. The operation can therefore range from several minutes to several days. At all times during the process samples are examined to observe the stage reached in the operation.

When the operation is considered complete the mixture is pumped through filters to the coater or storage tanks to remove any agglomerates or foreign matter present in the mixture.

Before coating it may be necessary to redisperse the mixture if it has been stored as re-agglomeration may occur. There is also a possibility that the thermosetting resins may start their cross-linking reaction even at normal temperatures.

Coating the video tape

A high precision tape must have a uniform coating of mixture firmly fixed to the base film and this must be done at a reasonably high speed to make production economically viable. The coating thickness limits are of the order of ±2.5% both longitudinally and transversely across the web. Severe limits of uniformity are, therefore, imposed on the manufacturers of the base film and various coating processes are used in an attempt to ensure a uniform coating of mixture independent of variations in base film thickness variations.

The most common method of coating is by the use of a knife. The blade of the knife extends across the web and the mixture is held behind it. A small gap between the blade and the base film allows the mixture to adhere to the tape to a thickness determined by the gap. If the gap is constant variations will occur in coating thickness depending upon the variations of thickness of the base film. This can be practically overcome by referencing the position of the blade to the top surface of the base film but the reaction time of the equipment does not allow it to follow high rates of change. The final thickness in this operation will also be dependent upon the mix viscosity and the speed of the coating line.

In an attempt to improve the method, various types of roll coaters are used. In the reverse roll coater the mix is applied as a thick layer to a very smooth surfaced and accurately machined roller known as an applicator. The layer is accurately metered and reduced to the required thickness by another precision roller or an accurately set knife. The base film passes under the applicator roller in the opposite direction to the roller movement and has a coating transferred to it as it passes the layer of mixture. The accuracy of such a system is dependent upon the imperfections of roller bearings and the machining of the knife, together with the viscosity of the mixture and vibrations associated with the operation.

A more sophisticated system uses for the metering action a finely grooved wheel which passes into the mixture and lifts out quantitites depending upon the depth of the grooves. This is known as a gravure roll. The uncoated tape passes over the gravure roll just after a blade has ensured that no excess moisture is adhering to the grooves. The tape is therefore coated across its surface with ridges of measured mixture. The tape is then passed beneath a smoothing bar to give the finished coated tape. Provided that the mixture has entirely adhered to the base film from the gravure roll the difficulties of the system lie in the smoothing operation. Fixed or rotating rods can be used to produce the uniform flow and the accuracy of the final coating is dependent upon this operation.

Orientating the magnetic particles

While the tape is still fluid it is necessary to orientate the magnetic particles on the tape in the direction of the head-to-tape movement, and this is very different for transverse and helical machines. The degree to which this is achieved considerably affects the magnetic properties of the tape. Imperfect orientation will be most noticeable at high frequencies where the output can be reduced. The strength of the magnetic field used, the dispersion and the viscosity must be carefully controlled if an effect known as 'ridging' or 'roping' is not to occur. When the external magnetic field is applied, the particles will tend to form chains as do iron filings around a permanent magnetic field. If the field is too intense the surface of the tape will become round and the head-to-tape contact will be affected causing losses.

Drying and curing

The tape, after orientation, must have the toxic and usually explosive solvents evaporated from it. This is done in ovens with a substantial air flow across the tape for thermoplastic resin binder materials. The thermoseting resins also require that the cross-linking action takes place at this time and this is known as curing. The action is dependent upon temperature and time and this requires extremely critical control over the length of tape in the oven and the rate of flow of the production line. The same control also applies to thermoplastic resins as the efficiency of the solvent evaporation is of great importance if the mechanical properties of the tape are not to vary in use as more solvent evaporates.

Surface treatment of the oxide (calendering)

In order to achieve the necessary head-to-tape contact, the surface of the tape must have a surface finish approaching 2–4 μin from peak to valley. Calendering is normally used and today is performed in line with the coating process.

The tape is passed between two rollers, one hard and highly polished, the other is softer which presses the tape against the polished roller. New calender materials such as nylon, Beltax and steel against steel are also used which result in a mirror finish on the oxide surface.

Slitting

All the preceding operations are carried out on large widths of base film known as 'webs', which are subsequently precision slit into the desired final widths (Figure 4.48). Almost universally used for this slitting process is a method using rotary knives which act

Figure 4.48. A web being slit into two before being slit into the desired widths of tape (Memorex)

like scissors. As they rotate they make intimate contact and slit the tape. The knives must be extremely sharp to avoid any tearing action, otherwise a ragged edge will result (Figure 4.48). Debris from the base binder and oxide materials can be produced and this will eventually cause dropouts if it clings to the tape. To avoid this precautions are often taken by fitting cleaners to the machine.

Other less precise methods of slitting are possible and these include razor slitting and scoring. With razor slitting the blade is held firmly in position and the tape is passed under it. In the scoring method a circular blade is forced through the web against a hardened metal lock-up roll.

When the tapes have been slit they will not be perfectly straight if unwound but will exhibit curvature. It is essential that the curvature is closely controlled as it can be an important factor on certain video tape machines to obtain accurate tracking and

Figure 4.49. Rotary slitters (Memorex)

programme tapes capable of being interchanged between machines. In the slitting operation it is also essential to avoid one edge of the tape being lower than the other.

Slitting tolerances have considerably improved in recent years. ±0.001 in (0.0254 mm) is generally accepted as a standard for 1 in (25.4 mm) and 2 in (50.8 mm) tape but ½ in (12.7 mm) video cassettes require a slitting precision of ±0.0004 in (0.01016 mm).

After slitting, the tape is usually tested in a meaningful fashion to ensure that it will perform to its expected specification. It is finally rewound and sealed in a clean room atmosphere.

Clean room atmosphere

The manufacture of any magnetic product must be carried out in an absolutely clean atmosphere. This requires considerable planning and factories are specially designed for this work. Elaborate ventilation systems use either the latest laminar flow systems or conventional systems are necessary, with limited entrance and exit facilities. Doors are guarded by small rooms acting as air locks to prevent any dust entering the clean room.

The staff use specially laundered clothing and have to pass through air showers and vacuum systems on the way into the manufacturing areas to remove any possibility of dirt being taken into the clean room atmosphere. The room is also temperature and humidity controlled – both of these factors are also very important in the use of the product.

One can begin to understand how difficult it is to manufacture a high quality video tape. Every stage must be critically controlled and any variation in the process from optimum conditions will vary the final product parameters and may even cause its complete rejection.

Care and handling of video tape

The general use of video cassettes in home and industry has made possible the use of video recording in environments which were previously unsuitable. Considerable damage to open reels of tape was attributable to handling and environmental dust which is now prevented by the enclosed cassette.

However, there are still many people in CCTV and broadcasting using reel-to-reel tapes with all the old problems. Obviously the conditions under which a precision video tape is produced cannot be reproduced in an everyday environment and the life of video tape therefore varies enormously depending upon the operating conditions.

During use the tape will slide over guides and tape heads causing frictional wear, and the very severe treatment the tape receives from the head will also cause wear so that after between 50 to 200 passes dropouts become so noticeable that the tape is no longer of any use. It is imperative that the head remains in intimate contact with the tape, and any separation when very short wavelengths are being recorded causes a considerable loss of signal. Separation of the tape from the head is not only caused by irregularities in the oxide surface, but by foreign particles becoming embedded in the tape. These can comprise atmospheric dust, tobacco ash, food particles and debris removed from the tape by the heads and guides and redeposited onto the tape.

It is therefore essential that the heads, guides and any parts of the machine with which the tape will come into contact are thoroughly cleaned before using the machine. Scratches can be caused by dirty guides on the polyester side of the tape. Small chips of polyester are removed and these can be trapped between layers of tape. The pressure between layers after rewinding is high and the particles can become permanently embedded. This is even more important when the particle is in the inner layers of the tape as a ridge formed in this area will cause distortion throughout the reel.

Tape should not be left lying ready on a machine for a considerable period as it is at these times that it is most vulnerable to dust. The tape should only be loaded prior to use. Some dropouts caused by dust are only temporary and can be removed from the tape by successive playings, so that it is essential before discarding a video tape to ensure that the defects are permanent.

The importance of cleanliness in video recording cannot be stressed too strongly. It is also important when cleaning the equipment that the correct cleaner is used, otherwise permanent damage can occur both to the tape and to parts of the recorder.

The most common cleaners which will not damage the magnetic tape or rubber components are:

Freon
Carbon tetrachloride
Ethyl alcohol
Methyl alcohol

Of these Freon is recommended, as ethyl alcohol and methyl alcohol are both flammable and carbon tetrachloride is dangerous to health in a closed environment. Cleaners which will damage the tape and MUST NOT be used are:

Acetone
Heptane
Naphtha
MEK
Trichloroethylene
Xylene

It has been shown how important is the contact between head and tape to avoid any loss of signal. The dropout rate can therefore increase not only due to debris and oxide imperfections, but by worn heads causing insufficient contact. Obviously the greater the tip penetration the higher will be the rate of wear on both the head and the tape and if excessive it can also permanently deform the tape. If, however, the contact is allowed to lessen both the visible noise and dropouts will increase markedly. The setting must therefore be a compromise, and a tip penetration of between 1 and 4.5 thousandths of an inch (0.0254–0.1143 mm) is permissible depending upon the type (quadruplex or helical) and make of machine.

The electronic set-up of the recorder will also affect this problem. The RF signal after recovery by the heads is passed through a limiting circuit to minimise any amplitude variations from causing visible deterioration of the picture. If, however, this circuit's effectiveness is decreased due to any failure or incorrect setting, then the dropout rate will be seen to increase. The amplitude and duration are also greatly affected by the transient responses in the RF amplifiers and these should be regularly checked to avoid unnecessary problems.

Cinching of video tape

Often in tape libraries one can find reels of tapes where interlayer slippage has occurred and 'windows' appear in the tape. The tape will often give the impression of several layers being buckled and very often this permanently damages the tape.

Inevitably the problem is initially caused by winding on the recorder. When being fast rewound the reel of tape has considerable momentum and if abruptly stopped several layers slip upon themselves and produce a buckle in the tape. It is therefore essential when stopping a recorder that the tape is stopped gradually, the brakes work evenly and the correct tension is maintained in the reel of tape. Also, if a tape is rewound with insufficient tension the resulting tape layers are loosely packed and then subjected to either vibration or abrupt changes in environment the tape will again cinch. This is why tape can sometimes be taken from libraries in a cinched condition although the problem did not exist when the tape was initially stored.

The mechanical condition of the recorder is therefore of paramount importance when this problem occurs and the brakes and winding tension should be thoroughly checked.

Operator handling

Every time a tape is threaded onto a recorder, oils and salts are transferred from the operator's hands to the tape and recorder.

This is usually unavoidable unless the operator is wearing gloves. The oils and salt hold any foreign particles to the tape and these can ultimately cause problems.

This becomes a greater problem when tapes are physically edited and in this situation it is essential for the editor to wear cotton gloves. During physical editing the tape is developed so that the recording tracks can be seen together with the editing pulses. It is essential that all traces of the powder are removed from the tape after editing or dropouts will occur. In electronic editing, or even for cueing purposes, operators use marking pens to write on the back of the tape. These marks must be allowed to dry before any further winding takes place otherwise the ink will be transfered to the oxide in the next layer and cause dropouts or head clogging.

Transporting video tape

Before shipping any video tape it is essential to ensure that the tape is wound under the correct tension, otherwise the tape will cinch when exposed to temperature variations or vibration. It should be insulated and transported in a properly constructed fibreboard or plastic container.

When receiving such a tape, a careful examination of the reel should be made to ensure that no damage occurred in transit. Severe damage can occur and this usually affects the edges of the tape. This type of damage will affect the edge tracks and possibly cause dropouts when the tape is wound and the edges are scraped across the flanges of the reel.

Conditions for storage and use

Although tape is made under very exacting temperature and humidity controls, its ability to operate over a very wide climatic range adds to its versatility as a medium. The design of the tape ensures that its maximum efficiency occurs when it is operated under similar conditions to those prevailing when it was manufactured, i.e. 15–25°C with a relative humidity of 50 ±5%.

Permissible operating temperature, however, can range between 5 and 32°C and humidity can vary between 20 and 80%. This does not, of course, mean that there will not be problems associated with some tape at these extremes. The abrasiveness of tape increases with humidity, which shortens the head life. The possibility of the heads clogging with the consequent loss of signal also increases. At lower humidities the coating plasticiser can evaporate resulting in a shortened tape life. Electrostatic charging will also be more pronounced and will tend to increase, resulting in a greater attraction of dust and an increase in dropouts. Whenever tapes have been exposed to extreme temperatures and humidity changes they should be allowed to acclimatise before use.

Reels should always be stored on their edges to avoid the weight of the tape falling on one flange and possibly damaging one edge of the tape.

Rules for increasing tape life and obtaining the maximum efficiency from the system are simple but need considerable attention to detail. However, the increase in the technical performance and the financial savings should make it worthwhile to observe the following rules:

To avoid dropouts
1. Clean the recorder thoroughly.
2. Operate in a clean atmosphere.
3. Do not smoke or eat near the recorder.
4. Do not thread the tape before needed.
5. Ensure that the limiters and RF circuits are correctly aligned.
6. Handle the tape as little as possible.
7. Ensure that head tip penetration is correct.
8. Apply cueing and editing marks with caution.

To avoid tape deformities
1. Ensure that the mechanical parts of the recorder function correctly, especially checking winding tension and brakes.
2. Avoid extreme climatic changes.
3. Avoid damaged reels.
4. Prevent debris being wound between layers of tape.
5. Store the tape on its edge.

To increase head life and minimise the risk of head clogging
1. Operate at the recommended temperatures and humidity.
2. Operate at the correct tip penetration.

Conclusion

Video tape manufacture is one of compromise and presents the most difficult challenge to the tape manufacturer.

The two significant advances in video recording in recent years have been the introduction of the 1 in helical scan format into broadcasting and home video cassette recorders. Both have been made possible by advances in tape development. High energy particles and extremely smooth tape surface have allowed high frequencies to be reproduced. Chroma noise has been reduced with better dispersion techniques. Improvements in the base film have been obtained and resulted in much smoother surface and thinner tape which has allowed greater lengths to be fitted into a cassette and yet still retain its strength to withstand the head penetration. The lubricant used in the tape assists in reducing this problem and must be chosen to reduce the wear caused by the extreme pressure of the head but at the same time to have some abrasiveness to prevent head clogging.

Improvements in magnetic particles has allowed very high frequencies to be recorded but the same particles had to be selected to also allow low frequency audio to be reproduced satisfactorily.

When digital techniques become available for video recording the degradation due to multiple copies, wow and flutter, print-through and other common recording problems will cease to exist. The ultimate performance of any recording system, however, will always depend on the video tape manufacturer, who must produce suitable media if the advances possible with modern electronics are to be realised.

Chapter 5

Disc Recorders and Players

Although all press publicity seems orientated towards the domestic disc recorder which has still to make an appearance in meaningful numbers, the professional disc recorder is now indispensable in many fields such as broadcasting, medicine and industry for analysis of momentary events.

In the broadcast field the introduction of the HS 100 by Ampex gave the broadcaster the facilities of slow motion, fast motion, stop motion and reverse motion frequently used in sports programmes.

In the medical field, disc recorders are incorporated into x-ray systems and the doctor can considerably reduce the amount of x-rays given to the patient by recording a picture immediately on exposure, which can then be examined for as long as desired. This feature is important when needles or instruments are being inserted into the patient and their position must be monitored continuously.

In industry, events often occur only momentarily after long periods of testing and these periods must be recorded and be capable of continuous replay for analysis.

All these systems are very short term recording systems with similar characteristics. Apart from the medium of the disc and the mechanics of the transport, the electronics and signal processing are the same as a professional VTR.

Discs for domestic use, however, are all 'replay-only' systems and again their signal processing is similar to the domestic VTR. The differences between the systems are the medium chosen and the way the signal is recorded on the disc. All are designed for mass duplication, as the systems only become viable to the manufacturer if sufficient programmes can be produced to attract sales of many thousands, similar to the audio disc business.

Whether the public is prepared to pay sufficiently for such programmes is the question that has held back the exploitation of this technology. As more and more normal TV channels become available to the public, whether by normal transmissions, satellites or cable, then the public could become saturated with choice, especially since the normal person can devote only so much time to TV. Unlike listening to music, which sometimes assists the performance of other work and repetition is often enjoyable, video requires complete concentration and repeats are not usually welcome, however good the programme.

Broadcast video disc

The video disc (Figure 5.1) is not a substitute for normal recording methods but is solely used for effects. For this reason the time that can be recorded is limited to 30 seconds and the system relies on

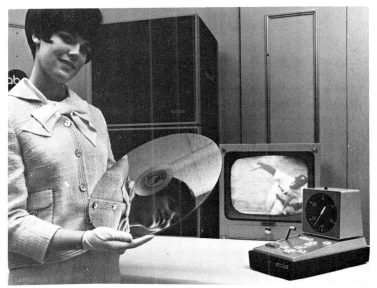

Figure 5.1. Ampex HS100 slow motion disc recorder. There are two discs and both sides are used for recording. The machine records the last 30 seconds of programme. Each TV frame can be held for 'stop' motion or repeated several times for slow motion

recording the last 30 seconds of any action until an event that is wanted for analysis occurs, when the machine is stopped.

The machine is equipped with two discs and recordings can be made on either side by separate heads (Figure 5.2). It is arranged that each head records one complete field of the picture in turn. Each head is capable of recording, playback and erase and the sequence for any head is to record a complete field in one revolution then move during the next two fields, erase the recorded information on its new track and again record for the fourth field. The complete sequence for all four heads is shown in Table 5.1.

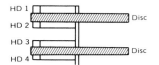

Figure 5.2. Head arrangement on the HS100

Table 5.1. Head movement and recording sequence of HS100

	Field 1, 5, 9, etc	Field 2, 6, 10, etc	Field 3, 7, 11, etc	Field 4, 8, 12, etc
Head 1	Record	Move	Move	Erase
Head 2	Erase	Record	Move	Move
Head 3	Move	Erase	Record	Move
Head 4	Move	Move	Erase	Record

The tracks are arranged as concentric rings around the 16 in diameter disc and in total 1800 fields can be recorded. Each head moves for two tracks before recording. When the heads reach the centre of the disc they return towards the perimeter and record on the alternate tracks which were passed on the inward travel. Using this method a continuous even motion is achieved without any large head movement being required. Each track is spaced 0.01 in. As a complete field has been recorded on each track, stop motion is achieved by simply repeating the output signal on replay from the same track. Slow motion is achieved by repeating the same track a number of times before advancing to the next.

In the replay mode the erase and record circuitry are disconnected and the recovered signal is passed to the processing electronics. As shown in Chapter 1 the difference betwen two fields is a half line displacement of the line sync pulse in order to produce an interlaced frame. When stop motion is used, therefore, and one field is continuously repeated, a half-line delay is alternately inserted and removed to provide the correct waveform timing.

The chrominance subcarrier frequency is an odd multiple of one half the line rate in the NTSC system and in the PAL system it is further complicated by the PAL switching of the phase relationship.

In the NTSC system the phase of the unmodulated subcarrier alternates between 0° and 180° at the beginning of each line because the frequency is an odd multiple of the half line frequency. Therefore, in frame one, the odd numbered lines will have a chrominance phase of 0° and the even numbered lines will have a phase of 180°. In frame two the opposite occurs, even numbered lines having a phase of 0° and odd numbered lines 180°.

If we reproduce field two from field one, the half line delay will cause the odd numbered lines in field one to become even numbered lines in field two and, therefore, the phase of the chroma will be incorrect. If, however, the chrominance is removed and inverted by 180° before recombining it with the luminance signal the chrominance will be correct.

If the field is repeated a third time to become the first field of the second frame, the half line delay is removed but the chrominance phase inverter remains in circuit. When the field is repeated a fourth time to become the second field of the second frame, the half line delay is inserted, but in order to give the correct chrominance phase the inverter is removed. The inverter and half line delay are, therefore, continually switched in and out to reproduce a fully interlaced and correctly phased colour signal.

In the PAL system an extra delay line is inserted in the chrominance path and the switching is arranged so that the correct line is inserted to obtain the correctly phased signal at any time.

Although the signal system is similar to the FM systems of the professional recorders, a second 30 MHz modulation system is used for the half-line delay function, which incorporates an ultrasonic delay line. The signal therefore has to be amplified, modulated, delayed and demodulated to provide this correction.

Channel equalisers also have to provide correction for the position of the head on the rotating disc. The writing speed obviously decreases as it approaches the centre of the disc and the apparent speed is reduced from 76 000 cm/s (3000 in/s) on the circumference to 3352 cm/s (1320 in/s) on the inner track (60 Hz systems).

The rotational speed of the disc depends upon the field rate of the recorded signal and through a servo is locked to the external vertical synchronising pulse.

The disc is a precision made item and the aluminium substrate surface is lapped to an accuracy of approximately four millionths of an inch (0.1016 µm). The surface is electroplated with a thin layer of magnetic nickel cobalt alloy and finally plated with a few

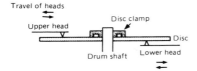

Travel of heads

Time chart for concentric recording process

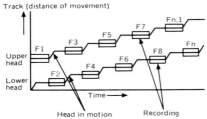

Track pattern for endless recording

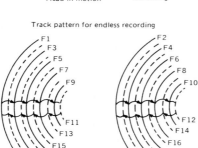

Upper surface of disc   Under surface of disc

(F stands for field)

- Upon receiving a command, each video head starts moving intermittently (stepping) radially. Each field is recorded on the disc in the form of a circular track. One head is held stationary while the other steps to the next track. Recording or playback is performed utilising the head that is being kept stationary. Switching between different recording or playback modes is performed by controlling the number of steps, the direction and the period of stepping.

- While the disc is rotating, the video heads are not in contact with the disc surface, but hovering above it with a minute clearance.

- Storage capacity of the VM-1200LU Series is 1200 television fields (600 frames if the frame recording mode is applied), corresponding to 20 seconds of recording in the normal full-zone recording mode.

Figure 5.3. JVC disc recorder

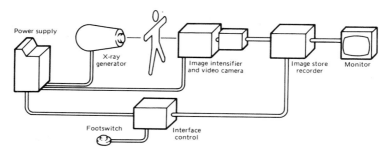

Figure 5.4. Electronic radiography system by VAS

micro-inches of rhodium to prevent surface corrosion and ensure a smooth surface for the heads.

Although the broadcast machine uses two discs other manufacturers use one but obviously a shorter recording time is available. The pattern for the JVC VM 1200 LU series of disc recorders is shown in Figure 5.3 while a system using a disc recorder for x-ray recording is shown in Figure 5.4.

Domestic video disc systems

Possibly more literature, conferences and lectures have been produced on domestic video disc systems, without any successful product appearing, than any other subject relating to television. The Telefunken/Decca TeD system, which was the first system and was sold in limited areas, was not be successful.

Unlike other television equipment the product is only of use if the associated software is attractive to the customer. If the product is ever to be a success, therefore, it may be that the combination of a technical company capable of mass production and a programme producer of films or television shows is the combination to succeed. It is, therefore, interesting to observe the merging of interests between the competing systems. At the time of writing (changes are made very regularly) the following were competing.
1. LaserVision, originally called VLP, developed by Philips and MCA. (MCA are amongst the largest producers of programmes in the world.)
2. SelectaVision developed by RCA.
3. VHD (video high density) developed by JVC.
4. Thompson CSF developed by Thompson. Although not supported by others the French tend to go their own way and are often successful.

It must be assumed that the systems which used a pressure-sensitive stylus in a groove technique are no longer competitors. These include 'TeD' and 'Visc' manufactured by Matsushita. It is generally recognised that the failure of TeD could be attributed to the short playing time of 10 minutes and the lack of choice of programmes available for the system. Discs were also easily damaged.

VLP system (video long player)

This system, now called LaserVision, is backed by the right combination of partners in that Philips' wide business interests include a large number of products for its worldwide domestic market and MCA own most of the software that would be of possible interest to the public. Similar systems were initially separately developed by both companies before they joined forces in 1974.

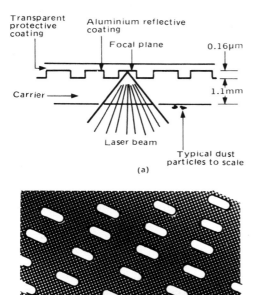

(a)

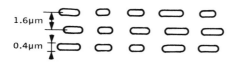

(b)

Figure 5.5. (a) Section through the disc; (b) electron microscope view of the disc surface with pits arranged in a row on the tracks

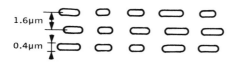

Figure 5.6. Spacing of the pits on the disc

The system uses a rigid disc on which the information is encoded in the form of tiny pits in the surface of the disc (Figure 5.5). The surface of the disc is coated with an aluminium reflective material and the signal is recovered by scanning the disc with a small laser. The reflected beam is modulated by variations in the beam caused by the pits in the disc surface and a light sensor converts the variations in intensity into electrical signals (Figure 5.7). In order to protect the information on the disc, the surface is coated with a transparent acrylic layer for protection, producing a completely smooth disc (Figure 5.5).

The disc is mounted in the player (Figure 5.7) so that the laser shines from beneath the disc and is focused below the surface coating so that dust has little effect. Initially the disc rotated at 1500 or 1800 rev/min, depending upon the TV system, allowing 30 minutes of programme to be recorded on either side. In order to increase the playing time to one hour per side the system has been redeveloped to provide a variable rotational speed which reduces from 1500 rev/min while on the inner track to 500 rev/min when on the outer track. This produces a linear velocity between the disc and the laser beam. When constant velocity is used each rotation contains two fields and therefore the machine is capable of stop motion and other effects. When the machine is adapted, however, for the longer play discs the relationship no longer applies and

Figure 5.7. The LaserVision disc player (Philips)

these effects are not possible. Machines will be manufactured to allow both types of discs to be played.

Normal VTR technology is used for signal processing with the exception that the two sound circuits provided on the system use separate FM carriers to the video and the combined signals are separated and demodulated by the processing electronics. The two sound circuits will allow either a second language track or stereo as an option.

The beam must be kept accurately aligned and focused on each track (Figure 5.8). In order to do this tilting mirrors and a focusing lens are used which are servo controlled by signals produced from the returned beam. The accuracy of tracking must be 0.2 µm radially and ±1µm for focusing accuracy. The mirrors act by magnets in a fashion similar to a galvanometer and focusing is provided by a movable objective lens (Figure 5.9).

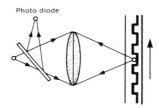

Figure 5.8. Modulation of the reflected light by means of 'pits' passing the light spot and resulting in a corresponding signal on the photodiode

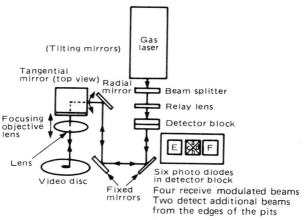

Figure 5.9

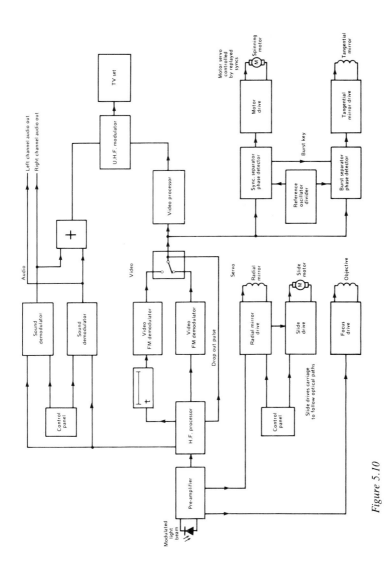

Figure 5.10

The returned beam is detected by four photodiodes and the signal output is the sum of the four signals produced. If the beam is correctly focused each detector receives the same signal but if the beam defocuses it becomes eliptical and different signals fall on each of the diode detectors. From this information correction signals can be generated for the focus control.

Two additional diodes are used within the detector to receive signals from two additional beams produced by the beam splitter and these are spaced 20μm before and behind the main beam. These beams normally read the edges of the pits and are received by the additional detectors. If the beam is off track unequal signals are received and from comparison of the two signals correction signals are produced (Figure 5.10).

At present this system is the most expensive of the competitive systems to produce and it will require reduction in the cost of components for it to become a profitable product for the manufacturer.

Thompson video disc

The disc system designed by Thompson-CSF is almost identical to the Philips/MCA system with the modification that the disc is transmissive instead of being reflective.

SelectaVision

After several abandoned attempts to have its own product in the consumer video market, RCA has developed a video disc which relies on signals being generated by variations in the capacitance between the disc and the metal electrode in the stylus while running in a groove. The groove is used, unlike TeD and Visc, solely for tracking purposes and the modulation is obtained from tiny pits along the bottom which causes the capacitance between the disc surface and the stylus to change. When first demonstrated in 1975 the disc had a coated metal surface but now they are made of a special PVC and no coating is required. However, unlike the Philips/MCA optical disc the RCA disc can be easily damaged by scratches, dirt, dust and finger marks each of which would modify the capacitive signal. It therefore has to be kept in a plastic holder called a 'caddy' which is housed in a rigid sleeve.

Playing time is at present 30 minutes each side of a double sided 12in disc. A version enabling a playing time of 60 minutes each side is being developed. At present only one audio track is possible with the system.

Because of the rotational speed of 450 rev/min, stop motion and other effects are not possible for the same reasons as for the long play version of the VLP. However, there is the possibility of a digital memory being developed which would allow a single frame to be reproduced for stop motion. Although no one has committed themselves to manufacture at the time of writing, licence options have been taken by BSR, Clarion, Mitsubishi, Nippon Electric, Pioneer, Sharp and Toshiba.

VHD

In a similar manner to RCA, the system developed by JVC also uses the variations of capacitance between the disc and the stylus to generate the signal. However, the JVC disc has no grooves and, therefore, the pickup electrode can slide over the surface; this may possibly lead to a longer life.

The pickup is kept on track by interlacing the programme tracks with a spiral of tracking signals also obtained from pits. If the pickup wanders off the signal track, variation in the tracking signals allows the correct servo to operate to compensate and bring the pickup back on track. Because of the nature of the signal modulations the JVC disc is easily damaged by dust and handling, and in a similar manner to RCA the disc must be kept in a caddy.

The JVC disc rotates at 900 rev/min and provides a playing time of one hour per side. Because of this speed a single frame memory is required to provide a freeze frame.

Conclusion

In order to be successful a video disc system must fulfil the following requirements.
1. The player must be cheap to produce.
2. A wide choice of software must be available at reasonable prices.
3. Replay equipment must be very reliable.
4. The disc must be capable of the usual mishandling and still work satisfactorily.
5. Production of the disc must be cheap and yield a high proportion of acceptable discs.
6. Technical performance must match that of a domestic VTR under subjective viewing tests.
7. Many retail outlets must be available with servicing facilities.
8. Large quantity sales must be guaranteed.

None of the systems at present meet all these requirements and this may mean more development of the complete system is required. Unfortunately for disc systems, the VTR is improving and becoming more acceptable to the public all the time. The VTR also maintains the one advantage to the owner that he can make his own recordings and with eight hours of recording available on a single tape the cost of recording a considerable library of programmes will mean the cost of a disc will have to be very competitive.

It should be noted, of course, that the main competitors for the video disc market are also the same competitors for the VTR market. Success in either field will affect the market for the other product. It could be this fact, amongst others, that makes each manufacturer have his system ready in case a competitor makes a launch, but each is waiting for the other to make a positive move.

No doubt reports of systems, mergers and dropouts in this field will continue for many years to come.

Chapter 6

Post Production

Video tape editing

Modern video tape editing has revolutionised the production of television programmes over the last 20 years and today the editing suite in a modern studio performs all the same operations as its counterpart in a film studio.

Prior to the ability to edit, a television programme had to be produced as a continuous production. Today programmes are made in parts and edited to add effects, sound tracks, produce accurately timed programmes and improve the dramatic effects, or eliminate mistakes and the less interesting parts of the live programme. Even sport benefits as a football match or an afternoon athletic meeting can be considerably condensed and include only the most interesting parts.

In addition many of the visual effects seen on the television screen are possible only by electronic manipulation of the picture and are never actually seen live in a studio.

However, although editing is a technical process it also requires considerable artistic flair. Today, editing systems range from those which allow simple edit insertions of material into a programme for CCTV, to computer systems operating several recorders and obtaining the audio and visual content of the finished programme from several sources to produce a major drama or variety programme.

With the advent of ENG (Electronic News Gathering) cameras and VTRs, television techniques have moved into direct competition with film. Even though higher initial capital costs are involved, the escalating cost of film production and the availability of sophisticated editing facilities and new electronic visuals has made the broadcaster start to invest in this technology for areas which in the past had been served by film.

131

Continuous shooting of an indoor production requires a large studio with many cameras and staff. Large amounts of scenery have to be built and a long time schedule is inevitable. To reduce these costs advantage is being taken of the new technology by shooting the programmes on location, using a 'rehearse then record' method, and producing a completed programme in many parts. This inevitably leads to a greater requirement for sophisticated editing suites to make the completed programme.

Editing suite requirements

The CCTV user and the broadcaster have considerably different requirements due to the scale and versatility required. Capital costs, in addition to the need for the operational flexibility, determine the specification of the system.

Usually, in CCTV either helical scan machines, such as IVC 800 series or the cassette recorder, usually in the form of a U-matic, are the only recorders available. The same replay machines are also often used to record the original programmes and are, therefore, part of a CCTV system incorporating sync pulse generators, monitors, vision and sound mixers and sometimes a timebase corrector.

Figure 6.1. JVC editor and U-matics

The additional editing unit is usually incorporated between two recorders in such a system and the recorders are suitably modified (Figure 6.1). These units are relatively small and incorporate either push button or joystick control (Figure 6.2) of the recorder's transport and electronic switching.

Two modes of operation are required; these are 'assemble' or 'insert' mode and the choice of editing affects the way the signals are recorded.

In the 'assemble' mode new material is added to the end of existing material and the video, audio and control tracks are all recorded as new signals on the tape.

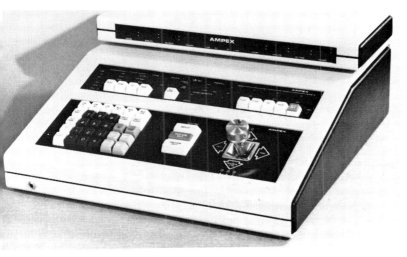

Figure 6.2. Editing control unit with joystick control of tape movement

In the 'insert' mode new material is used to replace existing material on the tape for a determined duration of time. In this mode only the audio and video are recorded and the old control track is left to act as the reference of tape speed and position. Often, when assembling, an editor will record a new control track for the full length of the new master tape and treat all the assembled parts as inserts in order to improve the stability of the completed programme tape.

It is essential, of course, that the incoming and playback signals are close to synchronism and each VTR must, therefore, be equipped with a vertical reference capstan servo.

Such systems usually provide rehearse facilities before the actual recording is committed and this allows minor timing changes if required. Separate sound editing is also possible.

A modern editing suite for the broadcaster is usually a self-contained operation with its own control room separate from the noise of the machines. This, of course, is not always possible but is desirable (Figure 6.3).

Figure 6.3. Professional editing suite using computer-controlled system (courtesy Television International)

Such suites must handle all categories of production and equipment formats, including fast compilations for news, sport and current affairs to the creative editing of a drama taking several days. Within the studio complex the recordings are made on quadruplex or 1 in professional helical machines while exterior material may also be available on film or U-matic (Figure 6.4). The video disc also allows effects and analysis for sport and drama.

The vision mixing console, especially for the production of commercials, is usually very complex since the effects, using electronic zoom and multiple picture generators, compete with the optical effects possible with film.

Sound is as important as the video and often more difficult to edit. The programme may require music, applause, effects, timed commentaries, lip sync on a reinsertion of a sound track or the elimination of sound that should not be audible. Often sound editing is completed after the video editing and a special audio suite may be required. Multi-track audio recorders synchronised

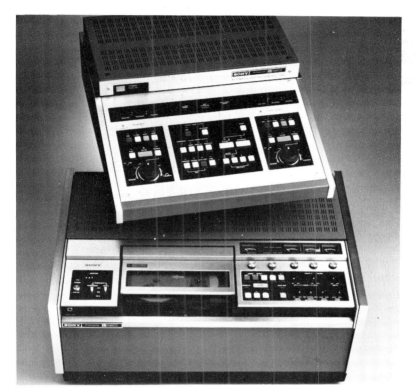

Figure 6.4. Sony GVE500 editor with BVU200 highband U-matic

to the VTRs together with audio mixers are, however, necessary for even a simple editing suite.

Electronic techniques of editing

As shown in previous chapters the format of the signals recorded on a tape varies considerably according to the mechanical arrangement of the system. The very first form of editing on a quad format consisted of identifying the position of the edit, developing the magnetic pattern of the signals with iron particles suspended in a liquid so that the individual tracks could be recognised and then physically cutting the tape with a splicer or razor blade. The tapes were then joined with splicing tape. Absolute cleanliness was required, for the remains of any particles or finger prints would seriously spoil parts of the programme. This procedure was possible with transverse recorders as the tracks are almost at right angles to the tape edge. The tracks of a helical scan recorder, however, can have a length of 50 cm and are at an acute angle to the tape edge.

Although this form of editing is still the only way to edit two first generation masters together, in practice it is time consuming and once the tape has been cut it is usually of no further use for new recordings.

With electronic editing it is necessary to erase the old recording first. However, as the erase head and video head are physically spaced, if both are switched on simultaneously there would be a period of time on the tape in which the signal had not been erased before the new recording commenced. This over-recording will cause a moiré effect where the edit takes place until the erased part of the tape is reached. In a transverse (quad) recorder it is possible to switch on the erase head half a second prior to the recording head as the erase head can be aligned with the almost vertical tracks. This time period compensates for the erase head being 8 in before the video head (Figure 6.5).

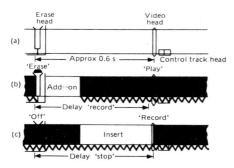

Figure 6.5. Relative positions of the erase and video heads in a quad recorder. The separation is equivalent to 0.6 second. In record mode a precise delay must occur in order to start the new recording at the end of the material already on tape. If the editing is an 'insert' the same delay must be applied to the 'stop' function of the VTR

However, because of the layout of the helical format, it is not possible to align such a head on helical machines, therefore a separate head for video erasure is fixed to the scanning wheel just prior to the recording head. This is called 'flying erase' and allows the minimum of over-recording to take place. If, due to the tape format, the erase head also crosses the audio track (as occurs on IVC machines) the level of the erase current is reduced as it crosses the auxiliary tracks to prevent partial erasure.

If the heads are to be switched so that the transition takes place in the guard band between the scans or tracks containing the vertical blanking signals, it is essential that the positioning of the tape and phasing of the head drum prior to the switching is such that the signal to be recorded is correctly phased with the signal already on the tape. By ensuring this relationship the timebase stability and signal continuity will not be disturbed.

Audio editing on VTRs

On all VTRs the audio and control tracks are recorded (and erased) by static heads in the same manner as an audio recorder. Some recorders have facilities for two or more audio tracks.

A timing process between the start of erasure and commencing recording must again be provided due to the physical spacing between the erase and record heads.

In order to avoid clicks when editing between two analogue signals it is necessary to gradually build up the erase and record currents and provide a quick mix rather than a cut. At the end of the insert the audio waveform must again be similarly contrived.

Editing operation

The facilities available will determine the method used in any editing situation. If a manual edit is made this simply involves previewing and marking the point of the edit on the master tape and the start of the insert on the tape containing the new material (slave). Marking is usually done with a chinagraph pencil; great care must be taken to ensure that the mark is subsequently removed and does not damage the oxide.

The tapes are rewound on the master and slave recorders (usually about 10 seconds) so that in 'Play' mode both tapes simultaneously arrive at the edit points with their servo systems fully locked-up and the reproduced picture stable. At this point the record or edit button is operated on the master VTR. This system, of course, is rather hit and miss and although a helical scan recorder will record within a few frames, due allowance must be made for the erase and record delay period on a quad machine.

The next stage of improvement to the system is to mark the edit point electronically with a blip on a separate audio track. The system is designed to sense the tone and automatically perform the edit. A 'rehearsal' mode, with such a system, becomes possible for until the edit point position is perfected the system only switches the monitor from master to slave at the edit point and does not perform an electronic tape edit until specifically instructed. A further refinement can be added by placing the tone prior to the edit point and using a variable delay network to give the facility of moving the edit point until the editing occurs on the precise frame required during a rehearsal. The electronic edit is then made.

Very often the video and sound edits are required at different times and to achieve this the video is controlled by the edit tone and the audio is controlled manually. Abrupt edits of audio, especially of applause or effects, are usually unacceptable. The new and old sound tracks, therefore, have to be mixed using a separate audio recorder and two channel audio mixer. The original audio track is first recorded on the audio recorder and is then used as an input to the mixer together with audio from the slave recorder on which is the new insert. The output of the mixer is fed to the master machine. Obviously the audio recorder must be in synchronism with the VTR. Prior to the edit the sound is taken from the audio recorder and sustained before the sound is mixed across to the new audio to give a continuous effect through the edit point.

Time code editing

To further automate the editing process, the EBU in 1972 standardised a digital code which allowed each frame to be identified on a separate audio track (Figure 6.6). The code also identifies hours, minutes and seconds and the use of wide-band replay amplifiers aallows the code to be read over the range of spooling speeds encountered. When recording, the time of any sequence can be noted and in the editing suite control systems can be set to search and find the particular insert automatically. A visual display can also be provided to allow manual search.

When the time code is recorded on the master machine, systems can be produced to store addresses, control rehearsals and edits and operate to a programme of instructions. If the stores are large enough the audio can be treated differently to the video and edited at different times.

When shuttling two VTRs for rehearsal and editing, the lock-up and repeatability can vary by ±4 frames which, for precise editing, is inconsistent. The time code, however, can be utilised to synchronise the VTRs and so the edit points for the slave and master become consistent.

To provide synchronisation and automatic parking of the reels on the VTR it is essential for the master tape to have a continuous and time sequential code written on it. If time does not allow this,

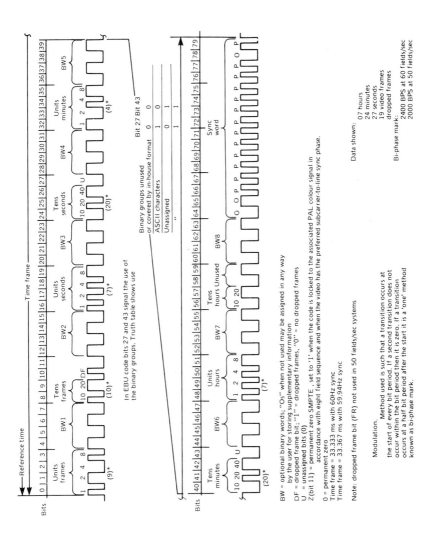

Figure 6.6. EBU/SMPTE editing code

the 'insert' mode cannot be used and the edited tape is 'assembled'. The cue track is then assembled at the same time as the video and the time code generator has to be synchronised with the old code before the edit point so that the final track is time sequential. This type of generator has the capability of 'slaving' or 'jam sync'.

The computer stores used for the control of the master and slave VTRs are loaded from the tape code as it is playing back or a keyboard which allows the editor to modify the data. Other editing systems making use of the code load from cassettes, paper tape or floppy disc and this allows data to be introduced from other sources where editing requirements have been predetermined such as by off-line editing systems.

Off-line editing

Due to the considerable expense of such editing suites it is obviously more economic if editing decisions can be made elsewhere at leisure and only the physical editing takes place in such areas. This has been made possible by the introduction of the cheaper helical scan recorders which allows the producer to view all the parts of the programme with the time code inserted in the picture. The producer is then able to select the combination of inserts to produce the final programme. As an extension of this method an editing system comprising two CCTV VTRs and an edit controller can compile a programme either as a 'rough out' or as a completed programme. The information taken from this tape can then either be used to speedily produce a master broadcast programme in the editing suite or in some instances can be used to automatically produce the edited programme. The economics of this system can be understood when it is realised that a modern editing suite can cost about £500,000 while an off-line system may cost about £20,000.

One disadvantage of the SMPTE/EBU time code is that it can only be displayed while the tape is moving. Helical scan machines often allow a still frame to be produced, which assists editing. Equipment has therefore been produced which places hours, minutes, seconds and tenths of seconds into the vertical interval and provided that the vertical interval is not too distorted it will produce an identifiable code on a still frame.

Multi VTR control

Often the parts of a programme are recorded on several tapes and to eliminate the continuous need to change tapes several slave

VTRs may be incorporated into the system (Figure 6.7). The additional machines also allow visuals such as wipes and split screeens to be produced. Extra master machines may also be provided to produce keying signals for visual effects.

Figure 6.7. Sony BVE5000 production editor control unit controls up to four players

When such systems are incorporated with video discs, electronic zooms and colour synthesis it becomes logical that the controls can be computerised. Systems are therefore in operation where the editor sits at a console and instructs the computer with typed instructions or light pens on the computer display screen. The physical work is therefore being removed from modern editing and more emphasis is being placed on creativity (Figure 6.8).

Conclusion

It now seems almost impossible to produce a programme without the aid of the VTR editor. This is a big change since the days when all programmes were transmitted live. The possibilities of modern systems are enormous and obviously will increase over the next decades. It is essential, however, that with all the technology available the use of it should either produce a better or more economic programme. It would be easy to adopt a method of operation solely because of available technology and possibly a belief that programmes have to be made in a certain way to be successful.

Figure 6.8(a). CMX 340X editor's display. A computer controlled editing system capable of being expanded with customer's needs. Inputs can be keyboard, teletypewriter, floppy disk or paper tape. A large number and variety of machines and effects can be controlled (courtesy F. W. O. Bauch)

Figure 6.8(b). The Edge (CMX). A simpler system than the 340X editor, The Edge can be used for editing with ¾ in and 1 in machines

Duplication of prerecorded tapes

Until the introduction of the video cassette recorder there had not been a great demand for duplication of programmes recorded on video tape. The demand was easily satisfied by machine recording methods in professional broadcasting and by the users of helical scan recorders.

The impact, however, of the cassette recorder radically changed the situation and produced a considerable need for duplicating facilities. The ease with which these machines can be operated has allowed their introduction into many places where people would be unable to operate a normal VTR. Machines which have only the ability to replay prerecorded tapes are being extensively used for the entertainment of ships' crews, training of staff, company communications and as an aid to selling sophisticated products. The introduction of the Betamax, VHS and Philips home video systems has also produced a new market for the prerecorded video cassette of feature films and specialist programmes.

At present the main advantage which film and ultimately the video disc systems retain over video tape recording is the ease with which the programme material can be duplicated at high speed.

Techniques of duplication

In theory there are four methods which could produce systems but at present, systems other than machine to machine recording, are rarely used.

The four systems are:
1. Machine to machine recording.
2. AC transfer method (Ampex ADR-150).
3. Thermal transfer systems (originally manufactured by Consolidated Video Systems) and tried by others – no system available at present.
4. A combination of methods 2 and 3 (development carried out by 3M but stopped. System was known as STAM – Sequential Thermal Anhysteretic Magnetisation).

Machine to machine recording

Most large scale users of CCTV or any broadcasting station will have at least two machines and, therefore, can make their own copies. The format can easily be changed by playing the tape on one type of recorder and recording on a different type. Different formats can obviously also be recorded simultaneously by using several different machines, and as many copies can be made at one time as there are machines available.

While recording the copy tape foreign language captions or different sound tracks can easily be added by normal production methods as the duplication takes place in real time.

However, there are disadvantages, for a copy of a one hour tape will take one hour to produce and is therefore expensive in both equipment and labour.

The quality of the transfer is also affected as the replay errors of the master machine are added to the record errors of the slave and both these are recorded on the copy tape. The errors include timebase instability, frequency and phase distortion, noise and a variation in the chrominance luminance delay. The copy is therefore, always inferior to the master and its acceptability depends on the added amount of electronic distortion, the quality of the original master and the standard accepted by subjective viewing. For the same amount of electronic distortion and the same standard of subjective viewing copies made from a high quality master may be acceptable while those from a lower quality master may not, although both masters when viewed by themselves would be classified as good. The added distortions in copying is sufficient to bring the copy from the lower quality master below acceptable limits while the same amount of distortion added to the good master would not (Figure 6.9).

Playing the master and rerecording at high speed as is normal when duplicating audio tapes is not possible with video, due to the

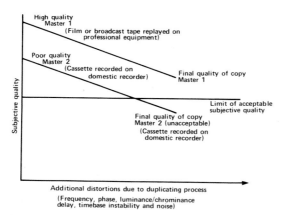

Figure 6.9. Although both masters are themselves of acceptable quality the poor quality master will produce unacceptable copies after the distortions have been added in the duplicating process

very high frequencies involved. This would make the equipment extremely complex and prohibitively expensive.

High speed programme duplication

Both the AC system and the thermal duplication method rely on the master and the copy being in contact, oxide to oxide, at the time of transfer and any method devised for the tape transport for the AC system can be similarly applied in the thermal duplication method. The principle, however, whereby the video informaton is transferred from the master to the copy is entirely different in the two systems.

AC transfer system

This method relies on the master tape being recorded on high energy tape of approximately 72 000 A/m (900 oersteds) and when duplicating this is placed in contact with a normal ferric oxide tape while applying an AC magnetic field. The field strength is made sufficient to agitate the domains of the low coercivity tape while leaving the master less affected. When the field is removed, the domains of the copy tape will settle to a pattern determined by the signal on the master tape. The efficiency with which the information is transferred from the master to the duplicate depends on the strength of the transfer field, the coercivity of the master tape, the magnetic characteristics of the copy tape and the efficiency of the duplicating equipment. This system is generally inefficient at long wavelengths and requires that the audio and control tracks are recorded on the duplicate by conventional heads transferring the information from the master. There is also a loss of FM, on which the video is modulated, of 3–8 dB in the possible output of the conventional ferric oxide tape when duplicated. This is due to tape separation and also that at the time of transfer the copy tape still retains its full magnetic properties which oppose the transfer process.

Thermal method

The thermal process relies on the fact that the Curie point of chromium dioxide is very low compared with that of ferric oxide and at temperatures between 120 and 125°C chromium dioxide loses almost all its magnetic properties.

If a master tape of normal ferric oxide is placed in contact with a chromium dioxide tape, on which is going to be recorded a duplicate, in an environment that raises the temperature to the

Curie point of chromium dioxide and then immediately cools the tape, the video information will be transferred from the master to the duplicate under extremely favourable magnetic conditions.

In this case the chromium dioxide responds to even the weakest signals from the master tape due to the low particle interaction fields of the chromium dioxide and also due to the extremely low opposition to the magnetic transfer from the chromium dioxide tape itself. At the time of transfer it is estimated that the coercivity of the chromium dioxide is about 400 A/m (5 oersteds) so the magnetism fed back is about 3–4 millitesla (30–40 gauss) which is negligible. As the chromium dioxide, now a duplicate copy, returns to normal temperature its coercivity rises from 400 to 40 000 A/m (5 to 500 oersteds) and it regains its entire magnetic properties. Note that it is a higher energy tape than the original master and can therefore, have a higher output than the ferric oxide master.

Using this method it was found that both the audio and control tracks could be transferred with the video without the need for separate record heads. The chromium dioxide duplicate, therefore, has both a higher output and a flatter response over a wider bandwidth than a duplicate made by an AC transfer system.

Production of a mirror image

In describing the duplication process it was stated that the transfer takes place for both the AC and the thermal method while the master and the duplicate are placed oxide to oxide. If the duplicate

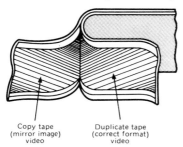

Copy tape
(mirror image)
video

Duplicate tape
(correct format)
video

Figure 6.10. In order that the final duplicate is of the correct format it is copied from a duplicating master which is a mirror image of the original recording

tape is to be played on a conventional recorder, the master tape must therefore be a mirror image in order that the duplicate is of the correct format (Figure 6.10). Production of the mirror image by a recorder requires considerable modification to the equipment.

The video tracks of the mirror image are reversed in the angle of the transverse scan, the audio tracks are along the top edges and

the cue and control tracks are on the bottom edge. The modifications therefore required for the quadruplex recorder are:
1. The video head drum rotation must be reversed.
2. The head tip connections must be changed for the correct sequence of head playback.
3. The tachometer signal system must be reversed.
4. The upside down female guide has to be fitted.
5. Cue heads must be located on the top edge of the tape.
6. The audio heads must be located on the bottom of the tape.
7. The recorder must be electronically capable of driving a high energy tape.
8. Heads must be efficient when driving such tape, which may mean special heads.

After these modifications the mechanical parameters of the machine must be preserved otherwise compatibility will be lost. Any duplicating system which can eliminate the necessity for such modifications obviously has considerable advantages.

To make a mirror image recorder for a helical scan machine becomes a major engineering project, sufficiently to prevent systems requiring such equipment from being produced.

The difficulties are caused by
1. The differences in the levels of the supply and take-up reels.
2. The tape tension variations which occur.
3. The timebase variations.

In quad machines the tension variations can be ignored, since the scan is at right angles to the tension vectors and tension variations result in nanoseconds of timebase errors.

In helical scan recorders, however, the scan angle is only a few degrees and tension variations cause microseconds of timebase error. The allowable tolerance very much depends upon the type of helical scan machine being used.

4. Tape guiding errors.

Due to the scan angle this is an extremely critical parameter in helical scan recorders and errors may require constant adjustment of the tracking control.

In the chromium dioxide thermal duplicating process the first duplicate to be made from the ferric oxide master is obviously a mirror image. If this chromium duplicate can be used as the new master, then copies made from it by the thermal process will be of the correct format and, provided the mechanical parameters of the tape are not altered, the new duplicated recording can be replayed on a conventional recorder. The system therefore eliminates the need to produce a master tape on a mirror image recorder.

Other chromium dioxide duplicates can be made in the same way by preheating the copy tape to its Curie point and immediately cooling it as it comes into contact with the new chromium dioxide master. Provided the master chromium dioxide remains at 20°C or more below its Curie point, it will be unaffected.

Throughout the duplicating process it is extremely critical that the tensions of the tape are maintained within specific design parameters, as this is fundamental to the correct format being correctly copied.

The advantages of the thermal system for duplication are therefore:

1. An extremely efficient transfer process which produces a very high performance duplicate.
2. The elimination of mirror image recorders.
3. The elimination of very high coercivity master tapes.
4. The audio and control track can be transferred simultaneously with the FM video without the need for auxiliary heads.
5. The possibility of duplicating all existing ferric oxide or chromium dioxide tapes without the need for prerecording on special high coercivity tape.
6. The duplicate is made on chromium dioxide whose characteristics of high efficiency can be exploited by equipment manufacturers.

Unfortunately, the AC transfer process does not allow the master tape to be transferred to a high energy tape as generally the master tape has to be three times the coercivity of the duplicate and with present day technology 80 000 A/m (1000 oersteds) seems to be the limit for the master tape. The present generation of cassette recorders use tapes of 40 000–48 000 A/m (500–600 oersteds).

Methods of winding

Two methods of winding the tapes have been developed, known as bifilar and the dynamic method (Figure 6.11). In the latter, the

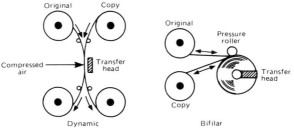

Figure 6.11. Two methods of winding tape in the a.c. transfer system

master and slave tapes are wound through separate paths and are brought together as they pass the transfer head. With this method it is possible to print as many as five slave tapes simultaneously from the same master and an hour programme can be copied in six minutes on the Ampex machine.

The bifilar method was developed to avoid tape slippage and a pressure roller eliminates any trapped air between the tapes before both tapes are fully wound onto the transfer reel. The reel continues to rotate as AC is applied to the transfer head and after the copy is made both types are rewound onto their separate reels. An hour long, half inch helical scan tape can be duplicated in about two minutes and, according to Matsushita, who developed this system, a signal-to-noise ratio better than 38 dB can be expected on the copy.

Stam system

Development of this system was carried out by 3M for a considerable time in the USA before the project was stopped. The initial object of the development was to provide the facility to copy from any type of master tape to any type of copy tape without the need for a mirror image recorder.

If this development had been successful any high energy, normal ferric oxide or chromium dioxide tape could have been used.

However, the initial specification had to be modified and if the master was a chromium dioxide tape it had to be transferred to a ferric oxide tape before being used on the duplicating machine.

The system used, within the machine, a proprietary steel transfer band which had a low Curie point but a very high coercivity. The ferric oxide master had its programme transferred to the steel band using a thermal process. Unfortunately the Curie point was too high to allow chromium dioxide master tapes to be used as they would have been erased.

After the transfer process the steel band carried a mirror image of the master and it then travelled to the other end of the machine where the signals were transferred to the copy tape by an AC transfer system.

The plan was to introduce a family of these machines for different formats and also to manufacture some machines with replaceable guides to allow different formats on the same machine.

Because of the difficulties experienced with both the AC and thermal methods it would have been a great engineering step forward if the two systems had been successfully combined.

Conclusion

If any copying system requires the master to be transferred to a special tape before high speed copying can commence, the advantages in time saving are lost as the new master can itself only be made in real time. The time taken to produce the new master can equally be used to make all the required copies on machine to machine recorders. However, if large quantities of copies are required there would be a considerable saving in equipment.

If several copies of different formats have to be produced simultaneously machine to machine recording is the only method.

Real time recording can also be utilised effectively for inserting foreign captions or new audio tracks in foreign languages.

Normally each process in duplicating degrades the picture in some way and the best quality picture is normally obtained by the least number of operations in making the copy. The secret of satisfactory commercial duplicating is quality control and as in any factory quality control should commence at the start of the system and should include all stages of production – it cannot be treated as something that is simple and straightforward. Quality control should include detailed examination of the recorders for noise, frequency and phase response, state of head, timebase stability and tension, since these parameters can vary daily.

It is essential that temperature and humidity are held to close tolerances as these affect the behaviour of tape. The area must also be extremely clean.

Before recording the replay machine or telecine must be accurately aligned and cleaned otherwise problems will arise; invariably this happens at about 50 minutes into a one-hour tape and causes a complete rejection of the run.

After recording it is essential that the tapes are, at a minimum, spot checked and at least one is checked from end to end for operational errors.

High speed video duplicating is still experimental, but so far has not proven successful, although systems, as explained, have been attempted by several major companies. Failure has been due to the mechanical problems of producing a mirror image in the AC system and tape shrinkage and deformation in the thermal system.

Unfortunately for the thermal process most domestic video cassette systems, where the real future for duplication exists, use tapes of 48 000 A/m (600 Oe) or more and chromium dioxide is not used.

Today, therefore, all major duplicating houses are using real time copying systems where one master can at times be recorded

Figure 6.12. Video duplicating centre recording on a large number of VTRs in real time (courtesy Rank Video Centre)

simultaneously on a hundred or more separate recorders (Figure 6.12).

Once, however, equipment is successfully produced for high speed duplication of video programmes onto magnetic tape, film and video discs will have lost one of their major advantages.

Anti-copying systems

Ever since the introduction of the video recorder producers and owners of feature films and television programmes have tried to find ways of protecting their investment. The pirating of films and audio records has become big business and immediately a television programme is broadcast many hundreds of copies are made either for personal use or for copying and exploitation. Although it is difficult to stop people copying off-air, the main worry for producers is the illegal copying of material given to duplicating houses for a limited number of copies to be produced for sale or for library use. Immediately one copy of this material is lent or sold the possibilities exist for innumerable copies to be made which obviously affects legitimate sales by the owner.

An important legal case is being fought in California between Sony and Walt Disney Universal Studios as to the legal right of Sony to produce equipment to record off-air programmes. After a lengthy court case the proceedings resulted in success for Sony but this was later overruled by the Appeal Court. It is, therefore, now illegal in the USA to record programmes from the TV. The case will now go to the Supreme Court or possibly legislation will be made whereby manufacturers of tape and VTRs will have to pay large sums of money to the copyright organisations for the owners of the programmes. This will considerably increase the costs of VTRs and tape to the customer. It will probably be several years before this case is finally settled.

However, development has resulted in systems being designed which allow a cassette to be replayed and viewed on a television set but make it impossible to re-record. To understand how this is achieved one must understand the video waveform and the servo system of a video recorder.

The frame pulses (see Chapter 1) are used by the television set to return the scanning beam to the top of the raster ready for the next picture.

When recording, the video machine locks the head drum to these pulses. If the pulses are not correct then the video tracks will not be laid down correctly and the tape cannot be replayed.

In replay the video recorder uses the control track pulses to lock the head drum and therefore the frame pulses are not required. Fortunately, the television set and the video recorder require different amounts of frame pulses to lock. Modern TV sets can lock on one or two broad pulses and display a synchronised picture. The video recorder, however, needs considerably more.

The systems, therefore, work by distorting the frame pulses sufficiently to prevent a video recorder locking but leaves the television set unaffected. This distortion can take the form of noise, movement, reshaping or adding waveforms to part of the vertical synchronising signals.

However, all television sets have different 'vertical hold' circuits and different video recorders have different servo systems. The systems, therefore, cannot be guaranteed to function correctly with all combinations of equipment. If sufficient distortion is added to stop all recorders recording then some television sets may experience vertical disturbances. If the interference is small enough to eliminate the possibility of problems with television sets then some recorders will record satisfactorily. The amount of interference must therefore be a compromise and accurately applied if problems are not to arise.

During the recording of a programme in a duplicating system the recorders must obviously be modified to record the initial recording as the interference is put into the system at this stage. Instead of the recorders locking their head drums to the vertical syncs of the television waveform (which will be distorted) a separate vertical pulse is provided which is in synchronism with the vertical syncs. If the master signal is being obtained from a telecine or VTR which is driven by a sync pulse generator then the vertical pulse from the SPG is used. If the master machine is not being driven from an SPG then a vertical sync separator is inserted into the signal path to obtain a synchronised vertical pulse before adding the distortion to the waveform.

Duplicating houses have had difficulty in operating these systems in the past due possibly to the experimental nature of the equipment, lack of knowledge about the amount of distortion required, variable equipment in the field or lack of care when applying the distortion.

It may, of course prove too critical a system to be used in practice but there seems no alternative that can be used without modifying recorders. The problem even then still exists, for wherever a correct waveform is reconstituted it can be recorded even if it is away from the recorder. Anti-copying systems may not be practicable so other solutions must be found.

Tapes can be identified electronically without a viewer being aware of the presence of the identifying signal. Although this will not stop people copying tapes it can help to trace the original source if pirated tapes are obtained, as the identifying signals would also be copied on all copies without the illegal duplicator knowing. This may help later prosecutions.

Perhaps a more practical solution is the one adopted in Germany where it is considered that it is not possible to stop people copying material. Instead a levy is imposed on all recording equipment in return for a blanket licence allowing the public to make single copies for their own use. It does nothing however, to stop the large scale pirate.

Chapter 7

Studio

Designing a closed circuit television studio

As a pilot uses a check list before take-off, so a prospective builder of a CCTV system has many questions to answer correctly before starting a project, otherwise the results can be very disappointing and perhaps rapidly become unusable for the intended purpose. Too often the responsibility for the design of a system is given to

Figure 7.1. A CCTV studio (courtesy Howden Management Services)

the staff who, although experienced in other work, have no television background. People are delegated because they occupy a particular position in an organisation, are given the budget for the college or company TV system and are expected to become experts in television by visiting a few retailers and exhibitions. So often a system starts with a choice of camera or VTR before all the problems of a particular customer have been analysed. Some of

Figure 7.2. A professional studio using Marconi Mk. IX cameras (courtesy Marconi)

the leading manufacturers are partially at fault for they are in business to sell their own hardware, and the installation of complete systems allows them to maximise sales to any single customer. However, hardware is only part of a correctly designed system and to utilise fully the potential of any hardware the remaining facilities for operation, post-production and maintenance must all be correct. These facilities cost money and with a restricted budget they may be obtainable only by buying less hardware.

All potential viewers of a CCTV programme in the UK will be used to watching possibly the highest standard of television production in the world and it is an unfortunate fact that unless viewers can concentrate on the contents of the programme without the distraction of poor technical quality or presentation, then the programme will have little value. Viewers quickly recognise an amateur production without necessarily understanding why they do so. Poor sound, meaningless camera shots, poor lighting and an amateur presenter result in a bored audience and no communication of information.

The television medium should provide visual information. If the programme conveys all the information equally as well if it is recorded on an audio casette, then the expense of television is wasted. An important part of any television system is the staff operating it: no matter how much the equipment has cost, without experienced technicians operating it, the results will be disappointing.

The first decision

Obviously, any company or group contemplating television production will know the type of programme they initially wish to make. The lower the budget the more simple must be the production. However, when designing the studio they should have in mind the type of programme they may wish to make as they expand, and when possibly more money becomes available. Space for extra racks, VTR editors, telecine, maintenance and extra storage will save money if initially planned, even though not immediately used. If the studio is successful and expands, careful initial planning may even prevent the studio having to be rebuilt in larger premises. Any easy-to-operate studio allows the staff to concentrate fully on the programme content. If, however, equipment is added over the years and has to be fitted in wherever possible, then the production will suffer and perhaps a greater number of staff will become necessary to operate the system.

The prospective buyer of a CCTV studio must, therefore, have clearly in mind the type of programmes to be made in the next five years, as any investment must at least last this period of time. The next major decision is whether the system will be colour or monochrome. If one starts initially with monochrome, with the intention to update in the future to colour, certain equipment should be purchased initially with this fact in mind to avoid too much obsolescence. Colour equipment is far more expensive, especially if one is using a multiple camera studio, as the cheaper range of colour cameras are completely unsuitable for such purposes.

Certain types of training programmes – such as medical, travel, design, cooking etc. – gain considerably from the use of colour, but training tapes which rely on interviews, facts and figures, can convey all the information in monochrome at a considerable saving. The problems associated with video duplication of the final programme for distribution are also made considerably easier if it is in monochrome.

Having decided on the type of programmes to be made initially and in the foreseeable future, and whether colour is necessary for the programme, the system designer is then in a position to start the detailed planning.

The studio

Generally the studio will be located in a building already occupied by the company and certain rooms will be allocated for conversion. In this case, as many of the ideal specifications for the purpose built studio should be matched as is possible.

The studio complex should be self-contained and isolated in order to avoid as much as possible unauthorised entry and interruption, as television is still a considerable magnet to the curious outsider.

As large a studio as possible should be planned and approximately 110 square metres will allow the construction of a versatile studio for two or three cameras. Smaller studios are obviously practical, but impose limitations on the amount of displays, demonstrations and scenery which can be introduced. However, large studios are of little use unless the ceiling is high enough to allow long shots to be taken without the lights becoming visible. This is often a problem in a converted building designed as offices. At least 7 metres should be considered the minimum height of any lighting grid.

The studio must obviously be sited in an area away from main roads, flight paths to airports, railway lines and other noisy environments, unless a considerable amount of money can be spent on sound insulation. Heavy insulation can make a room accoustically dead and reverberation time may have to be artificially increased to give satisfactory sound.

Large double door access should be provided into the studio for scenery and props and access from a drive should be easy for the loading or unloading of equipment. If the studio is not on the ground floor, then the lift must be large enough to take the largest and heaviest pieces of equipment, or the stairs must be wide and safe. Accidents can be very expensive in employee compensation and also in the possible loss for a long period of a valuable technician who is injured.

A studio requires storage space for scenery and props and this area must not be forgotten in the design of the studio complex. It may only be tables, chairs, microphone stands, lighting stands, lamps, drawing boards and a few demonstration aids, but the storage space required soon becomes fairly large.

If the studio is equipped with a cyclorama and a variety of curtains, then scenery for many programmes becomes minimal and with skilful lighting a variety of backgrounds can be produced, especially if the studio is operating in colour.

Ventilation in any studio is a major problem and a satisfactory solution can be expensive. When many lights are on and the studio has several staff working then the temperature quickly rises. The problem is to extract the air, and also bring into the studio fresh air, without the usual fan noise. Where budgets are limited, this is often an area where an unsatisfactory solution is tolerated.

Attention must be paid to the level of the studio floor. If there is a slope the heavy camera pedestals will start to move when the cameraman takes his hands off his camera.

Programmes need people, and changing rooms with washing facilities should be provided where participants may change their clothes in reasonable comfort and privacy. These need not necessarily be next to the studio, but communication is easier if they are. A room should also be provided with viewing facilities for people waiting to take part in programmes. This will avoid them wandering around and filling the control room and studio.

Control rooms

Control rooms are the nerve centre of the studio complex and the system should be designed for ease of communication with all areas and facilities to monitor all sources and outputs. All video sources terminate at the vision mixer from which the selected output becomes the programme and effects and captions can be added electronically or by mixing sources.

In CCTV systems, with good design, the whole system can be controlled by one person when making simple programmes. With a poor layout, however, the same equipment may require two or more people to operate it with a consequent increase in operating cost.

When the director is also a skilled operator he should in a small TV studio be able to operate the vision and audio mixers and have complete communication with everyone from the control desk.

In front of him should be a monitor on every signal source and also a vision mixer preview monitor and a transmission monitor. The height and distance from the director is critical for good

Figure 7.3. Director and mixing postiions (courtesy ATV Network Ltd)

operation. By moving only his eyes he should be able to glance at the audio and video mixer and all the monitors. If large movements of the head are required, then the operation will suffer. There should be sufficient space in front of him on the control desk for scripts and notes. Monitors should be spaced about six times the picture height from the viewer for viewing comfort, and preferably at or around head level when sitting. All operating equipment should be well lit with directional lighting to avoid any eye strain. Monitors must be matched and correctly set up. This applies especially to colour monitors and matching of cameras must take place on a single monitor.

There should be space so that an assistant can sit beside the director and operate the audio mixer or video mixer if the production becomes complex.

Telecine, VTR, slides, audio recorder and record players should all be operated remotely if possible from the control desk in small systems. This will not only reduce staff, but with experience will create a smoother operation.

In larger CCTV systems, where programmes are more ambi-
tious than the normal training programme, then the functions of
audio and video can be separated completely, but close contact
should be maintained and the same video monitoring system
should be visible to everyone.

With amateur presenters the director usually prefers to have
visibility through a window into the studio, although in professional studios this is no longer considered necessary and often the
position of the control room makes it impossible.

The main equipment racks are situated in the Central Apparatus
Room (CAR). In smaller complexes this may be an integral part of
the control room, or separate. On these racks are fitted the sync
pulse generator, providing all the different pulses to drive the
various pieces of video equipment and therefore keep all signal
sources synchronised (p. 176).

Each signal source is normally fed to a distribution amplifier
which allows five or six isolated outputs of the signal to be
obtained from the single input. These outputs feed the various
inputs to mixers, monitors and effects generators.

The main input sources to the various equipments are normally
taken through patch panels to allow various permutations of
equipment to be connected. This facility is invaluable to engineers,
as it permits them to apply test signals to individual pieces of
equipment or to by-pass the equipment if it is faulty. The correct
layout of both the video and audio patch panels can improve the
efficiency of any studio immeasurably and considerable thought
should be given to them during the design and installation stage.

Video tape recorders

Most studios exist to make video tape recordings and the masters
produced are either placed in a library for later showing or are usd
as the masters for the duplication of cassettes for distribution to
different parts of the company.

Before selecting the master recorder the final use of the master
recording should be fully understood. If the master is to be
duplicated, especially if it is colour, then the original recording
must be of the highest possible standard. This requires recording
on either a professional quadruplex format machine, an IVC 9000
or one of the high performance one inch helical scan machines
with direct colour recording (BCN B format or C format
machines, p. 74). However, these machines are possibly beyond
the budget for the type of studio we are discussing and the designer
will probably be limited to the higher grade of helical scan

machines capable of 5 MHz bandwidth but with separate colour processing and recording (IVC 900, 826, 871, Philips 87 series). With these recorders the master recording should, if possible, be transmitted through a TBC (timebase corrector) before being fed to a bank of duplicators. Many master recordings may appear satisfactory when viewed directly, but when further distortion is added in a duplicating process the final cassette may be of unacceptable quality. It is essential, therefore, that the original master is of the highest possible quality and cassette recorders should not be used for this purpose unless the master tape itself is to be shown. If any editing is to take place then the final edited tape will not be first generation and therefore, already not of the highest quality.

The area for a tape library should not be forgotten; this must be clean and of constant humidity and temperature (recommended 50% RH, 65°F, 18°C).

Cameras

Again, when making recordings the signal must be of the highest possible quality and when two or more cameras are used changes in quality should not be noticeable when switching between cameras. In colour this is not possible with simple one tube colour cameras and, to obtain matching between sources, three tube cameras must be used. In most cameras definition is improved by the use of enhancers, to give distinct edges to picture transitions.

Cable lengths on cameras are important, since high frequency loss and the timing of the signals to the mixer have to be corrected. When several signals are produced under the control of the single sync pulse generator it is essential, if timing shifts in the pictures are not to take place when switching between sources, that all the signals arrive at the mixer at the same time. The reference must, therefore, be the furthest source as each cable and the equipment will produce a delay. With this signal as a reference all other signals are delayed until their timings coincide. This is an important part of a studio construction, especially when the complexes are large.

Some manufacturers synchronise a multiple camera installation by genlocking (synchronising internally generated pulses in the camera with external pulses) each camera to a centrally generated signal. This has the advantage that only a single waveform has to be fed to each camera and allows a wide adjustment of timing range to be made.

Telecine

Most studios will include telecine facilities and the complexity and type will depend on the importance of film to the user. The subject is covered in detail in the next section.

Power

For lighting purposes three-phase power is brought into a studio complex and each phase should be balanced as well as possible. However, all technical equipment must be run from a single phase and when working on video equipment it must not be possible to go across two phases.

The technical earth is also of the utmost importance and this should be separated from all other earths and be connected to the structural steel of the building with a total resistance of less than 0.1 ohm. The earth should be taken to the racks and all technical earths should be connected to this. Earth loops must be avoided since they may cause hum bars to appear on the picture and hum to be heard on the sound.

Audio

However good the pictures, most of the information will be conveyed by sound and it is essential that this is of the highest possible quality. The art of balancing sound and the placement of microphones can only be learned from experience, although there are rules to be learned and followed (this also applies to the cameraman). However good the equipment, incorrect operation will produce poor results.

The centre of the audio system is an audio mixer, into which all the audio sources are routed. The output is controlled by faders permitting a single output or a mixture of several inputs which have been carefully balanced. Although level meters are used, balancing must be controlled by listening to the sound on a high quality loudspeaker.

In a similar manner to video distribution, sound distribution amplifiers are used to allow more than one output from any single source to be available for different uses throughout the studio complex.

Record players and magnetic tape recorders are also required to provide music, sound effects and pre-recorded inserts.

To avoid hum problems, the normal practice is to use balanced inputs, where the two wires carrying the sound are equally balanced about earth so that any induced hum or other interference will cancel out in the transformers. All the audio cables are

screened to avoid pickup of extraneous signals, and when installing care must be taken in routing the cables and ensuring they are
not adjacent to power cables.

Communication between everyone requires a fairly sophisticated talkback system. This will allow all cameramen and the floor
manager to listen to and talk back to the director, and communications should also be possible with telecine and VTR operators if
they are some distance away.

Test equipment

The engineers will need test equipment to keep a large installation
maintained and operating to the designed specification. This is
obviously far more expensive in a colour studio and the minimum
test equipment would be:

1. Test signal generator giving
   colour bars (normally provided in the encoders)
   graticule
   sawtooth
   grey scale
2. A good quality oscilloscope
3. Vectorscope
4. Voltmeters
5. RF generator
6. Audio generator

These are obviously expensive and to the non-engineer may be
overlooked when budgeting for the studio.

Cost of a studio

It is obvious that the cost of a studio can vary within wide limits,
but most studios have to be designed within a very restricted
budget. It should be clear, however, that a considerable amount of
money is spent on other than cameras and video recorders if a
system is to function correctly. In the USA most companies
entering video employ consultants to design and prepare the
specifications to suit the customer's budget and requirements. It is
then put out to tender and companies compete using the same
design and the same standard of equipment. Unfortunately this
generally is not the situation in the UK or Europe.

Using three colour cameras of acceptable performance, video
tape recorders, telecine, vision mixer, audio mixer, timebase
corrector, sync pulse generator, distribution amplifiers, microphones, dollys, patch panels, monitors, lights, control desk, test

equipment, coders etc., a hardware price of £80,000 plus is quickly reached before the cost of installation and studio space are added.

Conclusion

The design and building of a television studio should not be undertaken by inexperienced people. At the start, it is essential to know what type of programmes are to be produced and even if one starts small and progresses, it is important that one starts correctly, otherwise obsolescence takes place. As the amount of equipment is increased it may also be found that earlier equipment is incompatible. It may even be wiser to leave production to the professional studios who are both equipped and staffed. However, an in-house television system properly built and staffed can bring considerable rewards to a large company for training, communication both internally and with dealers and customers and can be used as a means of making a multinational company or widely dispersed groups of people within a country feel as if they have a common bond. This is being proved by many large companies, especially in the USA.

Some of the material produced by colleges is also exceptionally good and allows students to obtain the best lectures at their own convenience and the lecturers to always be seen at their brightest and best (subject to good editing).

However, the video must add to the information. If the message can be conveyed equally as well by audio only then the studio is wasted. Audio cassettes are far more convenient to salesmen and others who can listen at home, in a car or any other convenient place and production costs are only a fraction of the costs of a television programme.

Telecine

Film is still extremely important to the television industry for both programmes and commercials. Apart from ease of duplication it still has the advantage to a company selling the film worldwide that it can be played in any television standard without any form of standards conversion. The television standard on replay depends solely on the telecine, which can be PAL, SECAM, NTSC or any other system. With video recordings it is important to a distributor to know which television standards are being used in any particular country. The film distributor can ship the same product, without modification, to any television authority or cinema in the world.

The film used in television is either 16mm or 35mm with Super-8 used in exceptional circumstances where the contents are more important than the quality (as in news items). Super-8, however, is sometimes used extensively in CCTV although the cheaper range of ENG equipment will probably make this obsolete.

Film stock has improved enormously in recent years and whereas in broadcasting 35mm was used whenever possible, 16mm is now being used far more frequently.

Types of telecine equipment

A telecine system can consist solely of a projector showing the film directly into a television camera, but invariably most systems are

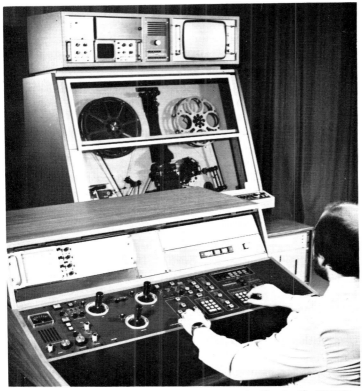

Figure 7.4. Foreground: operator at remote console (fitted with TOPSY panel); background: Cintel Mk. III flying spot telecine next to TOPSY floppy disc drive (courtesy Rank-Cintel)

more complex. The two main categories are those that use a television camera as the signal generating equipment (storage type) and the 'flying spot' system (non-storage), generating its signal from the scan of a cathode ray tube. The latter system is usually found only in broadcasting and high quality video duplicating systems as the equipment tends to be very expensive. Most of the systems in CCTV use a television camera with one or more projectors shining into it via a mirror system. However, these systems can also produce broadcast quality and at the top end of the quality range are just as expensive as the flying spot systems. More recent developments in telecine are using digital techniques and charge coupled devices (CCDs) for signal generation (p. 174).

Multiplexer systems and cameras

The projectors are arranged around the multiplexer so that each projector shines into its own individual input lens system (Figure 7.5). In a movable mirror system, mirrors are rapidly moved to

Figure 7.5. RCA telecine island using a multiplexer

direct the light from the required projector to the camera. The mirrors can be raised or lowered as required by the camera position or swing into position by electromagnetic or pneumatic systems (Figure 7.6).

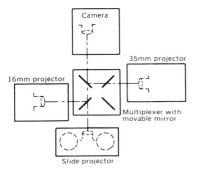

Figure 7.6. With this type of multiplexer the mirrors move in and out of the light paths as required to reflect the light to the camera. With four movable mirrors a wide arrangement of inputs and extra cameras can be devised

Different designs of multiplexers use different systems but most act quickly enough to produce an apparent video switch when changing projectors (Figure 7.7).

The mirrors used in the system are either totally reflecting or semi-transparent types. Some transparent mirrors are used in stationary mirror systems where it is necessary to totally reflect light from one projector and also allow light from a projector coming from a different position to pass through. The mirrors must be equally transparent to all wavelengths from red to violet or colour falsification will occur. The selection of the material for such layers and its evaporation onto the glass must, therefore, be performed with the greatest care. The precision and complexity of

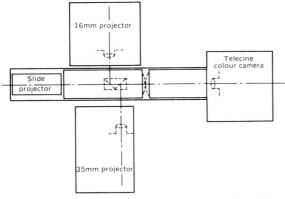

Figure 7.7. A prism multiplexer arrangement used by Philips

stationary mirrors therefore partially offsets the mechanical complexity required for moving totally reflecting mirrors out of the light path when not required. The transparent mirror is also affected by dust and its environment much more so than a reflecting mirror. The picture contrast can often become adversely affected as thin blurring layers are formed on the surfaces. These layers not only reduce the amount of light passed but also form reflecting layers which can result in ghost images.

In order to avoid the disadvantages of stationary semi-transparent mirrors and movable reflecting mirror systems, prisms of high quality glass have been developed which are insensitive to dust and atmospheric influences.

It is critical when installing such systems that the floor be perfectly level. If it is incorrect it will not be possible to align three or four separate inputs, which originate from different positions, so that the projected picture on the camera tube is exactly square to the tube face. If they are not square then trapezium distortion occurs on one or more inputs.

There are advantages to a multiplexer system over a flying spot system in so far that a variety of projectors can be selected instantly and in some multiplexer systems a preview facility can be incorporated by using an inexpensive monochrome camera. A normal complement of projectors in broadcasting consists of 35 mm and 16 mm projectors and a 35 mm slide projector.

Usually incorporated into the multiplexer is some form of control to enable the amount of light falling on the camera tube to be adjusted. Such controls have to be very fast and smooth in action if sudden large changes in picture brightness are not to occur when switching sources or when the density of the film is variable. Oscillation of the servo systems is also a possibility which must be avoided.

On the early monochrome telecines the projector lamp brightness was adjusted by a servo system sensing the amount of light being projected through the film. This tended to be slow in action and unsuitable for colour as the colour temperature of the lamp varies with the brightness and causes hue changes.

The system now adopted uses a variable neutral density filter, consisting of a wheel whose density varies around the perimeter and optically does not affect the colour of the projected picture. The neutral density filter is placed in front of the camera lens and the amount of light passing through the film to the camera is detected and the position of the filter is adjusted by an electronic servo. It is impossible to obtain satisfactory telecine pictures without such a system operating correctly.

The projectors used are normally standard cinema projectors made to operate at 25 f.p.s. when the TV system is operating at 25 pictures per second, instead of the 24 f.p.s. used in the cinema. The film image is focused onto the photoconductive surface of the camera tube and the projector flashes a picture during the field suppression period when the scanning beam is cut off and vertical flyback is occurring. Mistiming of this period can result in 'application bars' appearing on the picture (similar to hum bars).

Conventional projectors are an advantage over flying-spot projection systems in systems requiring different television scanning standards of 50 and 60 fields per second. Such systems are easily modified by using a two-blade shutter for 50 field working and a five-blade shutter for 60 field working. With flying spot systems the 60 field standard is generally performed by a sophisticated fast pulldown intermittent mechanism working on a 2:3 frame arrest principle, whereby alternate cine frames are exposed two or three times (Figure 7.8). Generally for 50 field working flying spot systems use continuous motion projectors.

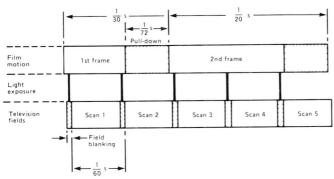

Figure 7.8. Pull-down arrangement required for 60 Hz projection

The choice of camera tube has a considerable effect on the final picture quality. There is usually no shortage of light which causes smearing in low light studio scenes when using vidicons. Telecines can be manufactured using any high grade camera and tubes and the visible results are determined by the sophistication of the camera and the technical standard of the film.

Comparisons with flying spot

An advantage of the camera type of telecine can be the amount of available light which can result in a superior signal-to-noise ratio over the flying spot system, especially when colour films of high density are shown and poor film quality has to be compensated by electronic means. When applying high gamma correction, extra black stretching and more contour correction than is normal, as much signal as possible is required. In a flying spot system, even with a high efficiency CRT, there is a limited amount of light available after splitting to the photomultipliers. This can result in a rather poor signal-to-noise ratio.

However, compensating for this problem is the fact that the noise from a photoelectric cell is proportional to the square root of the signal current. The photoconductive tube, however, has a constant noise output at all signal levels. Therefore, at black level the noise generated by the photoelectric cells at the beginning of the processing stage is less. The subjective results of the telecine depend, therefore, on the different factors from the various parts of the system.

In order to improve the apparent definition of the picture it is essential that enhancing circuits are incorporated which affect both horizontal and vertical contours (see Chapter 3). Independent units known as 'vertical aperture correctors' are generally incorporated into the system and have a considerable effect on the resulting picture.

A disadvantage of the camera and multiplexer type of telecine is the problem caused by the necessity for convergence of the three colour signals. The flying spot system has perfect registration due to its design principles. When three-tube cameras are used, however, routine operational attention must be given to ensuring the accuracy of registration and controls are usually made readily available. Small registration problems can be disguised to some degree by correctly operating enhancement circuits, but generally the picture quality produced by the telecine is considerably affected.

Flying spot telecine

The basic system of a flying spot telecine (Figure 7.9) uses the image of a raster produced on the screen of a cathode ray tube as the light source (Figure 7.10). The CRT must be specially produced and be of high brightness with a very short persistence time. Afterglow correction, usually in the form of high frequency boost, is generally applied to compensate for the finite decay time of the scanning tube phosphor. The light from the CRT spot is passed through a continuously moving film and the modulated light signal is focused onto a photocell. At any given moment the photocell signal is proportional to the optical transmission of the film.

In order to produce interlaced scanning, it is necessary to produce two separate images of the raster on the film. These are obtained by using either a split lens or two separate lenses producing separate rasters, one above the other, on the film. Each raster is scanned in turn while the other is blanked by a shutter synchronised to the frame rate. Both rasters are scanned in ½₅ second to produce the interlaced picture. As the film and scanning spot are both moving the scanning spot is made to move upwards

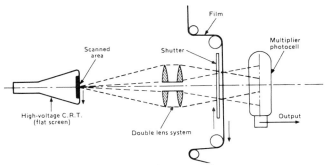

Figure 7.10. Principles of the flying spot film scanner

while the film moves down through the gate. The combined movement requires, therefore, for the raster to be reduced in height on the CRT to compensate, making the aspect ratio 4:1½ instead of 4:3.

In colour systems the spot of light, after passing through the film, is split into its red, green and blue component colours in a similar way to photoconductive systems, but in flying spot tele-cines the electrical signals are produced by three photocells.

Although perfect colour registration is obtained with flying spot systems there still remains the difficulty of ensuring that interlace is correct with perfect field-to-field registration. In the past this has necessitated meticulous optical and mechanical engineering. Recent developments have produced a digital technique which overcomes this problem and is available on the new Rank Cintel Mk. III telecines. With this method the film is scanned sequentially, stored and then the signal is converted to a standard interlaced signal.

Film shrinkage

When using a continuous moving projector, the accuracy of registration depends upon the sprocket holes. Positional errors of these holes causes jumping and lateral weave of the film. Film shrinkage of 0.5% is common and can often be two or three times this value. As the sprocket holes are positioned to feed the pictures at a constant number of pictures per second shrinkage will cause the velocity to be reduced. This can result in the film moving too short a distance and consequently if the reduction in distance is equal to a line pitch, the same line is scanned for both fields resulting in a loss of vertical resolution.

Special precautions have to be taken to avoid errors caused by film shrinkage which can involve moving the CRT field scan for alternate fields or moving one of the optical systems by the requisite amount. Recent digital methods used to overcome the problem of interlace due to the splitting of the fields (as previously explained) also eliminate this problem.

TOPSY (Telecine Operation Programming System – Rank Cintel)

To obtain consistent quality throughout the showing of a film the telecine must be equipped with controls which affect many parameters. These not only correct for often variable film quality but also provide a means of matching to other originating sources.

Previewing of the film is the only way the operator can be prepared for the various corrections to be made and obviously to obtain consistent results time and experiment is required.

TOPSY provides a microprocessor based system whereby adjustments can be made on preview until the operator is satisfied. The information relating to the series of events is then permanently stored on a mini-floppy disc. This system makes it possible for the operator to cue the telecine anywhere within the film. Adjustment events can be called from memory and displayed with their time of occurrence and can be transferred with a new frame number to provide identical settings for other parts of the film. On transmission the telecine is then controlled by the microprocessor and previously programmed corrections are made frame by frame. This new equipment renders obsolete the old system of 'Autocolour-grade', whereby information relating to correction for colour changes was programmed onto a punched tape.

The new system not only provides for colour balance correction but also for Cinemascope, panning, vertical aperture correction and audio levels.

Cinemascope

Many modern films made for the cinema have an anamorphic image which has a 2:1 width compression and an aspect ratio of

2.35:1. As the television aspect ratio is 4:3, the telecine scan must be modified.

If the viewer is to see the full width of the picture the film has to be transmitted in a 'letter box' mode. Unfortunately, only just over half the available picture height is utilised on the TV screen. If the full picture height is transmitted then the available information in a horizontal direction must be reduced. Fortunately most of the action tends to take place in the centre of the screen, but if action occurs in the parts of the film not being transmitted then it is necessary to pan by moving the horizontal scan of the CRT raster or camera tubes. Such scanning can be pre-programmed with TOPSY or manually operated on air. The anamorphic compression can also be corrected by scan adjustment.

Other aspects ratios of 35 mm film are used by the cinema and ratios of 1.65:1 and 1.85:1 non-anamorphic systems are encountered.

Combined and separate sound

The sound track used with film can be either magnetic or optical. The magnetic track is sensed by a static head in a similar way to all audio recording.

The combined optical track is recorded on the edge of the film and developed at the same time as the film. Two forms of audio modulation have been used, known as variable area and variable density. In both types a light shines through the audio track and the resulting modulated light is sensed by a photoelectric cell.

A *variable area* sound track modulates the light by altering the area of clear film through which the light shines. This alters the amount of light reaching the photoelectric cell and reproduces the sound.

A *variable density* audio track has a sound track whose optical density varies with modulation. The light passing through is similarly modulated. Such sound tracks, however, are susceptible to processing errors and therefore variable area sound tracks are preferred. When the sound track is combined with the film the system is known as COMOPT (combined optical) or COMMAG (combined magnetic).

Often where a foreign language sound track is used or news items are filmed with sound tracks, the audio track is separate from the film. This is known as SEPOPT or SEPMAG. These tracks can be found in the centre or at the edge of the separate sound film.

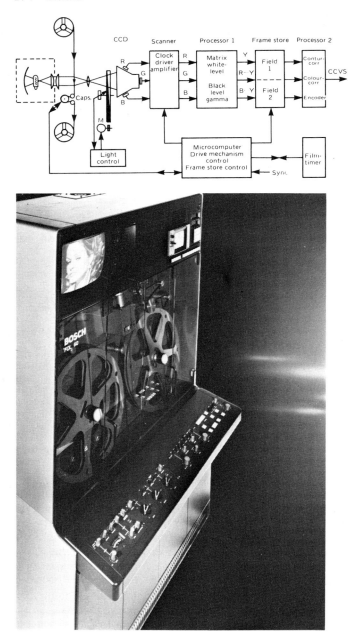

Figure 7.11. (top) Principles of the Bosch FDL60 digital CCD telecine; (bottom) the Bosch FDL60 telecine

When such sound tracks are separately run some means of locking the audio replay recorders with the telecine projectors has to be incorporated if synchronism and lip sync is to be maintained; the locking systems can be mechanical or electrical. The electrical systems can consist of fitting additional three-phase motors (Selsyn) to the projectors which drive them from motors locked to the audio recorder. The windings on the projector and recorder motors are connected so that as the first motor begins to move electrical fields are set up in the second motor which moves in sympathy.

Other systems have been developed which use pilot tones or the synchronisation of generated pulses to lock the movements of the projector and recorder.

In all cases synchronisation relies on the correct editing of film and sound track and accurate setting up by the operator, since the systems only ensure speed variations do not occur between the projector and audio replay machine once the start button has been operated.

Positive and negative film

Pictures can be transmitted from a telecine from either a positive or negative film. Rushed film news is often negative and consequently the operating parameters of the telecine have to be completley changed as the characteristics of positive and negative film are entirely different.

Apart from the necessary reversal, the contrast ratio of a positive film can be as high as 200:1, while for negative the ratio can be as low as 10:1. The gamma circuits therefore have to be altered to compensate.

Bosch digital CCD telecine

An entirely new technique for telecines has been developed by Bosch and Marconi which uses line scanning and digital storage (Figure 7.11).

The conventional film transport is continuous and is driven by a capstan motor. The picture information, however, undergoes RGB separation in the prism system and is scanned line after line by CCD (charge coupled devices) before being written into a digital frame store.

The frame store uses a 16 K RAM with component coding (see Chapter 10). Luminance and chrominance information is digitised separately and stored line by line as a full frame. The write and read processes are under the control of a computer. Interlace is achieved by reading out all 'odd' lines during the first field and all 'even' lines during the following field. As all the lines have individual addresses it becomes possible to obtain stills, forward and reverse operation, slow motion, fast motion and four different speeds.

After read-out the digital signal is converted to an analogue signal and encoded to produce a composite colour signal.

The advantages of the CCD sensors are:

1. Extremely long life and reliability.
2. No burn-in, afterglow or field lag.
3. Continuous vertical scan avoids shrinkage problems and flicker due to amplitude and positioning errors.
4. Constant vertical resolution due to the absence of any vertical deflection. All the scanning is on the optical axis.
5. Horizontal size and linearity adjustments no longer needed as horizontal read-out is generated by a shift register and not by beam deflection.
6. No twin optics jump scan or fast pull down – continuous sequential line scanning.
7. No EHT supply required but only low DC voltage for the CCDs.

This new development in telecine promises to produce excellent pictures for the future. Due to digital techniques being used the pictures have greatly reduced noise and will be easily engineered into the new digital studios of the future.

Conclusion

Although most publicity is currently given to improvement in VTRs, it is essential to a broadcaster that telecines also keep abreast of all modern developments. Modern cameras allow excellent telecines to be produced for the CCTV market and in the broadcasting field digital techniques are eliminating long-standing problems and producing considerable operational flexibility. The awards presented for the Rank-Cintel Mk. III telecine are recognition of this and are reminiscent of the awards to Ampex for their contributions to video recording.

Control room equipment

In a broadcast studio complex there are two types of control room. These are the studio control room, from which the director controls the programme production, and the master control room, which is responsible for all signal distribution throughout the complex and the broadcast network together with the station presentation and continuity to the local transmitter.

By the nature of the work involved the emphasis in the studio control room is on production while in a master control room (MCR/CAR – central apparatus room) the emphasis tends to be more on engineering, and presentation is solely one of switching and time-keeping.

A CCTV complex deals only with programme production and no transmitter or network exists. The roles of a studio and CAR are, therefore, usually combined and the equipment normally found in the CAR is incorporated in the studio control room.

Sync pulse generator (SPG)

The master timing source for the studio complex is the SPG. The pulses produced by this equipment are fed to every piece of equipment that produces a signal or whose operation must occur at precise times. Because of its importance, the SPG is normally duplicated and changeover in the event of failure is either manual or automatic depending upon the sophistication of the studio complex. Any interruption or variation in the performance of the SPG affects all areas and it must therefore be an extremely reliable

Figure 7.13. Sync pulse generator (courtesy Acron Video)

piece of equipment. Fortunately modern units are completely solid state and rely for their operation on frequency division and multiplier circuits, in the form of phase-locked loops, producing the required pulses from a master crystal oscillator which is mounted in an oven to provide a stable temperature. It therefore has all the reliability of digital equipment and usually requires no attention.

Monochrome television pulses

For monochrome operation four pulses are necessary:
1. Line drive (LD).
2. Field drive (FD).
3. Mixed synchronising pulses (MS).
4. Mixed blanking pulses (MB).

These pulses are sufficient to drive and time any monochrome studio complex and their timings will be related to the standard operating in any particular country. The master oscillator is usually locked to the mains frequency to avoid drifting hum bars within the picture but if the frequency is insufficiently stable then a crystal reference is used.

Gen-lock (slaving)

Often in a production it is necessary to mix between two sources whose waveforms are not synchronised. This is not possible until the local SPG has been synchronised with the external source so that the locally produced signals arrive at the mixer in synchronism with the external source. When this occurs mixing is possible and captions and credits produced locally can be superimposed on the remote pictures.

If synchronisation is not possible then mixing and superimposition cannot be performed and the signal can only be 'cut to' with a resulting disturbance in outgoing synchronising pulses which may cause frame rolls on monitors and certainly disturbance to any VTR machine which is recording the entire programme. Although the cut is momentary the VTR will require time to resynchronise its servo systems.

To overcome this problem the SPG is fitted with a gen-lock facility which allows the master oscillator to lock to the incoming waveform from the remote source, which then synchronises both waveforms. The gen-lock (slaving) must be performed before the programme commences as the initial operation will cause a disturbance to all areas being fed from the SPG. It is usually done when the signal is at black in a broadcast station so that momentary disturbances are not seen 'off air'. However, arrangements must be made in large complexes where studios are operating independently of the slaving area, to ensure that the studio and its signal sources (VTR, telecine etc.) are on a separate SPG. This can cause problems if they are recording a separate programme.

Once a source has been slaved to, the syncs must be maintained by the remote source until the programme is complete, or the SPG has been de-slaved, otherwise complete break-up of the station's pictures will occur.

When more than one remote source has to be synchronised to a local source a system such as 'Natlock' can be used. This technique compares the phases of the remote sources with the local reference and sends correction signals, usually digital, down telephone lines to alter the phase of the remote signal until it is synchronous with the local signal. A more modern method of synchronisation is a digital synchroniser (explained later).

PAL colour SPG

The PAL SPG has three more outputs than the monochrome SPG. These are:

1. Colour subcarrier, 4.43361875 Mhz, which is held within ± 1 Hz.
2. PAL ident which synchronises the R–Y vector switching.
3. Burst gate which allows the colour subcarrier to be placed on the back porch of the TV waveform.

In addition there may be an 'early sync' for any equipment requiring such an input pulse.

It is critical that the rise and fall times of the pulses are accurately produced if timings are to be correct and should be about 150 ns ± 50 ns.

Subcarrier and half line offset – NTSC

The NTSC subcarrier was chosen so that it was not a direct multiple of the line frequency, but of a half line frequency, so that at the end of a scanning picture one half cycle of subcarrier remains. On the next picture the phase of the subcarrier is reversed and the effect of the subcarrier on the screen is cancelled out over two pictures. In practice the cancellation is not complete due to incomplete retentivity of the eye over a picture period and the non-linearity of the CRT. A dot pattern can therefore be observed under certain circumstances.

Also, as the subcarrier is modulated by various colours over a picture area, its phase changes and the dots move. Provided that the hue remains the same over two pictures cancellation will occur. The magnitude of the subcarrier in PAL and NTSC is maximum only for saturated colours at full brilliance and does not occur on monochrome. Large areas of saturated colours are rare and in practice this reduced the chances of observation of the pattern.

The relationship of the subcarrier (f_{sc}) to the line frequency (f_H) in NTSC is given by

$$f_{sc} = (N - \tfrac{1}{2})f_H$$

N is a whole number and is chosen depending upon the line standard. In a 525-line system it is 228.

$$f_{sc} = 3.579545\,\text{MHz (USA 525-line NTSC system)}$$

The subcarrier in the 525-line NTSC system $= 227\tfrac{1}{2}f_H$ and is known as a 'half-line offset'.

SPG PAL system

In the PAL system the situation is further complicated by the reversal of the V axis on every line. The U axis behaves in a similar way to NTSC, but further modification must be made for the V axis patterning structure. With a half-line offset the dot structure will appear as straight lines in exactly the same position on each picture, resulting in lack of cancellation. In PAL, therefore, the half-line offset is made a quarter-line offset, which produces a U axis pattern which repeats every eight fields (fourth picture) and appears as a sloping line dot structure to the right which, although less visible, does not provide cancellation. The V signal, due to the 180° phase reversal on each line, produces a similar pattern but the dots slope to the left.

To produce patterns where the positions of dots of one field are opposite to those of the next field the waveform frequencies must be modified further and the frequency of the subcarrier must be altered so that it is a half-cycle different on each field. This represents one complete cycle per picture (25 Hz).

The subcarrier for the PAL 625 line system is therefore:

$$f_{sc} = (N - \tfrac{1}{4})\,f_H + 25$$

N in this system is 284

$$f_{sc} = (284 - \tfrac{1}{4})\,15\,625 + 25$$

$$f_{sc} = 4.433\,618\,75\,\text{MHz}$$

In a PAL colour SPG the crystal oscillator is the subcarrier and the broadcast specification relates the line frequency to the subcarrier by

$$F_H = \frac{f_{sc} - 25}{284 - \tfrac{1}{4}}$$

The SPG may also for certain purposes be capable of operating in two further modes.

1. Where the 25 Hz offset is not provided

$$F_H = \frac{f_{sc}}{284 - \frac{1}{4}}$$

2. Where the subcarrier is not related to the line frequency.

Pulse distribution

The outputs of the SPG are fed to individual pulse distribution amplifiers (PDA) usually at a level of 2 V. For every input the amplifier is capable of supplying a number of isolated outputs (normally six) which are fed to the various areas and pieces of equipment. In large complexes a number of amplifiers have their inputs looped to provide the necessary number of outputs. Amplifiers designed for pulse distribution must have good frequency and phase response so that overshoots and undershoots are not produced on the leading and trailing edges of the pulses.

Monosync pulse distribution system (Marconi)

Seven separate synchronising waveforms require to be distributed for a PAL studio and six for NTSC (ident signal not required). In a complex studio arrangement where pulse assignment systems are used a flexible system of pulse distribution must be achieved if costs are not to be too substantial. The monosync pulse distribution system generates all the necessary timing waveforms (Figure 7.14) and transmits these on a single cable to the various destinations. Both undelayed and delayed outputs of up to 3.15 µs are

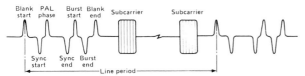

Figure 7.14. Monosync waveform (Marconi)

provided to permit the correct timing of telecines and VTRs for both the production and presentation control rooms. The selection of the correct pulses is provided by either an assignment system or patch panels. At the destination the train of pulses is converted to standard waveforms by a decoder and fed to the equipment in the normal way. Apart from a reduction of cabling, switching facilities and PDAs the timing of a studio is considerably simplified as a single delay at either the coder or decoder will give identical delay to all pulses. As shown in Figure 7.14, the monosync waveform pulses are coded in such a manner that both positive and negative sine^2 pulses are transmitted. Subcarrier is transmitted as two bursts each line to provide maximum stability. Peak levels of 1 V allow the signals to be transmitted through standard video distribution amplifiers and a bandwidth of 3.5 MHz is required.

Video distribution amplifiers

Similar equipment to pulse distribution amplifiers is used for the distribution of video where a single video source may be separately required in several studios, control rooms and recording areas for both monitoring and transmission purposes. Video distribution amplifiers must be capable of passing the complete PAL video signal without any deterioration and attention must therefore be paid to frequency, phase, linearity, noise, differential gain and luminance/chrominance gain and delay. The outputs are designed to supply 1 V into 75 Ω, although some have a level control allowing gains to be adjusted to overcome cable losses.

Several manufacturers have a DA suitable for either video or pulses and where a video DA is used for pulses it must be capable of the higher levels of 2 V (sometimes 4 V required) without overload distortion.

Equalising amplifier

In large studio complexes the cable runs may be very long, resulting in a loss of high frequencies. Equalising amplifiers capable of compensating for these losses will equalise cable runs up to 300 metres (typically 10 dB at 10 MHz, depending on the attenuation of the cable used). These usually have six isolated outputs and a single input.

Digital television field synchroniser

As previously explained the use of external non-synchronous picture sources within a studio centre presents many problems. Unless the studio has been able to slave then mixing, fades and other special effects are not possible and cutting to the source may cause frame rolls on the monitor.

Genlocking has the disadvantage that during slaving and deslaving the waveforms from the SPG are non-standard and elaborate assignment switchers and several SPGs may be required where other studios are making independent productions and therefore need to be separate and undisturbed. Digital techniques have, however, provided an elegant solution and by the introduction of one or more field synchronisers (Figure 7.15), the incoming signals can be retimed and treated in all respects as an internal signal source. The solution lies in the provision of a field store into which the incoming signal is written and it is taken out of store under the control of the station syncs. By this method the reconstituted signal is automatically timed to the station SPG.

Figure 7.15. NEC digital frame synchroniser

In the store the signal is in 8-bit digital format and the incoming signal must therefore first be converted by an analogue-to-digital converter (see Chapter 10). A 16K RAM (random access memory) is sufficient for a single field and when taken out of the store the digital signal is reconverted to its analogue form by a digital-to-analogue converter (DAC).

In the ADC the data is written into the store under the control of the SPG through clock and timing pulses generated from the SPGs syncs and burst waveforms.

As this type of equipment comes into more regular use the decision must be made concerning its uses and, therefore, the degree of sophistication. As we shall see, once an analogue waveform has been digitally encoded and placed into a store then a considerable number of effects can be produced and the unit can be incorporated into the production mixer. However, this causes a considerable rise in cost. There is, therefore, a debate as to whether the synchronisers should be simple units solely for synchronisation of signals or whether they should have a complete frame store and be capable of freeze frame and picture manipulation. If the market proves sufficiently large then perhaps both types of equipment will exist.

Timebase correctors

The final piece of equipment required to obtain standard waveforms and synchronism between sources is the timebase corrector,
which will be familiar to both broadcasters and CCTV engineers
(Figures 7.16 and 7.17). In VTR replays, tape and head speed
variations, equivalent to wow and flutter on audio recorders, cause
variations in the line duration of the replayed TV signal.

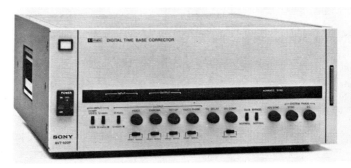

Figure 7.16. Sony digital TBC

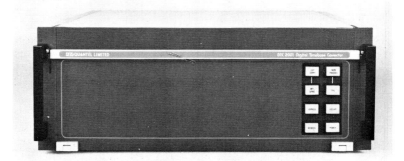

Figure 7.17. Quantel TBC

Quadruplex machines are capable of timebase errors under 1 μs
and even interchanged and dubbed tapes do not exceed a few
microseconds. However, the use of helical machines for non-
broadcast purposes require corrections of the order of 10 μs, and
with interchange of tapes, errors of ±1 horizontal line are
common. As the signal handling of these machines improved,

some broadcsters began to use them for transmission. Also, with the advent of ENG, the errors obtained from lightweight portable machines could exceed 100 lines.

Thus the particular problems of the customers to whom the manufacturer wishes to sell determine, to some extent, the performance and cost of the various pieces of equipment. Within the equipment the analogue waveform is first converted to a digital format, placed in a store and read by a clock synchronised from a stable signal source. The digital code is then reconverted to an analogue signal to produce a stabilised video output (Figure 7.18).

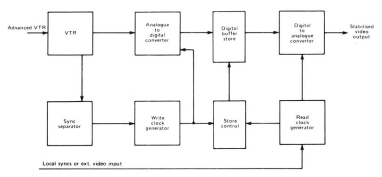

Figure 7.18. Digital timebase correction basic block diagram

The problem arises of how large the memory should be to cater for the amount of errors to be encountered. In practice, this may require between three and five lines of storage (window). If a drop-out compensator is incorporated, this will also increase the memory. If the errors exceed the store capacity a gentle vertical movement will be observed.

If the store has only three to five lines of storage, but is to be replayed with its output locked to the station syncs, it is necessary that the VTR maintains synchronism in a vertical lock mode. It is essential, therefore, that VTRs used with TBCs have a capstan servo, or a motor drive amplifier (MDA) which will act in a similar manner. This functions by comparing the input video vertical signal and output power signals in a phase comparator and producing a correctly phased sine wave to drive the VTR.

As there is a delay in the store of the TBC it is necessary to provide the VTR with an 'advanced drive' (early sync) so that the VTR will lock-up ahead of the point the video is required. If a capstan servo or MDA is not available a non-standard output is produced which varies according to the average frequency of the VTR transport.

The analogue signal is quantised (see Chapter 10) and reproduced as a digital signal of 8-bit words for the store. Each word represents one of 256 levels of analogue signal and each line is sampled at such a rate that it contains 771 digital words. The signal is written into the store under the control of a 'write' clock which is phase-locked to the phase signal from the VTR. On replay the information is read from the store under the control of the TBCs internal SPG (if it has one), local SPG or a composite video source fed to the TBC. Provided the memory is sufficiently large for the errors to be corrected, the replayed signal through the TBC, if fed with a broadcast SPG, will be of broadcast specification. Waveform levels can be adjusted in the output processing amplifier to provide the correct analogue amplitudes.

Analogue TBC

Analogue TBCs (Figure 7.19) correct for timing errors by adjusting the delay of the signal within a variable delay line. The sync timing of the replayed signal is compared with an internal or external SPG and a correction signal causes the delay to expand or compress the signal to correct the VTR jitter.

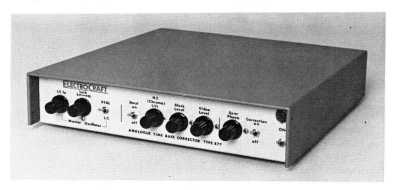

Figure 7.19. Analogue TBC

The 'Electrocraft' equipment produced to date includes a unit with a Fairchild CCD memory producing an approximate 30 μs window and a larger unit using the same memories but arranged to produce a two-line window and separate colour processing. The main advantage to the purchaser is price, which is far less than for digital TBCs.

Vision mixing

The equipment used to provide continuity switching and mixing between cameras or other video sources is the vision mixer (Figures 7.20 and 7.21). At the vision mixer position special effects are introduced either by the vision mixer itself or special equipment associated with it. In some countries the vision mixer may be called a 'production switcher'.

When mixing, wiping or superimposing two or more pictures it is essential that certain conditions relating to signal timing are met otherwise it is impossible for the mixer to perform correctly. These conditions require a timing accuracy of less than 50 ns for the syncs

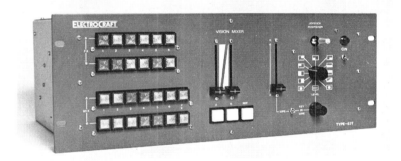

Figure 7.20. Electrocraft CCTV mixer

Figure 7.21. Ampex broadcast mixer

and a phase difference of less than 5° between the subcarrier reference bursts when transmitting PAL or NTSC. In order to attain this performance the various techniques previously explained are employed.

When mixing between two sources it is essential a non-additive method is used so that the mixed signal does not exceed the normal level. Although mixing can be achieved simply by the movement of two faders to which the signals have been directly applied, all modern mixers use DC controlled amplifiers. These provide low distortion and linear fades and have the advantage that the mixing controls can be operated from considerable distances, avoiding the need to run vision cables to the operational desk. The actual electronic mixing unit can, therefore, be left in the vision bays together with the remaining distribution equipment and the control of the fade amplifiers is simply performed by varying ramp generators.

Special effects

All but the simplest mixers have built in some form of effects generator which can take the form of a pattern generator to produce a variety of wipes (Figure 7.22), and chroma key. This latter effect is a technique which uses the colour differences to produce a keying signal for inserting one picture into another (see page 192).

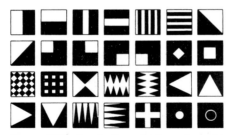

Figure 7.22. A selection of wipes obtainable from a combination of switching waveforms

Within the effects system there is a key signal selector and an effects amplifier. The key signal selector is used to switch any desired key signal to the effects amplifier to produce the required mix or superimposition. If the pattern generator is selected, linear ramp sawtooths or triangle waveforms together with non-linear parabola waveforms are generated. Each waveform is related to the television line and field waveforms. The manner in which these waveforms are combined produces the various switching patterns on the output of comparators which are then fed to the effects switch (Figure 7.23).

By adjusting the operational fader controls the generated waveforms are altered and this controls the mix between the two video sources.

The transistional edges to the wipe can be hard or soft. The latter is achieved by using controlled amplifiers rather than a hard switch. The comparator for the hard switch has a high gain while that for the soft edge has a low gain. The selected ramp waveform is fed into one side of the comparator and a fader controls the

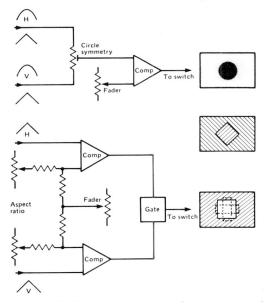

Figure 7.23. By combining the waveforms a variety of wipes is achieved

other input. If the gain is high the changeover will be abrupt as the switching edges will be steep-sided. However, if the gain is low the switching edge will have a long rise and fall time and will produce a soft switching edge due to the changeover taking several microseconds. In certain types of production this effect can be very attractive.

Outlining captions

When captions are superimposed over a picture, part or all of the caption is often illegible due to the captions blending with the background. In order to enhance the captions a black edge can be placed around the vertical edges or the colour of the captions can be altered. This is achieved by using delay lines and gates to stretch the caption signal (Figure 7.24). This signal is then used to operate an effects switch which produces a larger hole than the original captions in the background picture. If the original captions

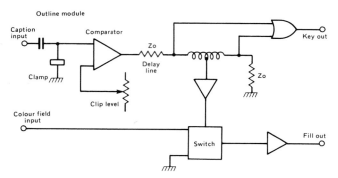

Figure 7.24. With the use of delay lines the hole for the caption is made larger than the captions so that when the captions are re-inserted they will have a black edge. Alternatively the hole can be filled with an output from a colour generator

are now reinserted they will have a black edge or alternatively the signal can be used to gate a colour field generator and fill the caption area with a selected colour. In order to produce an all-round edge effect it is necessary to shift the caption down the picture by one whole TV line, requiring two 64 µs delay lines in addition to the short delay lines. A variety of shadow effects can also be achieved by selection of the tap-off point from the delay line of the narrow caption signal.

Vision mixer layout

The complexity of a mixer is determined by the sophistication of its effects generation, the number of selection banks and the number of inputs to the mixer.

All mixers have a selection matrix on the input which can range from direct switching, relay switching or solid-state switching. The latter system is favoured in modern mixers and it is arranged that an input switches only in the vertical blanking period in order to minimise picture disturbance.

Simple mixers have two selection banks normally termed A and B, and mixing or effects is performed between the two banks. In addition, a preview bank may be added to allow the operator to view pictures prior to selection on the operational banks. When, however, mixes need to be performed between pictures which already contain captions or chroma-key insertions, a further bank is required giving the mixer an A, B, C selection (Figures 7.25 and 7.26).

A fourth bank D can also be added which will allow mixing between all four banks. The combined mixes can then be further mixed between A/B and C/D.

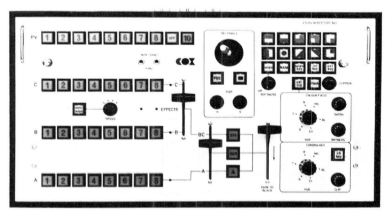

Figure 7.25. An ABC mixer by Michael Cox Electronics

On more complex mixers each input channel can drive its own mixing amplifier before combining on an output busbar, but elaborate electronics are required to prevent overload. Most mixers are fitted with a black input so that a correct waveform is transmitted when the pictures are faded down.

Colour synthesisers

A simple method of producing coloured captions and other effects from a black-and-white source is the use of a colour synthesiser. The synthesisers rely solely on an adjustable preset video level to operate a switch and usually two or three levels can be separated and used to operate colour generators and produce different colours. The switching signal is derived from a black-and-white camera looking at a caption or other item and for good edges the camera tube must produce good rise times.

Synthesisers can be used to colour the output of cameras looking at x-ray plates and this can help to highlight many details not immediately obvious when viewing in black and white.

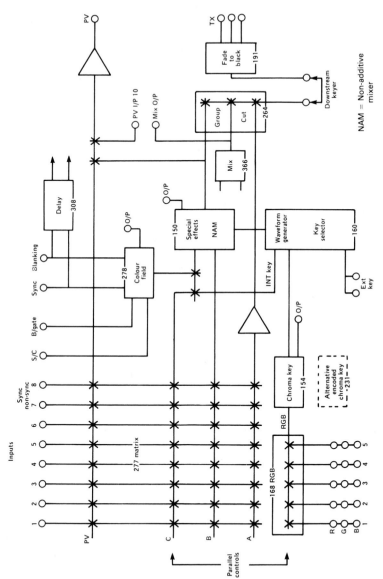

Figure 7.26. System layout of the mixer shown in Figure 7.25

Video typewriters

The development of ICs to produce electronic characters has enabled caption generators to be produced which operate from a normal keyboard. These are inserted in the signal path and automatically insert any letters typed on the keyboard if the transmission button is selected. These units normally have several pages of electronic memory which can be pre-programmed and inserted by the operator at the correct time.

Such systems can be used for a small number of captions or, if provided with large memories, for subtitling a programme in a foreign language.

A less expensive way of storing the large number of captions required to subtitle a complete film is to type all the subtitles on a large roll of paper and to arrange for these to be displayed in sequence in front of a black-and-white camera. At the appropriate time the subtitle is mixed with the programme and after display the roll moves on to the next subtitle, either by manual operation or automatically by coded pulses running synchronously with the programme and operating the mixing equipment.

Chroma key (colour separation overlay)

Normally all the colours in a scene pass through the television system, but it is possible to insert an electronic switch or filter which will block a particular colour. If a scene is then transmitted, wherever that particular colour exists no signal is produced and the area will be black. Normally the colour chosen to produce this effect is blue but other primary colours could be chosen. If the switching signal produced by the colour is then used to entirely blank the picture from another camera except in the area in which the colour appeared in the original picture, a picture will be produced which is identical in size and shape to the blanked area of the initial picture. If these pictures are mixed, the final picture will be complete but originate from two separate sources.

A simple application would involve an artist appearing against a blue background on one camera and a second camera looking at a picture or slide of a street scene. When these two pictures are used with chroma key the artist will appear on the screen as if he is in a street. The blue background can be produced by either blue painted scenery or a blue lighted cyclorama. In a long shot within a studio the blue backing is usually insufficiently wide or high enough and the lights are often visible. This is known as 'shooting off' and to prevent the light causing problems a blue mask is fitted to the front of the camera to eliminate the troublesome area.

To provide the illusion of artists appearing behind railings or windows which are in the picture into which the artist is to be inserted, black masks are placed in front of the artist to coincide with the railings or windows within the picture. All cameras must be locked-off and alignment is performed by using a mixed feed viewfinder on the camera which shows both pictures.

Scene sync

As the complete picture when using chroma key originates from two separate sources it is not possible under normal circumstances to move the camera on the artist without a loss of perspective due to the background picture being static.

To overcome this problem scene sync places the background picture on a special display stand linked by servos to the pan and tilt controls of the foreground camera. If the artist's camera is now moved the background picture moves in sympathy and therefore creates the illusion of being a natural background.

Digital effects generators

The introduction of digital techniques into broadcasting and the availability of computer technology have allowed the introduction of effects which would be impossible without this form of picture processing (Figure 7.27) for to process the video signal, for these new effects, in excess of 10 million computations per second are required (100 ns for each computation).

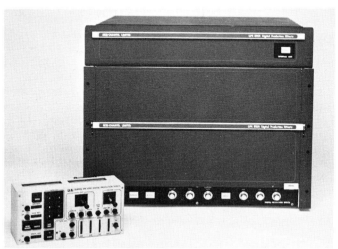

Figure 7.27. Quantel digital effects generator and control panel

As explained in Chapter 10 the analogue waveform can be satisfactorily reproduced by sampling 256 separate levels of the analogue signal. With this digital sampling the reproduced picture will not be detectable from the original picture produced with an analogue waveform. The sampling rate along each line will produce a broadcast quality picture at 700 samples per line. As there are 575 active lines in the 625-line system and 25 pictures per second the information stored is $25 \times 575 \times 700 \approx 10$ million pieces of information each representing a particular part of the picture.

The information is placed in a frame store for immediate access by the computer so that each storage point represents a particular position on the screen down any of the 575 active lines or along any of the 700 sample points on each line. The computer therefore has access to any particular part of the picture for manipulation.

The operational control panel works in conjunction with microprocessors and specially produced software. Freeze-frame is produced by continuously reading the frame of information held in the store when the button was pushed while a line reversal is achieved by reading the store from the right of the frame. Spinning and tumbling effects are produced by the computer reading the frame store information from the bottom and right side instead of the left. To produce scrolling effects the computer can be instructed to commence reading the frame store from any position. Electronic zooming in and out can also be achieved by several multiplications and divisions by the computer of the 700 line sampling points.

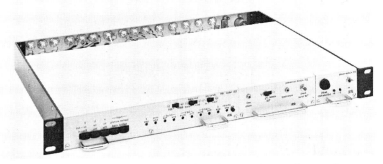

Figure 7.28. Michael Cox PAL coder. Signal generating equipment (cameras, telecine, etc) may only provide RGB outputs. These have to be coded to the colour system being used – PAL, SECAM, NTSC. The correct pulses from the SPG together with the RGB signals are made the inputs and the composite colour signal is the output. Colour bars may also be provided for test purposes

Audio equipment

In spite of the video complexity the audio is of equal importance to any programme. In the larger studio this can be separated from the vision and liaison between director, cameramen, vision control, audio engineers and other remote sources is maintained by a complex intercom system.

In the audio control room, in addition to the audio mixer, will be found record players, tape decks and a high quality audio monitoring system. Unfortunately, as this book is primarily about video, the complexities of audio must be omitted.

Figure 7.29. 16 × 4 switching matrix for routing signals to several destinations in a studio complex (Michael Cox Electronics)

Conclusion

The control room is purpose built and equipped to provide the opeational facilities required for the work it has to perform. No standard design is possible and the rapid growth of new equipment makes flexibility in the original design a major consideration. Above all, the control room is where people work for many hours in close proximity and often under considerable pressure and the designers of equipment and facilities must therefore always consider this fact.

Outside broadcast vehicles

The range of possible designs for outside broadcast vehicles is wide, especially since the introduction of portable cameras for ENG and EFP work. This is not surprising considering the range of programmes covered by the outside broadcast division, which include news items, sport in all environments, processions and ceremonies, concerts, theatres, churches etc.

The outside broadcast vehicle can range, therefore, from simple one camera mobiles with limited sound and recording facilities to vehicles capable of housing all the production and engineering facilities required for four or more cameras and audio mixing of the standard found in sophisticated studios.

To these requirements must be added telephone communications, talkback to cameras and engineering, heating, power, ventilation and recording facilities. Often VTRs are carried in a specially designed vehicle due to the weight, size and noise of conventional quad recorders.

To complete the necessary range of OB vehicles there are also those used by the micro-wave link engineers.

All the necessary equipment has to be installed in a vehicle whose maximum size and weight is governed by the laws of the country in which it will operate. The requirements of the law are especially important when the vehicle is operating in different countries. Such features as axle loading, lighting and visibility for the driver when driving on the opposite side of the road are important considerations. After a suitable chassis, capable of carrying the weight of all the equipment and allowing a reasonable spare weight capacity, is chosen, the specialist coach builder can make the body. The vehicle's engine must withstand hostile environments and four-wheel drive is used whenever possible, as the vehicle will often be situated in fields or on the road in such hostile weather conditions as snow and slush.

The designer of the mobile has all the normal problems of the studio designer to contend with plus many additional worries. The operating crews will spend many hours in the vehicle, very often without a break when the action is not controlled by the director. The limited space must not cause a feeling of claustrophobia and sufficient operating space for each position must be provided together with space for scripts or other necessary information.

The equipment must also be accessible for easy maintenance. This can be attained by fitting the standard 19 in racks to rollers so that they can be pulled out when access is required to the back.

Air conditioning must be effective especially as many operators smoke. The air conditioning must be capable of handling the range of temperatures likely to be experienced in both winter and summer. It is also essential that the equipment works quietly and does not distract the staff. All the technical equipment must be ventilated to keep it at a normal working temperature and while travelling and before the power is connected separate heating (possibly oil) is usually provided for both the operators and to protect the equipment from condensation. The coachbuilder usually provides bodywork with a double skin with insulation between the layers, which not only helps the air conditioning problems but also insulates the interior from the outside noise.

When all the equipment is fitted the vehicle must balance. The layout and springing of the vehicle is, therefore, important in order to achieve this state. At rest, jacks are usually provided to stabilise the vehicle.

Connections from the vehicle for cameras, microphones, audio, video, telephones, communications and power are made on an outside panel which must obviously offer some protection from the weather when static and when travelling.

The vehicle must be capable of towing its own generator when insufficient power is available on the site. In some small vehicles sufficient power to operate a small camera and video recorder can be generated from an alternator driven by the engine and connected to a 12 V d.c. to 240 V a.c. inverter to provide the necessary mains voltages. It is usually important to regulate the incoming mains voltage to the vehicle and often hum-stop filters are required when earthing becomes a problem.

Use is often made of the roof for camera mountings or, in the case of micro-wave links, for the mounting of the transmitter or

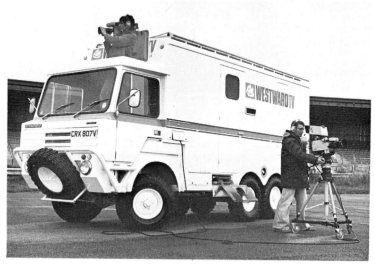

Figure 7.30. OB vehicle designed by Sony

receiver. In these instances the roof must be strengthened and access is by ladder. Usually some form of hoist is provided for raising and lowering the equipment.

All the equipment must be capable of being firmly secured when travelling and as much storage space as possible must be left for cameras, cables and other necessary accessories.

Typical examples of layouts are shown in Figures 7.30 to 7.33, although generally, as mobiles are customed designed, there are no two which are the same.

The design and building of mobiles is a very interesting and demanding form of systems engineering and a considerable amount of operational experience is required to be able to correctly specify the requirements. Invariably many compromises have to be made and for the need of half-an-inch of extra space, it can often require literally going back to the drawing board to try and make everything fit correctly. Invariably with the use of ENG and EFP cameras and video recorders the majority of mobiles will become smaller and far less complex. There will, however, always remain the necessity for the large scanners for all the big occasions

Figure 7.31. Control console inside OB vehicle

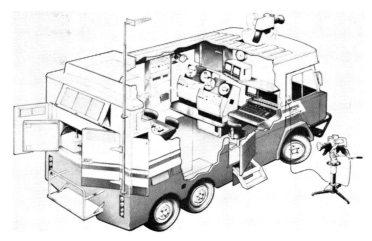

Figure 7.32. Two camera mini mobile – standard design (Marconi)

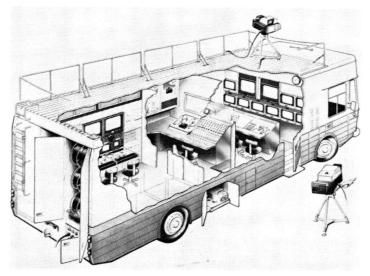

Figure 7.33. Four camera vehicle – standard design (Marconi)

and as the OB director will not want to be without the new effects being used in the studios the amount of equipment and system complexity will continue to expand and set new problems for the mobile designer.

Chapter 8

Transmission

British Telecom television distribution network

Most people, including staff working in television, seem unaware of the importance of British Telecom (the Post Office) for the reception of their television programmes. Unless closely associated with communications, it is little realised that all transmissions once they leave the studio until the time they are transmitted locally are under the control of British Telecom. The monopoly in communications given to the Post Office (as it was called) makes them the sole provider of radio and cable links within the country for telephony, data, music and television. Only outside broadcast links by microwave from the outside broadcast venue back to the studio are provided by the BBC or ITV companies and often British Telecom have to provide start links to a point from which the first microwave transmitter can operate. British Telecom also operates an outside broadcast microwave unit which can provide these facilities if required. Even if the television companies are providing the vision link for an outside broadcast British Telecom invariably provide the music circuits and the necessary control lines for communication with the outside broadcast vehicles.

The Eurovision network and reception and transmission to and from satellites are not exceptions to the British Telecom monopoly. The Eurovision network, rented to the BBC, enters the UK at Tolsford Hill near Dover while satellite transmissions operate from Goonhilly in Cornwall and Madley in Herefordshire.

Compared with the number of engineers and technicians who work for British Telecom, the staff operating these systems together with the inter city multi-channel telephone circuits is very small. In the London Telecom Tower (Figure 8.1), which is the main distribution point, there are about 60 staff to operate the switching centre and radio links for 24 hours every day of the year.

Figure 8.1. London Telecom Tower

In other cities such as Birmingham, Manchester, Carlisle, Glasgow and Bristol, where the switching requirements and circuits are considerably less, the staff is proportionately fewer. It is the smallness of this group of specialist technicians together with the fact that they never come into contact with the public that has made their important contribution to our television service relatively unknown.

Requirements of the distribution network

Three main circuits are required by the broadcasters to provide television programmes. These are the
1. Vision link.
2. Music or sound circuits.
3. Control lines for engineers and production staff to communicate with originating and receiving stations.

The vision links must be capable of transmitting a PAL 625-line signal without distortion and for this each vision circuit is equalised to 5.8 MHz. The normal sound circuits are high quality telephone circuits equalised to 8 kHz. British Telecom also provide circuits for stereo broadcasting equalised to 15 kHz.

The control lines are private telephone wires rented to a destination for a period of time. Where a company requires to be in permanent contact with another user of the network then a permanent private wire is provided. The circuits are normally ordinary telephone lines which have the commercial speech specification of 300 Hz to 3400 Hz. Different circuits are handled by different departments of British Telecom. The vision links are transmitted by radio links while the audio circuits are provided by the telephony side of British Telecom.

Subscriber's local circuits

The inter-city links are provided between British Telecom television and sound switching centres which are usually situated near the centres of main towns. In order to feed or be fed from the network it is essential for a company to have local ends between themselves and the switching centre for vision, sound and control lines.

These circuits are permanently rented by a subscriber and are very expensive. This is why most of the major TV studios and facility houses in London are close to the Telecom Tower. The longer the link the greater the expense and if a facility house requires such connections there is a very small area in which it can be situated before the cost of the links makes the whole operation uneconomical. Once a facility house or studio has local ends to the national switching centres they can be interconnected in order to share standards converters, record direct into duplicating facilities, transmit and receive from Eurovision or satellites, transmit CCTV anywhere within the system in the UK or abroad and transmit and receive normal network television programmes. Also connected to the London switching centre in addition to the BBC and ITV studios and transmitters are such companies as Television International, VisNews, NBC, ABC, and CBS London facilities, Rank, Audio and Video, ITN facilities and British Telecom's own Confravision CCTV studios in Euston. The latter studios allow conferences to be held and viewed simultaneously at all or any of the other British Telecom studios in Bristol, Birmingham, Manchester or Newcastle or any other point connected to the system. To ensure privacy the conferences, unlike all other programmes passing through the switching centres, are not monitored. At present about five conferences a day are transmitted on the network.

Requirements of BBC and ITV stations

Both BBC1 and BBC2 are national networks which normally transmit the same two programmes simultaneously to all parts of the country, making the BBC's requirements considerably different to those of ITV. For only short periods throughout the day do BBC regional stations take their transmitters off the national network and feed either local inserts into the news or local programmes. Consequently, for the majority of the time, the BBC national links can be left alone by British Telecom and the small amount of switching required can be left to the BBC. Most programmes are than transmitted via the BBC Television Centre in London.

The ITV network, however, is entirely different, for although major programmes are networked the originating source often changes for each programme as each of the network stations is responsible for transmitting its own network programmes. A separate company, ITN, is also responsible for networking all national news.

There are 16 individual companies at present on the ITV1 network and each is responsible for its own programmes and commercials in its own area. The operation of the company's contracts are supervised by the IBA who also control and staff the transmitters in each area, and are also responsible for providing the daily schedule of communication links to which the network and British Telecom operate. These are obviously closely checked by the communication engineers of each company who must ensure that video and audio lines are available at the correct time from each originating source in order to provide their area with a network programme.

During an evenings transmission the first network programme may come from London, the second from Manchester, the third from Anglia, the News from ITN and the fifth from Birmingham. For each programme British Telecom must rearrange the video and audio network links to ensure that the companies are connected to the correct source. Sometimes this can be arranged before the start of a programme but often switching must be done on a time cue to ensure that the circuits are connected on time. The switch is performed during the commercial break or announcement preceding the new programme. Of course, not all circuits have to be switched and different routings often require switches to be made at switching centres in different parts of the country.

Often more than one programme is transmitted on the network at the same time by using different links. It may be that Birmingham and Manchester are taking the same programme from London while the rest of the stations are taking programmes from Anglia. There is obviously a limit to the number of links, and this determines the permutations possible at any one time.

The switching is automatic once set-up by British Telecom network engineers. The actual switching equipment takes several bays and racks in the equipment room and is currently performed by uniselectors. However, the operational panel in the switching centre control desk requires the punching in of the time, circuit destination and source. A bell momentarily warns the engineers prior to the actual switch, after which the circuits are switched by the clock. Over-ride facilities are available for urgent alterations to the schedules. Due to the continual alteration of the network routing it is often difficult to allow ITV programmes to over-run

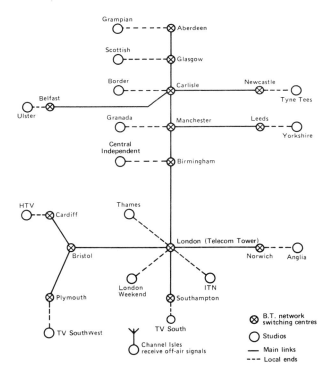

Figure 8.2. Network routing for ITN

and accurate start and finish times of programmes are absolutely essential in order to provide good station presentation.

When networking, the originating source provides a 'clean feed' of the programme. This means that only the programme is transmitted and it contains no commercials. The programme is then transmitted down the inter-city link and fed on local-end vision and sound circuits to the local TV station. The programme is then routed through the master control and presentation area where local commercials are added before feeding the composite programme back on out-going local ends to British Telecom who send it on the permanent circuits to the local transmitters. The 'clean feed' of the programme would also have been split at the switching centre and fed on other inter-city links to other switching centres where it is fed to local television stations; they may also split it and feed it on to another inter-city link. An example of an ITN news routing is shown in Figure 8.2.

London Telecom Tower

Although on a larger scale than other TV communications centres the tower serves as an example of other centres.

The tower has 36 floors to the top and the transmitting and receiving aerial dishes are fitted on the outside of the building between the 24th and 25th floors. The transmitters occupy floors 20–22, and handle telephony in addition to television. As the transmitters are wideband each link is capable of 960 or 1800 channels of telephony (depending on link) or a 5.8 MHz channel for TV. The difference between the TV and telephony channels is in modification to the pre-emphasis stages. In addition to the main circuits standby or 'protection circuits' are available which can be

Figure 8.3a. Control position, TV switching centre (Telecom Tower)

Figure 8.3b. TV switching control

switched to if any failure occurs. The links can be switched manually or a pilot tone failure, transmitted with the signals, causes automatic changeover. The network switching centre and base-band equipment is situated on the 14th and 15th floors.

It is with the staff at the switching centre that the liaison between British Telecom and the network subscribers takes place (Figure 8.3). At any one time there may be passing through the

Figure 8.4. Outside broadcast audio acceptance control

centre ITV programmes, BBC1, BBC2, possibly conference vision, closed circuit transmission between subscribers and satellite transmissions. The inter-continental satellites are used at present for about 20 transmissions each day by such companies as ABC, NBC, CBS and VisNews in addition to the BBC and ITV.

Outside broadcasts, if not fed directly to the studios, will also pass through the centre. A special control desk is staffed for the control of audio circuits for outside broadcasts (Figure 8.4).

The radio links transmit vision only and the music circuits go via Faraday exchange. The BBC, however, transmit sound in syncs but this is backed-up with normal land lines.

Radio links

The microwave links operate in the frequency range 6000 MHz (6 GHz). Two ranges are used known as 'upper' 6.5–7.0 GHz and 'lower' 5–6 GHz. Some links for telephony also operate in the 4 GHz range. At these frequencies radio waves travel in straight lines and to conserve power are radiated in narrow beams. The receiving station must be visible to the transmitter with no obstructions otherwise the signal will be stopped. This requires the

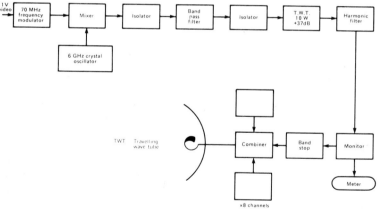

Figure 8.5. British Telecom radio link transmitter

signal to be received and retransmitted at regular intervals and to Birmingham intermediate stations are used at Harrow Weald, Dunstable and Charlwalton. At each intermediate point the frequency and polarisation is changed and also the direction of transmission. Figure 8.5 shows a block diagram of a transmitter.

The video signal initially frequency modulates a 70 MHz carrier before entering a mixer stage where the signal modulates a 6 GHz carrier. The pilot tones of 9.03 MHz or 8.51 MHz are inserted at this stage. The RF signal for transmission is generated by a travelling-wave tube to produce a power output of 10 W. Before leaving the aerial it is combined with eight other similar channels on different frequencies which can be either TV or telephony channels. Channel spacing of either 30 MHz (1800 channel telephony links) or 20 MHz (960 channel telephony links) are used.

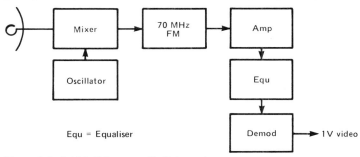

Figure 8.6. British Telecom radio link receiver

At the intermediate stations the signal is demodulated to the 70 MHz stage and is then remodulated to the 6 MHz range before retransmission. At a network switching centre the receiver demodulates the signal to the 70 MHz IF and finally demodulates this to the original 1 V video signal for distribution to the TV studios (Figure 8.6).

Testing television links

Every part of the link introduces some distortion to the TV signal and the longer the link the greater will be the distortion added to the signal. For those companies such as Aberdeen at the end of the link from London, it is of considerable importance that each individual link in the chain is operating at maximum efficiency. Each link is allowed a certain deterioration which will vary depending on the number of repeaters stations in the link and amplifiers in a local end. The total allowable distortion on any combination of links is, therefore, the total of all the individual link distortions making up the chain.

The links are tested by the ITV companies every week when a series of test signals are originated by either the IBA or a London network station. The main signals used for measurements of frequency, phase and delay distortion are pulse and bar signals which can be fitted into a special graticule on the scope and percentage distortion read directly for the various parameters. In the past these distortions have been directly correlated against picture imperfections judged by a group of experienced viewers. The measured distortions are, therefore, directly related to visible imperfections in the picture. Other signals such as grey scale for picture linearity tests, 50 Hz signals for low frequency tests (possible cause of streaking) and noise measurements are also included.

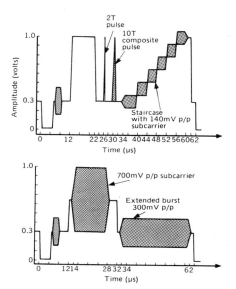

Figure 8.7. Insertion test signal lines 19 (32) and 20 (333) as used in the UK. The measurements of insertion test signals (ITS) are used for measuring
  sync amplitude
  low-frequency bar amplitude
  low-frequency bar tilt
  K factor on 2T pulse shape
  2T pulse-bar ratio
  luminance non-linearity
  chrominance differential phase
  chrominance differential gain
  chrominance/luminance delay
  chrominance/luminance crosstalk
  chrominance/luminance gain
  noise level
Measurements are made on oscilloscopes using specially marked graticules into which various waveforms fit. 'K' rating tests, using 2T pulse and bar, are related directly to visible picture imperfections based on subjective viewing

In addition to these weekly tests the ITA network also transmit test signals in the blanking period of the TV waveform and these originate at the network station transmitting the programme (Figure 8.7). The music circuits are also tested and use the normal frequency runs, noise measurements and harmonic distortion tests.

The BBC also perform similar tests on their network.

Conclusion

There have been considerable advances in the communication network since the introduction of ITV in 1955. The original ITV link from London to Brimingham was a 900 MHz radio link operating over five hops, while the BBC network was by coaxial cable.

Today 32 TV microwave channels operate from the London Telecom Tower alone. With the introduction of the fourth channel this will have to increase as will the rest of the network.

All the time equipment is being modernised although some equipment using outdated techniques is still in evidence. Obviously, however, with such vast investments required it is not possible to re-equip each time advances are made in technology.

British Telecom must, of course, be giving considerable thought to the transmission of digital video because it is in transmission links that the greatest benefit will be found. When a signal can be recreated in its original form at each network switching centre without visible distortion then the deterioration caused by long links will be a problem of the past.

Satellites for broadcasting

In 1945 Arthur C. Clarke, a British science fiction writer, suggested the use of communication satellites in a synchronous geostationary orbit, as a means of world communication. In a high-altitude orbit 36 000 km (22 300 miles) above the equator and with the use of only three satellites, coverage of almost the entire world could be achieved.

The satellites in this unique orbit require a velocity of 7000 m/h (11 300 km/h) in order to remain in this orbit. At this velocity and height they rotate at the same rate as the Earth and therefore appear to be stationary above a fixed point on the Earth. Orbits above or below 36 000 km require velocities, in order to stay in orbit, which make them pass over the Earth's surface and are therefore used for surveying and monitoring purposes (Figure 8.8).

Critics of Clarke's idea argued that the time delay of approximately 270 μs from earth to satellite and back, would be too great for telephone conversations. This was before the improvements in modern echo suppressors, and at a time when the British Post Office (as it was then) preferred medium altitude orbits.

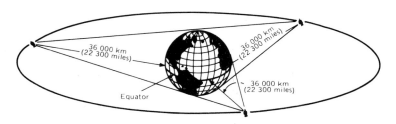

Figure 8.8. A synchronous satellite moves at the same velocity as the Earth in a circular equatorial orbit. It therefore appears to remain stationary over a fixed point on the equator. The unique position of 36 000 km (22 300 miles) above the equator allows three synchronous satellites to provide almost complete coverage of the Earth. This orbit is also known as a geostationary orbit

However, with the passing of time and the accomplishment of the idea, the use of satellites by television companies is controlled mainly by economics. The cost of a circuit is high due partially to the number of telephone circuits that can be placed in the same bandwidth as a TV signal and the profitability of the telephony channels.

The first earth satellite to be used by television was Echo I, an aluminium-mylar plastic sphere of 30 m diameter, which was a passive satellite and signals were simply bounced off it. Unfortunately it soon became deformed and unusable.

The first active satellite was developed by the Bell Telephone Laboratories and was launched on 10th July, 1962. This was named Telstar I and was used during its short operational life for a number of television transmissions between North America and Europe. However, its low-altitude elliptical orbit caused its visibility to vary from orbit to orbit, which limited the period of time for programmes and often it was not around when required. The Goonhilly receiving station was built to maximise the visible period and the aerial had to be designed to track the satellite when it came into view.

It was left to the Hughes Aircraft Company, led by Dr. Harold Rosen and supported by NASA and the US Defence Department, to prove the viability of the geostationary satellites when they launched the Syncom satellites during 1963–64.

The launching was achieved by first placing the satellite into an elliptical orbit with a perigee (closest approach to the earth) of about 270 km (170 miles). Because the satellite has a greater velocity than is required for such an orbit it assumes an elliptical orbit and with the correct velocity will rise to an apogee (furthest distance from the earth) of about 36 000 km (22 300 miles). At this point a motor increases the velocity to about 3000 m/s (10 000 ft/s) and the satellite then assumes a circular orbit. Small gas jets are installed for final correction and final positioning can take several weeks. An error of only 20 m in 35 000 km (70 ft in 22 300 miles) will cause the satellite to drift from a stationary position by 0.1° per year. If the orbit is also not circular, even if it is of the correct deviation, a cyclic variation resulting in a variation of the received carrier frequency will occur due to the Doppler effect.

In order to keep the satellite in its correct position considerable accuracy is required in the initial launch to minimise the later corrections. The operational life of the system is often determined by the amount of fuel required to keep the satellite in position, for once the fuel runs out the satellite can no longer be controlled.

The Syncom I and II satellites were installed with transposers of restricted bandwidth but in 1964 Syncom III was launched and was used to transmit the Olympic Games from Tokyo to North America.

The success achieved with the Syncom satellites led to the formation of the Intelsat organisation with the American Comsat Corporation as the managing company and other countries having shares in the organisation.

In April 1965 Early Bird, later to be renamed Intelsat I, was launched carrying two transposers which could be used for either television or multi-channel telephony. During the years 1965–71 continuous progress was made with the Intelsat satellites and their size and facilities increased considerably. While Intelsat I weighed 38 kg (85 lb) in orbit, Intelsat IV weighed 487 kg (1075 lb) (1112 kg, 2452 lb at lift off) and had 50 000 solar cells capable of an ERP of 1.9 kW for a 17° beam or 38 kW for a 4.5° beam. Spot beams had been introduced into the Intelsat satellites to provide direct broadcasting to individual countries and allowed the effective radiated powers to be increased to tens of kilowatts. Later Intelsat satellites IVA and V launches in 1975 and 1979 carried 20 and 27 transposers respectively. Intelsat V has the capability of either

12 000 two-way telephone circuits or 40–50 TV channels depending upon the way it is used.

Intelsat IV carried 12 transposers each capable of passing one or two 625 line television programmes in colour and using either wide beam or spot aerial beams on retransmission.

Russia also developed a series of Molniya satellites primarily for television distribution over her own territory. The orbits of these satellites, which form their Orbita system, are non-synchronous and highly elliptical, and so more suitable for the coverage required in the northern latitude without the need for fast tracking earth stations.

Canada also saw the advantage of satellites for domestic communications in distant and sparsely populated areas and began Telesat Canada in 1969. The Anik satellites were launched in 1972 and the systems are controlled from a purpose-built centre in Ottawa. Initially the satellites were used for telephony, data and telex, but later satellites carry radio and television. America also now offers circuits on the Western Union Welstar and RCA Satcom satellites to any customer.

Indonesia has expanded her television service by using a geostationary satellite situated 83° East and now transmits to over 50 stations throughout the country.

Direct broadcasting from satellites

Direct broadcasting to domestic receivers is also possible instead of only to a ground station. If sufficient power is available, one geostationary satellite can theoretically transmit to one third of the world's surface. However, as most of this would be sea or unpopulated land, restricting the beam widths to between 1 and 5° not only makes the distribution selective but also allows realistic transmitter power to be used. To allow for satellite drift and rotation the minimum practical beam is considered to be circular with a diameter subtending an angle of 0.6°. This, for many small countries, is larger than required and results in spillover into neighbouring territory.

During the period August 1975 to July 1976 the Indian government, with American aid, experimented with instructional television when 2400 villages in six states received programmes directly from a satellite stationed over Africa. A frequency of 860 kHz was used, radiated from a 10 m diameter parabolic aerial.

America also cooperated with Canada in 1976 in an experiment known as 'Hermes' when a satellite carrying a 12 GHz transmitter was launched. These experiments proved the feasibility of direct broadcasting and a further satellite has been launched by Japan.

In January 1977 the ITU World Administrative Radio Conference held in Geneva made frequency allocations for satellite transmissions. The United Kingdom was allocated five channels in Band VI 11.7 to 12.5 GHz from a geostationary satellite at 31°W, which is over the South Atlantic near the most easterly part of Brazil. The same position is allocated to Ireland, although it has a smaller beam, and Spain, Portugal and Iceland. Other groupings

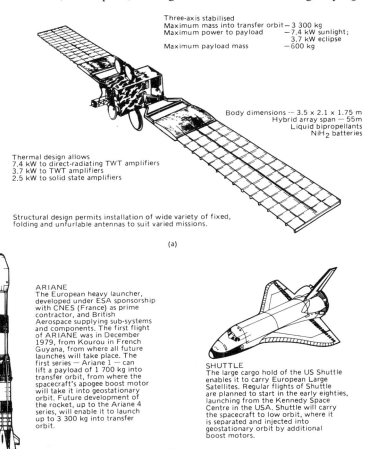

Three-axis stabilised
Maximum mass into transfer orbit — 3 300 kg
Maximum power to payload — 7.4 kW sunlight;
3.7 kW eclipse
Maximum payload mass — 600 kg

Body dimensions — 3.5 x 2.1 x 1.75 m
Hybrid array span — 55m
Liquid bipropellants
NiH$_2$ batteries

Thermal design allows
7.4 kW to direct-radiating TWT amplifiers
3.7 kW to TWT amplifiers
2.5 kW to solid state amplifiers

Structural design permits installation of wide variety of fixed, folding and unfurlable antennas to suit varied missions.

(a)

ARIANE
The European heavy launcher, developed under ESA sponsorship with CNES (France) as prime contractor, and British Aerospace supplying sub-systems and components. The first flight of ARIANE was in December 1979, from Kourou in French Guyana, from where all future launches will take place. The first series — Ariane 1 — can lift a payload of 1 700 kg into transfer orbit, from where the spacecraft's apogee boost motor will take it into geostationary orbit. Future development of the rocket, up to the Ariane 4 series, will enable it to launch up to 3 300 kg into transfer orbit.

SHUTTLE
The large cargo hold of the US Shuttle enables it to carry European Large Satellites. Regular flights of Shuttle are planned to start in the early eighties, launching from the Kennedy Space Centre in the USA. Shuttle will carry the spacecraft to low orbit, where it is separated and injected into geostationary orbit by additional boost motors.

(b)

Figure 8.9. (a) The European large satellite; (b) launchers – the European large satellite is designed for launch by Ariane or by the Shuttle (courtesy British Aerospace)

have been made for other European countries. As it will be impractical to redirect a domestic aerial to a different position, countries who are likely to view each other's programmes have been allocated the same orbital position.

Examples are

France, West Germany, Belgium, The Netherlands, Luxembourg, Italy and Austria

Poland, East Germany, Czechoslovakia, Hungary, Roumania and Bulgaria

Norway, Sweden, Finland and Denmark

Libya, Tunisia, Algeria and Morocco.

These allocations are for 15 years but it is doubtful whether there is any advantage to a small country already equipped with a sophisticated network in using satellites. The advantages of satellites seem to be for those countries with vast distances to cover and with systems in regular use or who have sparsely distributed populations.

The EBU have considered Eurovision and their requirements include coverage of Europe, eastern Mediterranean and North Africa. Transposers will be required for both PAL and SECAM and a high quality sound circuit must be provided together with 20 commentary circuits and service and control circuits.

The European space agency was formed in 1975 and is responsible for a series of eight European Communications satellites (ECS) which will start to become operational in the 1980s and one will possibly replace the present Eurovision network. Their design life will be about seven years.

At present an Orbital Test Satellite has been launched and is in a geostationary orbit at longitude 10° East. An experimental receiving station has been built by the IBA to make preliminary studies of the propagation and reception of the 11–12 GHz signals.

Mobile earth stations

It is possible to inject signals into the Intelsat network from transportable earth stations. This has made possible world-wide television from places which were once completely inaccessible and where no established communication links exist. Television transmission is now possible from the middle of the oceans as was proved with the Apollo landings.

Technical parameters

Although in the future some method of digital coding may be used the preliminary standard is for frequency modulation with a bandwidth of 27 MHz. A total of 40 channels spaced at 19.18 MHz has been planned in order to increase the number of channels allocated to each country although there is an increase in interference from adjacent channels.

Transmitters and receiving aerials must be closely controlled to reduce interference, especially of side lobes. The power that can be radiated is controlled by the power generated on the satellite where it is assumed that it will be possible to generate about 4 kW. In order to provide five national channels and allow for a free-space attenuation, which for European coverage will be typically 206 dB, it would appear that the maximum beam area will be about 1.1° to give acceptable pictures. However, oxygen, cloud and water vapour will increase the attentuation. At the higher latitudes where the elevation is lower this attenuation increases. Rain will cause a greater attenuation than most other factors in the 12 GHz band and IBA measurements suggest it is approximately 1 dB/km for a rainfall of 1 in/hour.

The satellite can be positioned with advantage to the east or west of the reception area as this reduces the beam area. However, during the Spring and Summer equinoxes when the sun appears to cross the equator the Earth will eclipse the satellite at about midnight and power will be lost from the solar cells for about 72 min. As broadcasters will wish to transmit after midnight it is necessary to position the satellite to the west to delay the eclipse. The delay obtained is equivalent to 4 min for every degree that the satellite is west of the service area.

Reception of satellite signals

The limiting factors for the reception of satellite pictures in the 11.7–125 GHz band are the aerial gain and thermal noise generated in the receiver. It is important, therefore, that the early stages of the receiver should not only have a low noise factor but also high gain sufficient to swamp the noise produced in the later stages of the set. The aerial will receive unwanted noise which considerably increases as the angle of elevation becomes lower. With the satellite positioned for the UK at 31°W, the elevation for the west of England will be about 27° while for the north of Scotland it will be about 17°.

The most effective aerial will be a parabolic reflector and for the power received it would appear that a diameter of about 1 m will be required with a receiver noise factor of about 8 dB. The surface of the aerial must be accurate, according to the IBA, to within ±0.0025 m of a true parabolic and positioned within 0.5° towards the satellite so as not to significantly worsen the signal due to loss of gain and directivity. A clear line-of-sight to the satellite is required, which in heavily built-up areas may be difficult and in blocks of flats may require communal aerials.

Microwave solid state techniques are developing reasonably rapidly and local oscillators at 12 GHz can be provided by the use of Gunn diodes. Microwave transistors using gallium arsenide in field-effect devices have also progressed. Suggested designs for receivers envisage two IF stages in the region of 1200 MHz and 140 MHz with the final FM signal being converted to AM for insertion into a normal TV. It is also possible that a dual-standard TV may be designed which will receive the normal UHF and VHF signals and FM signals converted by a front-end tuner to a range of 0.9–1.3 GHz. However, until transmissions become a reality it is difficult to prophesy how far development will have altered for different components. Those countries without an established terrestrial UHF service will be able to radiate in the Band V allocation of 620–790 MHz, which will ease some of the problems.

Conclusion

The demand for small communication satellites in geostationary orbits is growing so rapidly that it is predicted that within five years space will be saturated. These will obviously be used for purposes other than television as navigation, data and telephony requirements expand. It is reliably estimated that within 20 years there will be a requirement for about 200 large satellites, each of which may cost about £25 000 000.

Already satellites have overtaken cables as the major provider of international information links. Europe's largest is expected to be available in 1985 when the L-SAT is launched. The design of this satellite incorporates solar panels of 55 m (180 ft) span to provide the power, sufficient for 90 000 telephone circuits or the equivalent data or television circuits. Direct television broadcasting will also be possible.

Europe's OTS 2 satellite launched in 1978 was expected to last until at least 1982 with the ability to provide two television programmes and 5400 other circuits. This has paved the way for the medium size European Communication Satellites (ECS) of which eight are planned. These will have approximately twice the capacity of the OTS satellites. The first of these satellites will be marine communications satellites (MARECS) and three will be used for world-wide marine communications.

In the USA, the law has been changed to prevent monopolies and create the opportunities to rapidly advance the communication links. Companies are being formed to provide data links between towns and offices throughout the country.

Satellites have already had considerable effects on broadcasting with the ability to immediately receive live programmes from around the world. However, the advantages are always in an east-to-west direction due to time delays. Events occurring in the

Figure 8.10. Artist's impression of MARECS, a maritime communications derivative of the European communications satellite (ECS). Both ECS and MARECS programmes are led by the Space and Communications Division of British Aerospace Dynamics Group. Three MARECS spacecraft are being built (courtesy British Aerospace)

USA are invariably too late for inclusion on European TV. A recording can more easily be put on a plane and be in Europe for the next day's transmission at a considerably reduced cost. Whether in the United Kingdom and European countries served by an established terrestrial network there will ever be the need to broadcast directly from satellites remains to be seen. However, it is planned that the Eurovision network will be replaced by satellites and perhaps the Indian experiment will assist the third world to rapidly improve the educational opportunities of their people. Engineers are proving the feasibility of the systems but we shall have to wait for a demand and for it to be economically correct before the politicians will act decisively especially in countries where the government has a monopoly of communications.

Master antenna television and community antenna television

Master antenna television (MATV) covers any master aerial system feeding two or more receivers. However, the more complex systems involve blocks of flats, hotels, hospitals and other buildings being cabled to receive signals from one or more aerials placed in the optimum position to receive the best possible signals

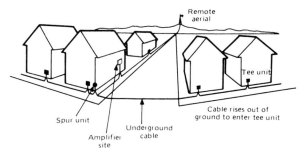

Figure 8.11. Aerial sited on hill and signals fed to a nearby housing estate

(Figure 8.11). Community antenna television (CATV) involves an area being fed by cable from a distribution centre where not only off-air signals are distributed but also possibly signals from stations normally impossible to receive which are brought to the distribution centre by a transmission network. Pay Television and community produced television are also possible as additional channels on the cable network. Naturally space for the extra channels is not restricted by the normally available transmission frequencies but solely by the capacity of the cable to carry the signals. These networks are rented to the subscriber but in areas where reception is poor due to topography, it is the only way to receive good signals. In Europe, especially in Belgium, many people can receive programmes from several countries by such networks. In America it has led to a considerable growth in 'Pay Television' systems where the subscriber is able to watch new films in his home.

Often in a block of flats the internal system can be a mixture of MATV and CATV, which can lead to some complexity in the system design.

Cable system

The basic system consists of a cable network which takes the signal from the aerial or distribution centre and incorporates amplifiers, equalisers, attenuators, splitters and outlets, arranged in such a manner as to carry the signals to the subscriber and to arrive at individual sets at the correct level for each channel with minimum interference from external sources or cross modulation within the cable system.

The decibel

To understand the design parameters of such systems it is essential to understand the definition of a decibel. Although the decibel (dB) is used when dealing with other equipment in television it is mostly used in transmission systems.

Our eyes and ears do not react linearly to stimuli but in a logarithmic manner. To hear or see an equal change in intensity the light or sound must double each time and not increase in equal steps.

Decibels are therefore a ratio of change and in order to know the actual intensity of a given decibel increase or decrease we must first know the reference level. In audio the level is 1 mW into 600 ohms; in video it is 1 V into 75 ohms and in MATV work it is 1000 μV across 75 ohms. However, decibels gain or loss are ratios and are the same irrespective of the reference.

The mathematical expression for the voltage ratio is

$$dB = 20 \log_{10} \frac{V_2 \text{ (output voltage)}}{V_1 \text{ (input voltage)}}$$

Amplifier gains and attenuations and cable losses are referred to in dB. This has the advantage that because we are working in logarithms, gains of amplifiers in dB can be added and losses in dB can be subtracted.

As an example, an aerial may receive 100 µV of signal (Figure 8.12). This level is −20 dB below the reference level for 0 dB (1000 µV across 75 ohms). If the signal passes through an amplifier with 20 dB gain the output signal will be 0 dBmV. If this is now fed to a cable with 6 dB loss the signal arriving at the television is −6 dBmV, which based on our reference is 500 µV. Table 8.1 relates the value of the dB to a reference of 1000 µV across 75 ohms. The problem arises of deciding how much signal should be supplied to the television and whether this is obtainable with a particular system. The limiting factors are noise, signal strength received and the picture quality acceptable to the viewer. As the signal-to-noise ratio decreases so does the picture quality.

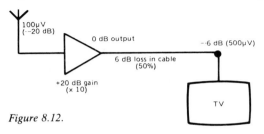

100 µV
(−20 dB)

0 dB output

−6 dB (500 µV)

6 dB loss in cable
(50%)

+20 dB gain
(× 10)

TV

Figure 8.12.

The approximate subjective picture quality ratings for various signal-to-noise ratios are:

45 dB	S/N	Excellent picture.
40 dB	S/N	Interference perceptible but good quality pictures.
33 dB	S/N	Acceptable pictures, interference not objectionable.
28 dB	S/N	Picture quality marginal, interference becoming objectionable.
22 dB	S/N	Poor pictures, objectionable interference.
Below 22 dB	S/N	Unusable pictures.

(These figures will vary and depend upon how the signal-to-noise ratio is measured.

Assuming therefore, that the lowest picture quality acceptable from a system must be rated 'Good' a 40 dB signal-to-noise ratio must be obtained.

Every amplifier has a noise factor which adds to the system noise. A typical figure for the 'equivalent noise input' to the

Table 8.1. dBmV/microvolt chart

dBmV	μV	dBmV	μV	dBmV	μV
-40	10	0	1 000	40	100 000
-39	11	1	1 100	41	110 000
-38	13	2	1 300	42	130 000
-37	14	3	1 400	43	140 000
-36	16	4	1 600	44	160 000
-35	18	5	1 800	45	180 000
-34	20	6	2 000	46	200 000
-33	22	7	2 200	47	220 000
-32	25	8	2 500	48	250 000
-31	28	9	2 800	49	280 000
-30	32	10	3 200	50	320 000
-29	36	11	3 600	51	360 000
-28	40	12	4 000	52	400 000
-27	45	13	4 500	53	450 000
-26	50	14	5 000	54	500 000
-25	56	15	5 600	55	560 000
-24	63	16	6 300	56	630 000
-23	70	17	7 000	57	700 000
-22	80	18	8 000	58	800 000
-21	90	19	9 000	59	900 000
-20	100	20	10 000	60	1.0 volt
-19	110	21	11 000	61	1.1
-18	130	22	13 000	62	1.3
-17	140	23	14 000	63	1.4
-16	160	24	16 000	64	1.6
-15	180	25	18 000	65	1.8
-14	200	26	20 000	66	2.0
-13	220	27	22 000	67	2.2
-12	250	28	25 000	68	2.5
-11	280	29	28 000	69	2.8
-10	320	30	32 000	70	3.2
- 9	360	31	36 000	71	3.6
- 8	400	32	40 000	72	4.0
- 7	450	33	45 000	73	4.5
- 6	500	34	50 000	74	5.0
- 5	560	35	56 000	75	5.6
- 4	630	36	63 000	76	6.3
- 3	700	37	70 000	77	7.0
- 2	800	38	80 000	78	8.0
- 1	900	39	90 000	79	9.0
- 0	1000	40	100 000	80	10.0

Definition of dBmV:
0dBmV = 1000 μV across 75 ohms

amplifier is -53 dBmV. This is the noise at the output of the amplifier with no input signal and the input is terminated with 75 Ω.

To produce a signal-to-noise ratio of at least 40 dB at the output the input signal must be at least 40 dB larger than the noise. This means the signal must be -53 dB $+$ 40 dB $=$ -13 dBmV. By calculation or by looking at the table, it is found that a signal of approximately 220 μV is required.

As amplifiers and other equipment are cascaded on larger systems, the system noise increases and the signal strength must be increased to produce the same quality of picture. It should also be stressed that a margin is required to allow for deterioration in performance with age or adverse conditions. Obviously, however, reception of a poor picture rather than nothing is often a determining factor, but these types of calculations and design parameters can allow judgements to be made and the correct equipment chosen.

Aerials

The most important item in any MATV system is the aerial, as this determines the signal level received. Its positioning also determines whether ghosting and multiple images occur. These effects are caused by the signal travelling over two or more paths before arriving at the aerial. The first signal path will possibly be direct but the signal will also reflect from buildings and hills before arriving at the aerial. Careful positioning of the aerial, together with the use of a highly directional array, can reduce these problems.

Different aerials are chosen for different systems because of their specifications for gain, bandwidth, matching characteristics, polar diagram and mechanical characteristics. Yagi aerials have high gain but narrow bandwidth; useful for single channel reception. Log periodic aerials have a wide bandwidth but moderate gain. A single aerial is therefore suitable for multi-channel reception. Parabolic reflectors can be used for UHF reception; these have high gain and are highly directional.

The gain and height of an aerial must be chosen to give the required signal strength for the quality of picture required, and it should be remembered that the aerial is the only element in the system which can increase the signal level without increasing the noise.

Precise impedance matching of the aerial to the system must also be provided otherwise reflections and loss of signal strength will occur as signals are reflected up and down the aerial lead.

Table 8.2. Typical dimensions and losses of coaxial cables used for CATV and MATV

Dimensions—metric									
Inner conductor	mm	0.81	1.27	1.67	2.33	2.33	3.05	3.05	
Outer conductor	mm	4.54	6.49	8.18	10.96	10.96	13.99	13.99	
Nominal overall	mm	6.34	8.39	10.20	12.26	13.10	15.04	16.99	18.07
Dimensions—imperial									
Inner conductor	in	0.032	0.050	0.066	0.066	0.092	0.092	0.120	0.120
Outer conductor	in	0.174	0.256	0.322	0.322	0.431	0.431	0.551	0.551
Nominal overall	in	0.250	0.330	0.402	0.478	0.516	0.587	0.669	0.705
Mechanical characteristics									
Minimum bending radius	mm	32.00	42.00	51.00	185.00	66.00	230.00	85.00	275.00
Minimum bending radius	in	1.24	1.65	2.01	7.21	2.60	8.97	3.35	10.72
Weight	kg/km	50	79	93	135	144	195	233	270
Weight	lb/1000 ft	33	53	62	90	96	130	156	180
Electrical characteristics									
Impedance	ohms	75	75	75	75	75	75	75	75
Tolerance on impedance	ohms	±2.5	±2.5	±2.5	±2.5	±2.5	±2.5	±2.5	±2.5
Attenuation in dB/100 m									
40 MHz		4.5	3.0	2.3	2.3	1.7	1.7	1.35	1.35
100 MHz		7.5	4.8	3.7	3.7	2.7	2.7	2.1	2.1
230 MHz		12.0	7.5	5.75	5.75	4.3	4.3	3.35	3.35
300 MHz		14.0	8.65	6.7	6.7	5.0	5.0	3.9	3.9
600 MHz		19.25	12.65	9.9	9.9	7.45	7.45	5.95	5.95
860 MHz		24.85	15.25	12.1	12.1	9.2	9.2	7.3	7.3
Attenuation in dB/100 ft									
40 MHz		1.37	0.92	0.70	0.70	0.52	0.52	0.41	0.41
100 MHz		2.30	1.46	1.13	1.13	0.82	0.82	0.64	0.64
230 MHz		3.65	2.29	1.75	1.75	1.31	1.31	1.02	1.02
300 MHz		4.27	2.64	2.04	2.04	1.53	1.53	1.19	1.19
600 MHz		5.87	3.86	3.02	3.02	2.27	2.27	1.81	1.81
860 MHz		7.57	4.65	3.69	3.69	2.80	2.80	2.22	2.22

Designing the system

The programmes on most systems will be distributed at several different frequencies in the range 40–860 MHz. Cable attenuation will cause signal levels to vary considerably between these limiting frequencies and so the starting point must be to ensure that the furthest television set from the head end receives sufficient signal at the highest frequency used. If the pictures are to be in the 'excellent' category and sufficient leeway is allowed for deterioration due to ageing or adverse reception conditions, then a level of 1 mV signal (0 dBmV) should be planned at the set. If cable lengths on large systems are so great that losses at the high UHF frequencies prevent the signals being distributed at their transmitter frequencies, then frequency conversion can take place at the head end to convert the transmissions to frequencies within VHF bands I and III. A maximum upper frequency of 230 MHz is then used. Equalisers have to be used to compensate for differences in cable losses between the high and low frequencies used. The designer must ensure that channel signal levels neither overload the amplifiers nor are sufficiently low to cause deterioration in picture quality.

The cable lengths to each television outlet must be accurately known to allow the losses at different outlets to be calculated (Table 8.2).

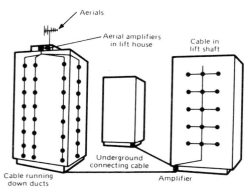

Figure 8.13. Aerial sited on top of office and examples of various methods of cabling large buildings

In a large building one or more main cables are fed from the head end and spur cables are taken off at each floor (Figure 8.13). Each spur cable has 'tee units' at the appropriate place to feed an

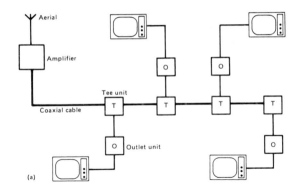

(a)

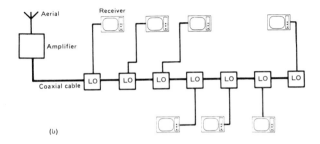

(b)

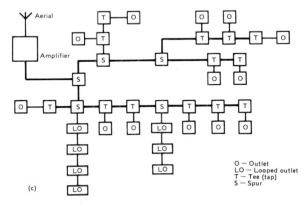

(c)

Figure 8.14. (a) Distribution of signals using taps from the main cable (remote outlets); (b) an economical cabling system whereby the outlets are in series on the coaxial cable; (c) a more complex system using spur cables and a combination of methods (a) and (b)

outlet (Figure 8.14). The units are directional and act as attenuators (taps). The correct attenuation value is chosen at each outlet to reduce the signal level to the correct level for the particular receiver since the signal had previously been made sufficiently high to overcome the losses to the furthest outlet. On large systems additional amplifiers are inserted into the spur cables to maintain the levels, as the maximum output of any amplifier is limited before overload distortion and interference signals due to cross modulation of signals occurs. Where additional amplifiers are used power must also be fed through the system.

By calculating the losses and signal levels at each stage the gain of the 'launch amplifier' or 'head end amplifier' can be calculated as can the signal strengths required to overcome the inherent noise of the system and to provide the required picture quality.

CATV

CATV systems are designed on the same principles as MATV, but on a larger scale, distributing programmes to whole communities or even complete towns. The main trunk lines need a low loss coaxial cable with repeater amplifiers spaced along the cable. AGC (automatic gain control) amplifiers also provide automatic correction for the level changes that occur due to temperature. The main trunk is kept as short as possible and is routed to as many distribution points as are required to feed the different circuits to the various communities. Obviously the higher the population density, the more economic such systems become. The length of the circuit that can be used is determined by the degradation of the picture due to noise, reflections, ghosting, cross modulation, equalisation and phase problems.

A bridging amplifier is normally used on the trunk cable instead of tee pieces (taps) in order to provide isolation. From this the feeder cables which themselves can require four to ten amplifiers, are run to the rows of houses or other outlets.

The individual houses are fed from taps inserted into the feeder cables at about 50 m (150 ft) spacing. Each tap usually has four outputs and is inserted into the feeder cable by piercing the outer sheath and making contact with the inner conductor. Taps can lead to ghosting due to reflections and are being replaced with directional couplers on more modern systems.

In the head end design the UHF channels are coverted to VHF to reduce losses on the cable.Each channel is individually corrected for picture and sound levels to reduce interference between channels and the sound carrier is normally reduced in level to prevent interference on the picture. All channels are then combined and frequency pre-equalised for the section of cable before the first main trunk amplifier. The pilot carrier for AGC operation is also added at this stage. The use of many channels on CATV systems requires the overload level to be reduced due to a severe form of interference called 'windshield wiper' effect, caused by the horizontal sync pulses of the different stations being unrelated in time. If cross modulation occurs due to overload then a vertical bar is seen to move horizontally across the picture.

Conclusion

CATV and MATV have been with us for many years and cable networks, where economic, are the immediate answer to enable an increase in the number of television channels available to the viewer when broadcast frequencies have been used. It will be interesting to discover the effect of fibre optics on such metworks, as their predicted cheapness and their wideband characteristics will probably allow installation to many homes for uses additional to television in the future.

Fibre optics

Cable systems and television transmission lines at present use copper or aluminium cables but experimental systems using fibre optics as the transmission medium are already in use. Since March 1976 Rediffusion has been using a 1400 m (4700 ft) span on a cable television trunk route in Hastings in south east England. The same company, with the co-operation of Delta Kabel in Holland, has also experimented since 1978 in Arnhem with glass fibre optics brought directly into the home. In 1976 Tele Prompter, who operate a Manhattan CTV system, also began experimenting with fibre optic cables in the trunk route. Experiments with normal telephone communications on fibre optics is also being actively investigated and over 100 systems in Britain, Canada and the United States are in operation. In Britain alone, British Telecom plan to have 100 000 km (62 500 miles) of fibre optic cable installed and being used between all the major towns before 1990.

It is expected that, with increased production, the cost of fibre optics will compare favourably with that of coaxial cable by the early 1980s. As copper becomes more difficult to obtain and the cost of energy to make aluminium becomes higher the quartz and silicon material needed for fibre optics will remain plentiful.

However, fibre optics possess several technical advantages over conventional cable, among which are smaller size and larger transmission capacity. The problem caused by cross coupling of signals in conventional cables laid together is eliminated as there is no significant coupling between fibres.

Coaxial cable changes its characteristics with temperature and elaborate pilot tone systems and equalisation procedures are a necessary part of operating coaxial links. The light signals, however, through a fibre optic system are stable with temperature changes. In addition, as the transmission signal is not electrical it is unaffected by external electrical fields and static discharges.

However, because it is a light signal instead of an electrical signal the system becomes more complex as the electrical signal has to modulate a light source and at the receiving end a light demodulation system has to be incorporated. This limits the possibility of bringing into the home a number of fibre optics and allowing the subscriber to select his own programme. The cost of transcoding the digital output of the light detector means that cable operators have concentrated on using fibre optics on super-trunks, where the equipment is common to all subscribers.

There are additional disadvantages at present to the use of fibre optics. In CATV systems it is common to carry power to the repeater amplifiers on the cable, but fibre optics are not capable of carrying power. The normal power of the light source is only of the order of microwatts. In CATV systems it is also necessary to tap into the cable to take feeds to houses or other distribution outlets. This is very difficult and expensive with fibre optics.

With present technology, splicing fibre optics is difficult. The ends are cut with a diamond stylus and aligned before fusing with an electric arc. Inconsiderate handling can break the fibres causing loss of light and therefore signals. These breaks are difficult to locate in the field.

Manufacture of fibre optics

Although made from the same constituents as ordinary glass, the fibre optic must be flawless and capable of transmitting light over several kilometres. It was only in the 1970s that technology advanced sufficiently to satisfy this requirement.

Previously the fibres had so many impurities and defects that the light was reduced to less than 1% while travelling less than ten metres. Current technology allows fibres to transmit more than 95% of the original light over one kilometre.

The process is begun by heating a one metre long small diameter tube of silica glass to nearly 1600°C (2912°F). The inside of the tube contains a chemical vapour which partially fuses to the inner wall to form a thin layer of glass. This vapour causes the glass formed to have a different refractive index and throughout the process the chemical composition of the vapour is changed to build up layers of glass,each with a different refractive index. The tube is then collapsed to form a solid tube known as a preform and, as this occurs, a glass core surrounded by the silica cladding is formed. The preform is then pulled to form hair thin fibres of 30–100 μm diameter to a length of 5 kilometres or more. Finally the fibre is coated with a fast-drying plastic before spooling onto reels.

Other methods are being perfected to produce fibres in which the light travels in a different manner. With the above method the light travels by being trapped by the cladding which acts as a reflecting surface and causes total internal reflection. The Nippon Electric Co. has produced a fibre for wide band operation by modifying the refractive index of the glass which then acts as a lens and focuses the light down the fibre. This has the advantage that all light rays from the object to the image cover the same distance and differential delay does not occur.

Transmission

For transmission in a fibre optic system the analogue signal is coded into a digitally modulated laser signal and for this purpose gallium aluminium arsenide lasers are built in arrays, together with the modulators, and are produced today about the size of a thumb-nail – the detectors are even smaller. The wavelength of light, itself an electromagnetic wave, is in the range of 400–700 nm (a blue-green light for example is 6×10^{14} Hz = 500 nm). The possibility exists therefore of modulation systems which can carry such vast amounts of information on a single fibre optic system that it is difficult to comprehend.

The modulation system used by British Telecom on its experimental link at Ipswich, which commenced operating in 1977, is 140 Mbit/s. This is not only adequate for telephones but also suitable for television transmission.

At present, due to the losses on the fibre optic links caused by imperfections in the fibre, repeaters are inserted in the links at 8 km spacing to reconstitute the signal. These amplifiers are expensive due to their complexity. Experiments now being conducted using infra-red as the light source allow signals to be transmitted up to 30 km before amplification as the longer wavelength signal is affected far less by the imperfections.

In Japan an experiment started in 1978 known as the Hi-Ovis project (Highaskio Ikoma Optical Visual Information System), which consists of a computer and transmission centre which is linked by fibre optic cables with about 158 homes. The occupants can view a number of television channels, operate the computer for home study, obtain train timetables and weather reports, shop at local stores by television and have fire and burglar alarm monitoring. Because of the immense volume of information that can be transmitted on the fibre optics transmission lines operating in both directions the system can be continually expanded. This would be economically, if not physically, impossible using conventional cable.

Conclusion

As copper becomes rarer, as all such raw material will, its replacement by fibre optics will bring a mass of information within the reach of everyone sitting in their homes and will rapidly change the way we live and work in the 21st century.

In broadcasting TV and sound studios all the signal generating and processing equipment will gradually become fully digital and obviously fibre optics will be able to reduce the mass of cabling currently used in the construction of such systems with the added advantage that possible electrical interference will be eliminated.

With a network of fibre optics the communications engineer will no longer be restricted to the amount of information he can transmit by his transmission lines and one fibre optic line will be used for many purposes.

However, a great deal of development has still to be done and a considerable amount of practical experience gained before the possibilities can be fully exploited.

Outside broadcast microwave links

A major problem faced by the outside broadcast planner is to provide the necessary links for the audio and video signals to the

Figure 8.15. A simplified example of the number of REC/TX required to send pictures back to the studio from an OB scanner when the topography prevents direct transmission

television studio. Sometimes this is unnecessary, if the programme is to be recorded and a mobile VTR is available. The mobile control room will, in these instances, simply feed directly to the VTR mobile. If for reasons of networking, live transmission or the need for immediate editing, this is not possible, then invariably microwave links operating in the range 2000 to 7000 MHz are used for the video. Audio is usually transmitted separately on equalised telephone lines by British Telecom.

At the frequencies used, however, the microwave signal travels only by line of sight. This may mean several links being temporarily installed on hills and buildings to receive and pass on the signal until it either arrives at the studio or a destination with a permanent link to the British Telecom network (Figure 8.15).

The planning of such links, therefore, requires surveys and tests before actual transmission. Although survey maps may show two points to be of sufficient height and distance that transmission should be possible, it often occurs that access to the area is not possible or buildings intervene between the transmitting and receiving points which prevent transmission. The routes then have to be replanned.

On remote sites where there is no electricity mobile generators have to be towed to operate the equipment.

Chapter 9

Reception

The colour television receiver

Previous chapters have shown how the televised image is converted to an electrical waveform carrying all the information about the picture's content, brightness and colour. The receiver decodes this information into signals capable of driving the cathode-ray tube and reproducing the information on the face of the tube.

To decode the signal the system must be designed to handle a method of coding appropriate for the transmissions it will receive. These systems can vary in the number of television lines and pictures with which the image is scanned each second and the coding used to transmit the colour difference signals. For a few specialist applications such as ships travelling around the world, multi-standard sets are produced which are capable of displaying pictures encoded in any standard. In areas of Europe and the Middle East, also, people situated on the borders of countries with different standards often desire to receive all the available transmissions and therefore require sets capable of receiving two colour standards. As the original TV colour encoding systems were designed so that a colour picture could also be received on black and white sets there are inevitably considerable similarities between parts of a monochrome set and a colour set. The latter can basically be regarded as a monochrome set with additional decoders for the colour signal.

Recently there have been considerable improvements in quality and reliability of colour sets mainly brought about by the introduction of integrated circuits and new CRT design. Additional facilities such as teletext and remote control have also been made possible.

In the home the viewer receives his signals from an aerial and his receiver is equipped with a tuner designed to tune to the particular

234

broadcast frequency required. However in CCTV and broadcast studios the signals to be monitored are at video and audio frequencies and so no tuner is required. These sets are known as 'Monitors' and although they contain fewer stages than a receiver they tend to be far more expensive due to limited production and the much higher performance specification required.

Receiver stages

Figure 9.1 shows a typical television colour receiver sutiable for PAL. The design of the set can be split into distinct areas many of which are common with a monochrome set, as follows.
1. UHF/VHF tuner.
2. IF (intermediate frequency) panel with vision and sound detection and sync pulse separation.
3. Timebase panel to generate the line and frame waveforms to drive the CRT deflection circuits.
4. Line scanning unit generates the line scan waveform for CRT deflection and the high voltage required for the EHT and focus.
5. Power supply that generates a stabilised supply for the electronics.

The circuits which are particular to a colour set are
6. Chrominance panel which demodulates the chroma signal and produces the three separate colour drive signals required for the CRT.
7. Convergence unit which in the shadowmask tube is required to supply correction waveforms to the convergence coils to ensure correct overlay of the three beams on all parts of the tube face in order to produce a composite picture. This unit is minimal with the PIL (precision in line) tube since alignment is an inherent part of the design and manufacture of the tube.

Tuner

In the UK the colour set will be fitted with a UHF tuner only as all transmissions are in these bands. However, in Europe, the USA and many other parts of the world the VHF bands are used which may entail the provision of both tuners.

Channel switching can be accomplished mechanically or by the touch sensitive ICs now available. Channel switching by remote control has also become common practice with either infra-red or ultrasonic beams being used to transmit the switching information from the remote unit to the TV set.

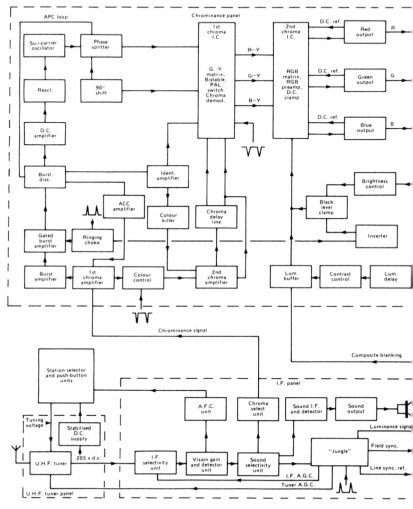

Figure 9.1. Block diagram of PAL colour television (Philips G8 chassis)

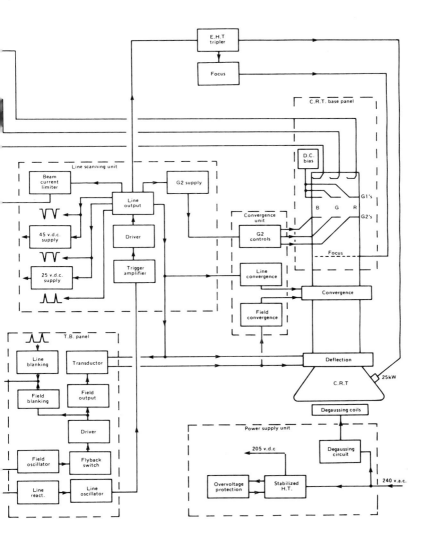

Tuning is usually performed by varying the voltage across a varactor diode with preset potentiometers selected by the tuner buttons. The diode then changes its capacitance to tune to the required frequency. AFC (automatic frequency control) voltages can be continuously fed from the IF detection stages to ensure that the station is accurately tuned. Arrangements have to be incorporated in the set to disconnect the AFC when manual tuning is required.

IF panel

The IF panel performs many functions. Its circuits must be tuned to accept the passband of the particular TV standard it is receiving (see multi-standard sets) and is responsible for most of the gain and selectivity of the set. In addition, the sound is separated from the video and both signals are detected, after which the sound can be amplified and applied to the speaker. Within the vision IF the colour subcarrier is detected and the chrominance signals are removed for separate demodulation.

Sync separators are also incorporated in order to provide the necessary pulses to synchronise the CRT deflection waveforms with the incoming video signal. This can now be performed by an IC but basically the sync pulses are separated from the video signal (luminance) by two separate integrating circuits, which are able to separate the line and frame syncs by the correct selection of *CR* time constants and detecting the differences in the occurrence of the pulses.

Timebase panel

The separated line and frame pulses are used to synchronise line and frame oscillators which produce the correct waveforms to drive the deflection coils. Blanking pulses of the correct time and amplitude are also generated for the chrominance decoder circuit.

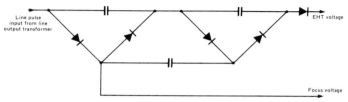

Figure 9.2. Typical arrangement of diodes and capacitors to form an EHT tripler unit

Line scan unit

The colour CRT needs a voltage of the order of 25 kV (depending on the size of the screen) in order to operate. To generate this, advantage is taken of the very high energy available in the line output transformer when operating at line frequencies to produce the line deflection waveform. Additional windings are placed on the transformer and the output is taken to a tripler circuit which produces the high voltages through a series of diodes and capacitors (Figure 9.2). Lower voltages and focus voltage are also produced for the set and correction waveforms used in the convergence circuits are additionally generated.

Power supply

The power supply has to generate one or more stabilised supplies and these are usually generated by a thyristor. These function by varying the switch-on point of the thyristor by monitoring the DC supply. If the DC rises the switch-on point is delayed. The thyristor is arranged to switch on positive half-cycles of the mains voltage and delay of this point tends to compensate for variations of the DC voltage.

These circuits incorporate an overload circuit which prevents the voltage rising above a predetermined level. This would not only cause possible damage to the set but would also increase the x-ray radiation from the CRT.

Chrominance demodulation (PAL)

The purpose of the chrominance demodulator is to recreate the three original colour signals from the two colour difference signals which were modulated on to the colour subcarrier. These signals are then processed and applied either as colour difference signals to the three grids ($R-Y$, $B-Y$, $G-Y$) and the luminance (Y) to the cathode or as RGB drives direct to the cathodes. In the latter method all matrixing of the colour signals is performed prior to the tube. Cathode drive is commonly used due to its greater sensitivity than grid drive.

It must be remembered that the bandwidths of the luminance and colour difference signals are very different and that all the detail in the picture is carried by the luminance signal, which is about 5.5 MHz in bandwidth while the colour signals are only ± 1 MHz in the PAL system. In the PAL system the $R-Y$ and $B-Y$ are amplitude modulated on quadrature phased carriers of the same frequency. In addition, the phase of the $R-Y$ signal is inverted on every line.

The system uses a suppressed carrier and therefore it is necessary to detect the burst in each line blanking period in order to synchronise in phase and frequency the oscillator used for the synchronous detectors. The phase of the burst alternates each line in synchronism with the $R-Y$ phase alternation and therefore from this burst (swinging burst) a PAL ident signal can be derived to ensure that the alternation of the $R-Y$ in the decoder is in phase with that transmitted.

When the $R-Y$ and $B-Y$ has been recovered matrixing circuits recover the $G-Y$ from the two previous signals and this is performed by resistively adding the signals in the correct proportions.

In all modern PAL sets an ultrasonic delay line is used to average out any hue errors due to phase errors. With such a delay line the hue will remain constant, as both vectors will be affected and only a slight variation in saturation will occur with the amount of phase error generally encountered.

A colour killer circuit is also incorporated in the circuit to remove the circuit whenever a monochrome signal is transmitted. This prevents patterning on a black and white picture. Usually the presence of the burst indicates whether the signal is colour or monochrome and this can be used for identification.

Decoder operation

A simplified diagram of a decoder is shown in Figure 9.3. Although alternative systems are possible the necessary operations which have to be carried out are illustrated.

The composite video is taken from a video stage in the luminance circuit and is fed to a chroma amplifier. Simultaneously the burst is gated, amplified, and is used as an input to a phase detector which controls the phase and frequency of the local oscillator. Invariably ACC (automatic chrominance correction) is applied to ensure the amplitude of the burst remains constant. The presence or absence of the burst is also detected to operate the colour killer circuit and, in addition, the phase of the burst synchronises the bistable switch for the correct phase of the oscillator input to the synchronous detector for $R-Y$ demodulation. This changes by 90° on each line. The oscillator output is fed directly to the $R-Y$ synchronous detector and through a 90° phase shift to the $B-Y$ synchronous detector for demodulation.

The chroma signal is passed to the delay line which not only corrects for hue errors but also separates the $B-Y$ and $R-Y$ signals (Figure 9.4).

In the PAL signal the $R-Y$ chroma signal is referred to as the V signal and the $B-Y$ chroma signal is referred to as the U signal.

The separation circuit uses the delay line together with an add and subtract network connected to both input and output. It must be remembered that the V signal will reverse on alternate lines.

In the examples shown the first line is assumed to be $-V+U$. This will be delayed and appear on the output of the delay line when $V+U$ of line 2 appears on the input. The add circuit will therefore have $(V+U) + (-V+U) = 2U$.

The subtract circuit will have
$(V+U) - (-V+U) = -2V$
Line 3 will have
$(-V+U) + (V+U) = 2U$ (add circuit)
and $(-V+U) - (V+U) = -2V$ (subtract circuit)

As the lines have also been averaged such a circuit provides all the requirements for PAL-D operation and a simple method of separation of the colour components (Figure 9.4).

The delay line provides a delay slightly less than a full line in order that the addition and subtraction of the direct and delayed signals correspond to an exact number of subcarrier half cycles. If a period of $64\,\mu s$ were chosen it would not correspond and, therefore, for a PAL subcarrier of $4.43361875\,MHz$ a $63.934\,\mu s$ delay is used.

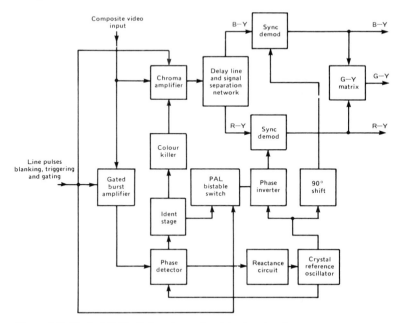

Figure 9.3. Typical PAL-D decoder and matrix signal paths

After separation the U and V signals are applied to the synchronous demodulators. These provide an output only when the reference signal and the signal to be demodulated are simultaneously applied. The reference signal must be of the correct frequency and phase as the original suppressed subcarrier. A synchronous demodulator can be regarded as a sampling circuit, where the circuit is switched on by the peaks of the local reference oscillator for short periods of time. If, therefore, there is misphasing between the chroma signal and the reference oscillator the demodulated signals will be incorrect.

As the V and U signals are 90° apart the reference oscillator input to the demodulators must be similarly phased. As the sampling rate is faster than the colour modulation changes, the demodulated output is a faithful reproduction of the original transmission.

A synchronous detector is constructed basically of a diode bridge to which the modulated signal and the reference signal are

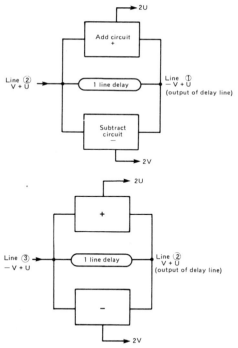

Figure 9.4. Operation of PAL delay line for separation of colour components and averaging of colour errors

fed – the reference will open the diode bridge on positive peaks. This circuitry is now an IC which incorporates other functions.

The decoded R − Y and B − Y are passed to the matrix to provide either RGB or R − Y, B − Y and G − Y for the CRT drive. Again this matrix can now be an IC.

SECAM and NTSC

NTSC and SECAM sets follow the same layout and their differences are found in the decoders. NTSC being very similar to PAL does not require the PAL switch as the R − Y axis does not change, therefore no delay line is used as hue correction by this method is not possible. The subcarrier is on 3.58 MHz when working on 525 lines 60 Hz and the bandwidths of the luminance and colour signals are different to those of PAL on 625 lines 50 Hz.

In SECAM an FM demodulator is used on each R − Y and B − Y modulated signal to recover the chroma signals. As only one colour difference signal is transmitted on each line, a delay line is used to store and have available two colour signals R − Y and B − Y for each line, although obviously one actually occurred a line earlier.

To ensure that the colour difference signals appear in the same order as transmitted the set is synchronised either each line by a subcarrier burst or each frame when special synchronising signals, (known as bottles because of their shape) appear in the vertical interval. However, because of the requirement to use the frame synchronising period for teletext services, some countries have adopted a SECAM standard whereby the sets are synchronised at line rate (see Table 9.1). As an FM signal is used, pre-emphasis and de-emphasis are used to improve the signal-to-noise ratio.

Multi-standard sets

A set capable of being taken anywhere in the world follows the same requirements as other sets but must duplicate and triplicate many of the electronic circuits.

Throughout the world there are many transmission standards in addition to line, frame and colour standards. These standards affect the audio and video spacing on the transmitted signal, the bandwidths required for transmission, the type of vision and sound modulation and the polarity of modulation. Table 9.1 shows these standards.

Table 9.1. World television systems

Parameter	System code								
	A	M (N)	B	C	G (H)	I	D K (KI)	L	E
Lines per picture	405	525 (625)	625	625	625	625	625	625	819
Field frequency (Hz)	50	60 (50)	50	50	50	50	50	50	50
Line frequency (Hz)	10 125	15 734 (15 625)	15 625	15 625	15 625	15 625	15 625	15 625	20 475
Video bandwidth (MHz)	3	4.2	5	5	5	5.5	6	6	10
Channel bandwidth (MHz)	5	6	7	7	8	8	8	8	14
Nearest edge of channel relative to vision carrier (MHz)	± 1.25	− 1.25	− 1.25	− 1.25	− 1.25	− 1.25	− 1.25	− 1.25	± 2.83
Sound carrier frequency relative to vision carrier (MHz)	− 3.5	+ 4.5	+ 5.5	+ 5.5	+ 5.5	+ 6	+ 6.5	6.5	± 11.15
Width of vestigial sideband (MHz)	0.75	0.75	0.75	0.75	0.75 (1.25)	1.25	0.75 (1.25)	1.25	2
Vision modulation polarity	positive	negative	negative	positive	negative	negative	negative	positive	positive
Sound modulation,	am	fm ± 25 kHz	fm ± 50 kHz	am	fm ± 50 kHz	fm ± 50 kHz	fm ± 50 kHz	am	am
f.m. pre-emphasis (µs)		75	50	50	50	50	50		

SECAM V. System where vertical synchronisation is used.

SECAM H. System where horizontal synchronisation is used.

Country	Colour	System	Channels
Afghanistan	PAL	D	
Alaska (USA)	NTSC	M	A2–13
Albania	SECAM (H)	B	
Algeria	PAL	B	E5–11
Andorra	PAL	B	
Angola		I	E9
Antigua & Barbuda	(NTSC)	M	A7–10
Antilles	NTSC	M	A3–13
Argentina	PAL	N	A2–13
Ascension Is		I	
Australia	PAL	B	Aus:0–11
Austria	PAL	B	E1–12
	PAL	G	21–68
Azores		M	A5
		B	E7–9
Bahamas	NTSC	M	
Bahrain	PAL	B	E4
Bangladesh	PAL	B	E5–11
Barbados	NTSC	N	A3
Belgium	PAL	B	E1–12
	PAL	G	21–68
Bermuda	NTSC	M	A8,10
Bolivia	NTSC	N	A7,10
Botswana		I	
Brazil	PAL-M	M	A2–13
	PAL-M	M	A38
Brunei	PAL	B	E5–8
Bulgaria	SECAM (V)	D	R7–12
Burma	NTSC	N	
Burundi		K	
Cambodia (Khmer Rep.)		M	A8–11

Country	Colour	System	Channels
Cameroon		K	
Canada	NTSC	M	A2–13
	NTSC	M	A15–30
Canary Is	PAL	B	E3–10
Cape Verde Is		I	
Central African Empire	B		
Chad		K	
Chile	NTSC	M	A2–13
China	PAL	D	Special Channel (57.75/64.25 MHz) + Channels R1–5
Colombia	SECAM (V)	M	A2–13
Comoro Islands		L	
Congo	SECAM (V)	D	R7
Costa Rica	NTSC	M	A2–12
Cuba	NTSC	D	A2–13
(US Navy)		(M)	(A8)
Cyprus		B	E6–11
Czechoslovakia			35–38
	SECAM (V)	D	R1–12
	SECAM (V)	D	R21–39
Dahomey		K	
Denmark	PAL	B	E3–11
Diego Garcia		M	A8
Djibouti	SECAM	K¹	K5
Dominican Rep	NTSC	M	A2–13
Ecuador	NTSC	M	A2–10
Egypt	SECAM (V)	B	E3–11
El Salvador	NTSC	M	A2–20
Ethiopia		B	E7
Fernando Po		B	

Table 9.1 (contd)

Country	Colour	System	Channels
Fiji	PAL	B	E1-12
Finland	PAL	B	21-68
France	—	G	F1-12
	SECAM (V)	E	21-68
		L	K3,10
Gabon	SECAM (V)	K	E2-11
Gambia	PAL		21-60
W. Germany	PAL	B	B
E. Germany	SECAM (V)	G	22-34
E3-12			
Ghana	SECAM (V)	G	E2-5
Gibralter	PAL	B	E6,11
Greece	PAL	B	E5-11
		B	23-49
Greenland	NTSC	M	A8
Guadeloupe	SECAM (V)	K¹	K5-8
Guam	NTSC	M	A8,12
Guatemala	NTSC	M	A3-13
Guinea Bissau		I	
Guinea Dem Rep		B	E2
Guinea. Rep	SECAM (V)	K¹	
Guyana, Fr.		M	
Guyana, Rep		B,G	K4,6
Haiti	SECAM (V)	M	A2-5
Hawaii (USA)	NTSC	M	A2-13
Honduras		M	A3-13
Hong Kong	PAL	I	E1-2
			E21-36
Hungary	—	D	R1-12
	SECAM (V)	K	R24-32
Iceland	PAL	B	E3-10
India	PAL	B	E4-7
Indonesia	SECAM (H)	B	E4-10
Iran	SECAM (H)	B	E3-11
Iraq		A	E5-11
Ireland, Rep	PAL	I	B1-11
			A-J, 29-43
Israel	PAL	B	E5-11
Italy	PAL	G	24-56
		B	It:A-H 21-34
		G	21-34
Ivory Coast	SECAM (V)	K¹	K4-10
Jamaica		M	A7-13
Japan	NTSC	M	J1-12
	NTSC	M	J28-62
Jibuti	SECAM	K¹	K5
Johnston Is	NTSC	M	A10
Jordan	PAL	B	E3-9
Kenya	PAL	B	E2-10
Khmer Republic (Cambodia)		M	A8-11
Korea, N		D	R5-12
Korea, S	NTSC	M	A4-13
(US Forces)	(NTSC)	(M)	(A2-13, 49-75)
Kuwait	PAL	B	E5-11
Lebanon	SECAM (V)	B	E2-11
Leeward Is		M	A7,8
Lesotho	NTSC	I	
Liberia	PAL	B	E6-10
Libya	PAL	B	E5-11
Luxembourg	PAL	C	E7
		L	21
Macau	SECAM (V)	I	
Madeira	PAL	B	E5

Country	Colour	System	Channels
Madagascar		K	
Malaysia	PAL	B	K5
Malawi		B	E2–10
Malta		B	
		G	E10
			21
Martinique	SECAM (V)	K'	K4–8
Mauritania		K	
Mauritius	SECAM (V)	B	E4–1
Mexico	NTSC	M	A2–13
			A14–45
Midway Is	NTSC	M	A4
Monaco	SECAM (V)	C	E10
	SECAM (V)	L	E30
	SECAM (V)	G	E35
Mongolia		D	R?
Morocco	SECAM (V)	B	M4–10
Mozambique		I	
Netherlands	PAL	B	E1–12
	PAL	G	21–58
New Caledonia	SECAM (V)	K'	K4–8
New Zealand	PAL	B	NZ:1–9
Nicaragua	NTSC	M	A2–13
Niger		K	
Nigeria	PAL	B	E2–10
Norway	PAL	B	E2–11
	PAL	G	44
Okinawa	NTSC	M	
Oman	PAL	B	E5–12
		G	
Pakistan	PAL	B	E4–10
Panama	NTSC	M	A2–12
Paraguay		M	A9
Peru	NTSC	M	A2–13
Phillipines	NTSC	M	A2–14
(US Forces)	(NTSC)	(M)	(A8, A34)
Poland	SECAM (V)	D	R1–12
		K	21–37
Polynesia, French		K	
Portugal	PAL	B	E2–11
		G	25–46
Puerto Rico	NTSC	M	A2–12
(US Forces)		(M)	(a44–56)
Qatar	PAL	B	E9,11
Reunion	SECAM (V)	K'	K4–9
Rhodesia		B	E2–6
Romania		D	R2–12
Rwanda		K	
Sabah & Sarawak (Malayasia)	PAL	B	E2–10
Samoa	NTSC	M	A2–12
Saudi Arabia	SECAM (H)	B	E5–10
(Aramco)	(NTSC)	(M)	(a2)
Senegal	SECAM (V)	K	K7
Seychelles		I	
Sierra Leone	PAL	B	E2
Singapore	PAL	B	E5,8
Society Is (Tahiti)	SECAM (V)	K'	K4–8
Somalia		B,G	
South Africa	PAL	I	14–13
	PAL	I	21–68
	PAL		B
Spain	PAL	G	21–65
		B	E2–11
Sri Lanka		B	
St Helena		I	
St Kits	NTSC	M	A2–13

Table 9.1 (contd)

Country	Colour	System	Channels
St Pierre et Miquelon		K¹	K4–8
Sudan	PAL	B	E5–7
Surinam	NTSC	M	A7–12
Swaziland		I	
Sweden	PAL	B	E2–11
	PAL	G	21–68
Switzerland	PAL	B	E2–12
	PAL	G	21–63
		B	E4–9
Syria	SECAM (V)	K¹	K4–8
Tahiti	NTSC	M	A7–12
Taiwan	PAL	B	E21
Tanzania	PAL	B,M	A2–13
Thailand	PAL	D	R
Tibet			
Togo	SECAM	K¹	K6–8
Trinidad and Tobago	NTSC	M	A2–13
Trust Islands of the Pacific (Micronesia)	NTSC	M	A8,10
Tunisia	SECAM (V)	B	E5–12
Turkey	PAL	B	E5–10
Uganda	PAL	B	E5–10
United Arab Emirates	PAL	B	E2–11
United Kingdom	PAL	I	22–66
		A	B114
		K¹	K6
Upper Volta		N	A3–13
Uruguay		M	A2–13
USA	NTSC	M	A14–83
USSR	SECAM (V)	D	R1–12
		K	21–68
Venezuela	NTSC	M	A2–13
Vietnam		D	R6
Virgin Is	NTSC	M	A7–13
Yemen Arab Rep		M	A5–12
Yemen Dem Rep		B	E4–10
Yugoslavia	PAL	B	E2–12
	PAL	H	21–68
Zaire	SECAM (V)	K	K5–9
Zambia	PAL	B	E2–4

A multistandard set therefore must fulfil the following or its use will be restricted to certain areas of the world.

1. Operating voltage and frequencies to be variable. This usually requires the set to operate with either 50 or 60 Hz mains (with considerable variations) and voltages of 110 V, 115 V, 120 V, 127 V, 220 V, 240 V, many of which will have poor regulation.
2. Operate in PAL, SECAM, NTSC and PAL-M in parts of South America. This usually requires the provision of separate decoders although parts of a PAL decoder can be used for SECAM when on the same line standard.
3. Operate with AM and FM sound modulation.
4. Operate with all the normal broadcast standards. This requires modifications to the IF and possibly line and frame timebase oscillators and waveforms as each standard is selected. Under these conditions the EHT and focus must be stable.

Obviously all these variations need complex switching arrangements. Although, until recently, these have been mechanically switched, circuits have been developed to examine the incoming signal and automatically adjust the set for the correct operation.

Professional monitors

The professional monitor still invariably contains the shadowmask tube in order to provide the definition required when viewing coded signals.

Due to both the individual selection of tubes and components together with the relatively low volume of production the cost is invariably high when compared to a TV set. The set, however, must be robust and invariably is housed in a metal case with handles. The effective screen area compared with size of the front of the monitor is of importance where space is often at a premium, especially in OB units. It is generally recognised that an ideal viewing distance for such a monitor is four times the diagonal screen size and this, therefore, can set the minimum screen size in any particular situation.

Usually at least two inputs to the monitor must be available for switching and all set-up controls must be readily available from the front. The phosphors on the tubes must be matched in a bank of monitors and, at least in the ITA network, the white when displayed must be of a certain specified standard. In addition to a coded input it is often necessary for the monitor to accept RGB inputs direct. Particular attention has to be paid to heat dissipation, as often studios are hot and the monitors are in banks.

Reliability is essential and it is esimated that during the life of a monitor its servicing will cost several times the purchase price.

In a similar way to all electronics the reliability of professional monitors has increased in recent years with the introduction of new components and lower power dissipation.

The professional monitor is an important tool to the broadcaster as all final assessment and alignment will involve looking at the displayed picture.

PLUGE (Picture Line-Up Generator)

The PLUGE generator provides a waveform for setting up both colour and monochrome monitors. The waveform consists of a pedestal with two narrow pulses and a wide bar on the right-hand side.

When adjusting the monitor the brightness is adjusted until the black pulse is about to disappear and the white pulse is just visible. The pulses are shown in Figure 9.5. If the brightness is too high then both the black and white pulses will be visible but if the brightness is too low neither bars will be seen. After the correct adjustment of the brightness the contrast is adjusted to produce the desired brightness of the peak white bar.

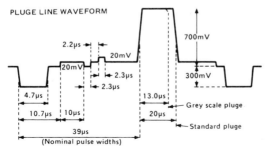

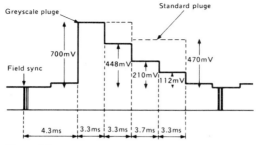

Figure 9.5

Conclusion

The reliability, picture quality, operational features and the intro-duction of new facilities such as teletext, has shown the consider-able amount of development time and expense the manufacturers continue to give to the television set. Much is owed to the component manufacturers and their ingenious ICs that are reduc-ing the size and power requirements of the sets.

Although outwardly the set is still chosen as a piece of furniture by the layman he should also be aware of the remarkable advances that have occurred inside the set in recent years.

Colour television displays

Television receiver development has depended more on the evolution of the cathode ray tube than on any other single factor. Today the shape, size and electronics of television sets are all controlled by the display tube and any great change in viewing habits will probably be brought about by major technical advances in the display system. This may take the form of flat panels, miniature or very large colour tubes or even three-dimensional TV. However, the cathode ray tube has dominated the industry for the last 50 years in various forms and an alternative is very unlikely to appear during the next 20 years.

The early work on cathode ray tubes was performed by such men as Ferdinand Braun (Braun tube) in Germany in 1930. From this work was developed the gas focused tubes used in the first BBC television transmission in the 1930s. V. K. Zworykin in 1929 combined for the first time the two essential parts of the cathode ray tube – the small thermionic cathode and an electron optical lens system. Zworykin, who was working on iconoscopes and cathode ray tube receivers in the USA, was also granted the US patent for electronic television in 1921.

RCA's shadowmask tube, which until recently was used exclu-sively in all colour receivers, resulted from the labours of many individuals and is an item few people believed could ever be produced on a production line when it was first developed. The design was based on proposals by A. N. Goldsmith and A. C. Shroeder and was first successfully produced in the RCA research laboratories in 1950. In recent years we have seen the develop-ment of the Trinitron by Sony Corporation and the precision in-line gun tubes originally developed by RCA and Thorn. Other manufacturers have now entered the market and tubes with such features can now be obtained with 110° deflection angles (necessary to produce the modern slim television set) and screen sizes up to 66 cm.

Principle of operation

The operating principle of all current tubes, irrespective of their type, is that almost any colour can be produced by additive mixing of red, blue and green light in the correct proportions – a principle similar to the Dufay photographic process. The tubes must produce a complete picture of the original scene in each of these primary colours and, provided the pictures are coincident, the eye will see a complete picture of the original scene in all its natural colours. The problems arise in making the three pictures coincident and in obtaining a bright sharply focused picture. It is the method of improving these features which has led to the new generation of tubes.

Shadowmask or tricolour tube

In the neck of the shadowmask tube (Figure 9.6) there are three elecron guns separately driven by the red, blue and green signals. The guns are arranged in a triangular formation where, looking from the screen, blue is the top gun, green is on the right and red is on the left (in some sets blue can be on the bottom).

The screen for a 63 cm diagonal tube is made up of a mosaic of phosphor dots which are grouped in triads so that one emits red and the others blue and green. These total about 1 300 000 dots which cannot be resolved by the eye at normal viewing distances. Between the screen and the electron guns is the shadowmask in which there are about 440 000 holes, each one aligned with a triad of phosphor dots.

When manufacturing the tube, the phosphor dots are photographically positioned using the shadowmask of the particular tube as the optical mask. The screen is coated in turn with a photo-resist material containing one of the colour phosphors. A powerful point source of ultraviolet light is then positioned where the gun relating to the particular colour is to be centred. This is known as the colour or deflection centre and is the position the beam appears to come from when the deflection coils are deflecting the electron beam. The ultraviolet hardens the photo-resist where it passed through the mask and hits the tube face. This is where a dot of the particular phosphor is required. The mask is removed and the remaining photo-resist and phosphor are removed leaving the dots of phosphor only where they are required. The process is then repeated for the other two colours.

Figure 9.6. Cutaway view of a 110° shadowmask colour TV picture tube, complete with (right to left) scanning coil, convergence yoke and associated neckware. Inset is shown the section of the shadowmask (courtesy Mullard)

The shadowmask is positioned about 12 mm behind the screen and this is produced from a master negative by a photo engraving process. Each hole is aproximately 0.25 mm diameter and the spacing is 0.6 mm. Each hole is tapered, as the thickness of the mask is about 0.2 mm and the electrons hitting the inner surface of the hole would be deflected over the screen and cause a loss of definition and saturation. It should be realised that the beam from the guns covers several holes simultaneously in the shadowmask. The holes in the shadowmask constitute only about 15% of the total mask area and therefore 85% of the possible electrons which could hit the screen are prevented from contributing to the brightness of the mask. In order, therefore, to approach the same brightness as a monochrome picture the beam current has to be considerably higher in a colour tube. In high ambient lighting the contrast and colour saturation of the colour tube are considerably reduced, partially due to the reflected light from the aluminium backing (used to stop effects of ion bombardment and also initially used to produce greater light output) and the unused parts of the phosphor. A reduction in desaturation can be obtained by using a glass face of reduced light transmission. Although the light output from the tube is reduced, the reflected light has to pass twice through the glass and is considerably reduced. A compromise obviously has to be reached between contrast and light output.

A different approach to obtaining greater contrast is to use a black non-reflecting material between the phosphor dots instead of the highly reflecting aluminium backing. Normally the phosphor dots are made larger than the hole in the screen to give tolerance to the beam landing on the phosphor and to improve purity. Again, this unused phosphor will cause reflections. If these dots are now reduced, the beam falling outside the phosphor will fall on the black surface and will create no illumination. Using this system, up to 50% of the screen can be covered by the black material. As the reflections are now far less, the light transmission of the glass can be increased to improve the picture brightness. It is also possible with this arrangement to make the different coloured phosphor dots different sizes in order to allow the separate beam currents to be made almost the same.

Modern development in colour tube design has allowed light output to be increased by the use of improved phosphors and the appearance of the set has been considerably enhanced by ultra-rectangular tubes and use of metal rim-guards. Safety glass protection against tube implosion is no longer necessary, as, during manufacture, a metal band is pressed while hot around the tube face. This puts the face plate under compression when it cools and, should the tube be broken, the glass will not fly out.

Problems of convergence

To achieve a colour picture, it is necessary for all three colours to be deflected horizontally and vertically with great accuracy in order to avoid imperfection in the final registration of the beams on the phosphors. The problem arises in the shadowmask tube that, because all three beams do not originate from the same source, they will be affected differently by the deflection circuits and this will result in a displacement of the colours on the screen. The effect is compounded by the flat screen which also introduces pincushion distortion.

Correction is achieved by additional components mounted on the neck of the tube which receive complex electrical waveforms to correct the position of each beam and therefore permit the convergence of all three beams at any point on the screen. In addition to the electrical waveforms, a blue lateral magnet is used in order to move the blue beam horizontally to ensure coincidence with the red and green beams.

Typically, fourteen controls are necesary to achieve the required results and these must also control very stable circuits if convergence is to be maintained. It was the manufacturers' desire to improve this feature which would not only simplify production but result in a better converged set with all the associated improvements in definition that led to the Trinitron and precision in-line tubes.

Trinitron tube

This was a development by Miyaoka of Sony Corporation in 1968 and is now used in all their receivers. In this tube (Figure 9.7), three separate cathodes for the red, green and blue beams are constructed within a single gun in a horizontal arrangement instead of the delta system of the shadowmask tube.

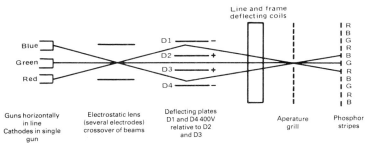

Figure 9.7. Simplified Trinitron picture tube (top view)

The aperture grill which replaces the shadowmask consists of a series of vertical slits (corresponding to phosphor stripes on the tube face) of red, green and blue. In the 32 cm tube there are approximately 400 slits and in the 45 cm tube approximately 466 slits. The beams pass through an electrostatic lens which focuses them and causes the beams to cross over. Without the deflection, the green beam passes down the centre of the tube while the blue and red beams are deflected by deflection plates which cause all three beams to pass through the grill aperture and hit the appropriately coloured phosphor. The grill is welded to a frame which holds it in tension. Its position is obviously critical if the stripes and slits are to remain correctly positioned relative to each other.

The advantages claimed for the Trinitron are extra brightness and ease of convergence. Sony maintains that the gun produces a 50% greater beam current than the shadowmask gun and in addition the grill has a transparency almost 1.33 times greater than the shadowmask. The combination of these two effects is to produce a picture twice the brightness of a conventional shadowmask tube.

Precision in-line tube

The advantage of using an in-line gun arrangement instead of the delta arrangement of the shadowmask tube was widely recognised and development proceeded in several parts of the world. The first tubes appeared in 1972 and by 1975 the first successfully mass produced in-line tubes became available in 90° and 110° angles and in a range of sizes incorporating 45, 50, 55 and 66 cm. Although the differences in the picture appearance would probably not be observed when compared to a correctly converged shadowmask tube, manufacturers' and service companies' problems are greatly reduced due to the fewer components and adjustments required.

The neck of the tube is still the standard size of 36.5 mm but, because of the elimination of the pole pieces required for dynamic convergence corrections, the neck length is reduced by 20 mm compared with the shadowmask tube, allowing a slimmer set to be designed. The electron guns are mounted horizontally with the green gun in the middle and the red and blue guns inclined towards the centre. As the eye is more sensitive to convergence errors between red and green and blue and green this reduces the effect if manufacturing tolerances leave residual convergence errors. The self-converging deflection field used with the PIL tube also has an important effect on focus. In the normal deflection field of the shadowmask, the spot which is focused at the centre of the screen will become blurred when deflected to the side. The special deflection field developed for the PIL tube, however, maintains focus of the spot in a horizontal plane but extends the vertical haze of the spot with deflection. To reduce this effect, a plate with a horizontal slit is placed in the second grid to reduce the height of the beams. This reduces the vertical haze on the spot but causes a larger spot at the centre of the screen. This, however, can have a beneficial effect as it can reduce Moiré interference patterns.

The screen consists of vertical phosphor stripes behind which is a slotted shadowmask. Each slot of the mask corresponds with a group of three stripes and for stability the slots are bridged at regular intervals. In order to reduce the Moiré effect, the bridging interval as displayed on a 66 cm screen is made 810 μm and for strength the bridges are staggered from slot to slot (Figure 9.8).

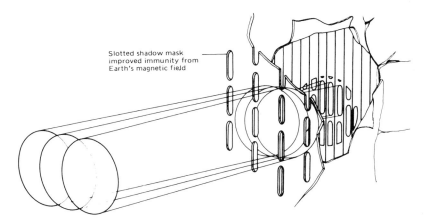

Slotted shadow mask
improved immunity from
Earth's magnetic field

Figure 9.8. Slots in a PIL tube

Colour purity is independent of beam landing in a vertical direction due to the stripes. In order to obtain the same horizontal definition as the conventional shadowmask tube, the stripes have to be horizontally spaced so that the three stripes cover the same horizontal space as three phosphor dots (Figure 9.9). This creates a width size for each colour stripe which is approximately half the diameter of the phosphor dot. In the 66 cm tube, the centre spacing of the phosphor stripes is 265 μm and the centre of each group of three stripes is spaced by 795 μm. The horizontal landing requirements are therefore far more stringent although of course the vertical landing tolerance is unlimited due to the vertical

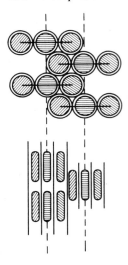

Figure 9.9 Dot structure of a shadowmask tube compared to a stripe structure screen of equal fineness

stripes. Colour purity in a vertical direction is therefore independent of the beam landing tolerance and only horizontal correction has to be applied.

The tube is constructed with an internal magnetic shield and advantage is taken of the unlimited vertical landing tolerance by rotating the degaussing coil through 90° compared to the shadowmask and completely eliminating the normal vertical component of the residual magnetic field which causes the horizontal errors. Because of the vertical continuity of the mask, the lines of magnetic force are uninterrupted and therefore the demagnetising force can be reduced, resulting in a smaller degaussing coil.

The design of the deflection system forms an integral part of the precision-in-line tube and is different from that of the conventional shadowmask tube. In 1954 J. Haantjes and G. Lubben were granted a US patent and proved it was possible to eliminate convergence errors by the use of in-line guns and a specially designed deflection system.

The characteristics of a deflection system which decide its convergence performance are:

 1. curvature of the image field,
 2. astigmatism,
 3. coma (in a delta gun arrangement, this effect causes the blue beam to be displaced in the direction of deflection relative to the red and green beams).

However, the curvature of the image field causes most convergence problems with deflection, since the three beams each have a radius of curvature which is less than the surface it is sweeping across. On a flat screen this causes the beams to form an equilateral triangle of colours at the screen.

In addition, astigmatism errors cause the convergence beam to split into two focal lines one of which is parallel and one is perpendicular to the direction of deflection. Either of these focus lines can be used, but it is the vertical focus line that is required for the system to work.

The result of combining the astigmatism error and curvature of the image field in a delta gun arrangement is to make the image spots form isosceles triangles instead of equilateral triangles caused by curvature errors only (Figure 9.10). These effects are corrected in the shadowmask tube by dynamic convergence waveforms which generate correcting fields around the neck of the tube.

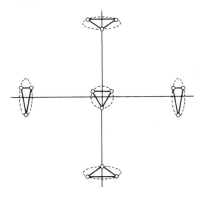

Figure 9.10. Convergence errors on a flat screen caused by curvature of field and astigmatism after vertical and horizontal deflection in a delta-gun arrangement

Haantjes and Lubben found that the convergence errors caused by the curvature of field could be compensated by increasing the astigmatism error and this would eliminate miconvergence in one direction at the expense of the other. If the astigmatism is increased in such a way as to compensate for the curvature of field and eliminate the misconvergence in the horizontal direction it has the effect of making the vertical focal line coincide with the flat screen over all the angles of deflection (Figure 9.11). Misconvergence in the vertical direction increases but in a PIL tube this vertical line becomes a point and perfect convergence is obtained over the entire screen.

However, if the vertical and horizontal deflection fields are the same and only rotated through 90° it is found that it is the horizontal focus line and not the required vertical line that coincides at all parts of the screen. It is necessary therefore to alter

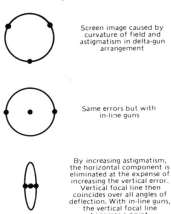

Screen image caused by curvature of field and astigmatism in delta-gun arrangement

Same errors but with in-line guns

By increasing astigmatism, the horizontal component is eliminated at the expense of increasing the vertical error. Vertical focal line then coincides over all angles of deflection. With in-line guns, the vertical focal line becomes a point.

Figure 9.11

the shape of the raster to achieve the automatic convergence. The horizontal deflection field is made pincushion shaped and the vertical deflection is made barrel shaped in the parts closest to the screen (Figure 9.12).

Already considerable improvements have been made in the PIL tube since its introduction. The original 20AX tube has been replaced by the 30AX (Figure 9.13). Alignment in manufacture has now eliminated all operational convergence controls and

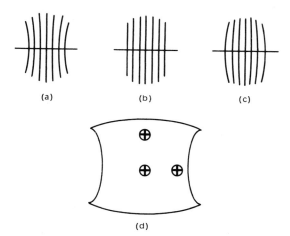

(a)   (b)   (c)

(d)

Figure 9.12. Types of field distribution: (a) barrel; (b) homogeneous; (c) pincushion. The field distributions shown in (a) and (c) produce astigmatisms of opposite sign and are used for vertical and horizontal fields respectively. (d) The field applied to a 20AX tube

manufacturers and service technicians no longer have to worry about a problem which affected the performance of many older sets.

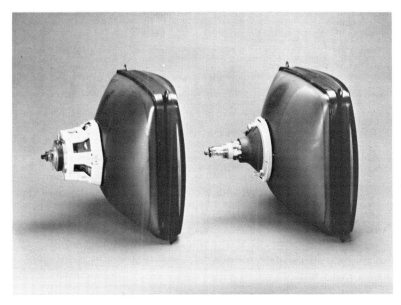

Figure 9.13. Mullard 20AX colour television tube (left) compared with 30AX type (right) (courtesy Mullard)

Flat-panel display systems

In recent years, considerable progress has taken place in the development of flat-panel TV displays, but major breakthroughs are still required before suitable prototypes can be used in the home. Colour systems have been demonstrated but have suffered from low resolution and brightness. Most major manufacturers of video equipment have experimented with a variety of matrix image displays, mainly using monochrome systems, but some have produced colour. The mechanisms for producing the picture have included incandescent lamps, plasma cells and liquid crystals.

The picture is formed in a flat panel display by using a two-dimensional matrix of light-emitting or light-controlling cells. One line of the television picture is produced by one line of cells and, therefore, about 480 rows of cells are required. In a colour display the cells are arranged in patterns of red, green and blue. A minimum of 250 cells of each colour in each row appears to be required giving a total of approximately 360 000 cells for a TV picture of good resolution. Each cell is connected to a horizontal and vertical bus bar in the matrix so that individual cells can be switched on by providing the driving voltage to the correct row and column. Fractions of the drive voltage will be applied to other cells due to this arrangement and it is essential, if these unwanted cells are not to be switched on and cause loss of contrast and resolution, that the threshold of operation of each cell is carefully controlled by having a non-linear response to the control voltage.

Plasma cells, which operate by creating a continuous gas discharge while the voltage is maintained, are most suitable for these types of matrices and these can also be made to produce the primary colours for a colour display by using the ultra-violet light they radiate to illuminate colour phosphors. The colour TV panels produced all had low brightness attributable to the inefficient production of ultra-violet by the xenon gas discharge normally used in these cells. Experiments using mercury vapour appear to be capable of better results and development work is proceeding.

If, of course, flat screen displays do become feasible then the problems of the TV set being restricted by the display tube will become history as the screen will be separate and hang on the wall like a picture. Convergence problems will no longer exist.

Conclusion

The television display tube as we know it today will remain with us for the forseeable future. The shadowmask will be replaced by precision-in-line tubes for domestic sets and, although further improvements will take place, it is unlikely that the average viewer will know the difference if he has a good receiver at present.

Although RCA must take the credit for the shadowmask tube, British companies can be proud of their record in the early development of cathode-ray tubes and their contribution to the development of the PIL tube.

With television sets looking externally much the same in the future, we shall probably have to rely on the introduction of teletext services as an excuse to buy a new receiver if our old one is still working.

Teletext and viewdata

Development engineering in Britain by the broadcasting authorities and British Telecom has brought a new dimension to the television set. It is no longer solely restricted to the display of conventional television but, with the correct additional decoders, the viewer has a number of valuable information services readily available in the home or office (Figure 9.14).

The BBC and ITV have similar services collectively known as teletext and individually known as 'Ceefax' and 'Oracle' respectively. These services provide the viewer, equipped with the

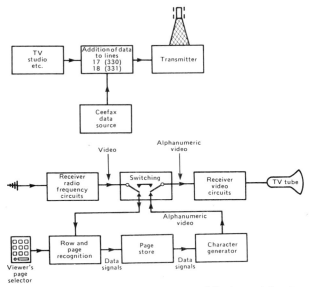

Figure 9.14. Transmission and reception of Ceefax and Oracle

necessary teletext receiver, with additional information relating to many subjects simultaneously with the normal televised programmes.

The British Telecom viewdata system is known as 'Prestel' and has the facilities to provide much more information as the viewer's television is directly linked via the telephone line with British Telecom computers. Due to the direct linking via the telephone line, the viewer using the 'Prestel' service also has the facility of a two-way conversation with the computer. The system can therefore be expanded to passing messages, direct shopping, direct debiting by credit card, booking seats on planes and trains and question and answer sessions with the computer. The 'Prestel' service, however, costs the user a payment depending upon the information supplied or the service obtained in addition to the normal telephone charges. The 'Ceefax' and 'Oracle' systems are a free service supplied by the broadcasting organisations.

Transmission of information

A standard has been agreed for the coding of teletext signals and many countries are co-operating with British Telecom in order that the viewdata systems will become international. The French, characteristically, have adopted their own system known as 'Antiope' which is incompatible with the other systems. The French system does, however, allow accented characters to be used and improved graphics at the expense of more complex coding. These features could also be incorporated into the Prestel system if necessary. Canada has also produced a different system called 'Telidon'.

As explained in Chapter 1, the television signal contains a frame blanking period in which no picture information is transmitted.

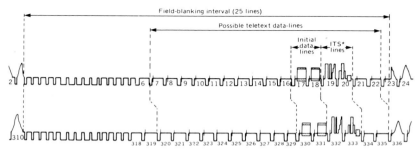

Figure 9.15. Teletext data lines

Modern receivers no longer require such a long period in which to recover after the vertical synchronising signals so that into this period can be fitted additional pieces of information. At present these are the ITS (insertion test signals), used to monitor the performance of links, and the teletext services (Figure 9.15). As can be seen from the diagram, two line periods are used during each field. These are 17, 18 and 330, 331.

Teletext page

A page of teletext, whether 'Ceefax' or 'Oracle', can have 24 rows of information with up to 40 characters on each row. The characters are tailored for a 7 × 5 matrix.

Each page is headed by a special row known as a 'page header' which is restricted to 32 characters. This line details the page number, date and time and is used by the receiver as a signal to indicate the start of a page and also which page is being received at any particular time. When the page number coincides with the page the viewer has requested the information is displayed on the screen.

Due to the available space, not all the information can be transmitted simultaneously. Each teletext line, therefore, has the information relating to one row of teletext data. As each field contains 2 rows and there are a maximum of 24 rows of information on a full page it takes 12 fields, at $\frac{1}{50}$ th second per field, to transmit a page or 0.24 seconds. Normally to improve legibility the number of rows is less than 24 on each page and therefore the time is reduced.

Pages are transmitted in sequence and, if 100 pages are used, it could take a maximum of 24 seconds after selecting a page before it is received and displayed. For the most commonly requested pages, such as the index, the time requirement is reduced by transmitting them more often. More economical use can be made of time where several pages are required for the information requested. In this instance the pages need only be repeated at a convenient reading pace of perhaps a minute or more. Other pages can be programmed to appear only at specific times of the day at which time the teletext decoder will receive the signal and store it for later viewing. The repetition time depends considerably on the update requirements of the information transmitted.

The teletext services originated out of development work to enable captions to be transmitted for deaf viewers. The service, therefore, allows this possibility in addition to foreign language subtitles and news flashes to be superimposed over the television picture as they occur.

The material transmitted is arranged in groups of pages of up to 100 and is known as a magazine. Each page carries a common magazine number in the range 1–8 and up to eight magazines can be transmitted in sequence or independently on a television programme channel. Access time for such an amount of information would be approximately three minutes but at the present time the full capacity is not being used.

At present the BBC1 and BBC2 services complement each other as the BBC2 service is updated less frequently and carries the overflow material from BBC1. The ITV service is independent of the BBC and has its own originating suite in a London ITV station.

Reception of teletext

As the teletext signal is digital it is not affected by noise. The signal is either available or there is no output as the noise exceeds a certain level. At this stage the normal television picture would also be of a very low standard. Digital transmission is, however, very susceptible to reflections, phase distortion and frequency distortion. Reflections produce extra pulses which completely modifies the information transmitted. Therefore, where reception is not excellent problems can arise even though an analogue TV signal may be acceptable.

The majority of the television sets in use today have IF stages comprising coils and capacitors and their response is not generally good enough for excellent digital transmission. The future generations of sets will possibly use surface acoustic wave filters (SAW filters) in the IF stages. The basic idea is shown in Figure 9.16. In

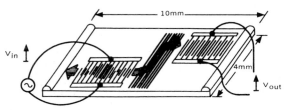

Figure 9.16. A basic SAW device

construction SAW filters consist of an aluminium pattern deposited on a piezoelectric material. When a signal is applied at the input it produces mechanical vibrations which travel along the surface of the material at an acoustic velocity. The variation in the spacing of the fingers and the amount of overlap causes additions and subtractions to the wave and alters the response obtained on the output transducer. A response similar to Figure 9.17 is obtained and by computer design this can be tailored to the required IF response. These filters eliminate the requirement for a

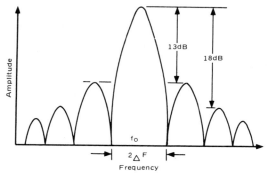

Figure 9.17. Waveform obtainable from a SAW device

large number of coils, together with their critical adjustments, and are therefore satisfactory for the response required in teletext and Prestel sets (Figure 9.18).

With the appearance of a new facility invariably add-on units are produced for existing equipment. Separate teletext units can therefore be purchased which decode the signal and remodulates the alphanumeric signals onto a carrier which is injected into the aerial socket. This method suffers from the decoding and remodulation process and restricted bandwidths.

Figure 9.18. An RCA technician prepares circuitry for installation of a high precision SAW filter, used in the company's newest line of TV transmitters for worldwide applications. The filter (in the foreground) replaces components weighing more than 230 kg (500 lb) in older model transmitters, and is used to shape and control visual response for enhanced picture quality

Obviously the best reception is obtained with a purpose-built set where the alphanumeric signals, after being decoded, are injected directly into the video stages.

Teletext decoders are now produced as a purpose built I.C.

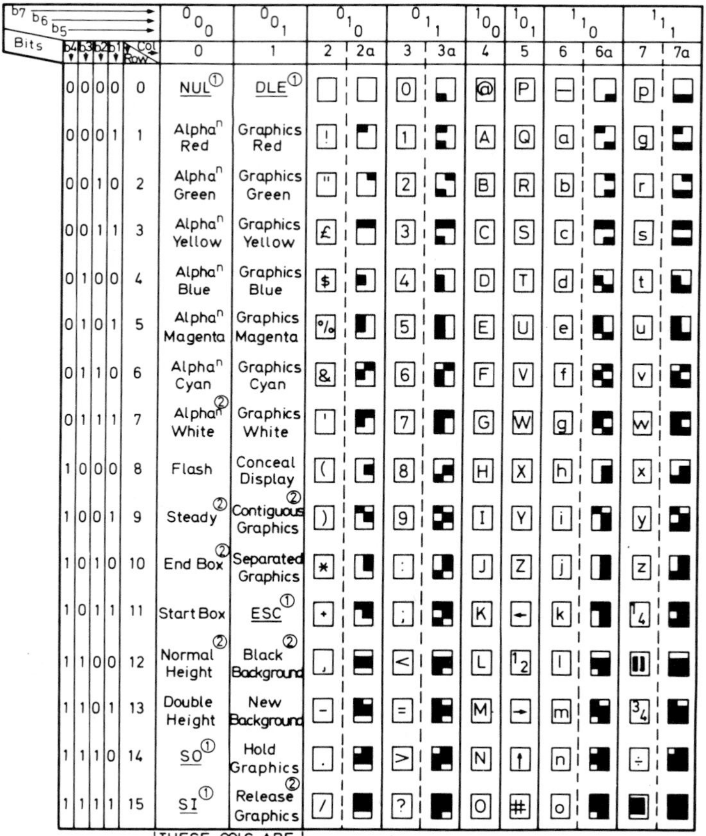

Bits (b4 b3 b2 b1)	Row	0	1	2	2a	3	3a	4	5	6	6a	7	7a
0000	0	NUL[1]	DLE[1]			0		@	P			p	
0001	1	Alpha^n Red	Graphics Red	!		1		A	Q	a		g	
0010	2	Alpha^n Green	Graphics Green	"		2		B	R	b		r	
0011	3	Alpha^n Yellow	Graphics Yellow	£		3		C	S	c		s	
0100	4	Alpha^n Blue	Graphics Blue	$		4		D	T	d		t	
0101	5	Alpha^n Magenta	Graphics Magenta	%		5		E	U	e		u	
0110	6	Alpha^n Cyan	Graphics Cyan	&		6		F	V	f		v	
0111	7	Alpha^n White[2]	Graphics White	'		7		G	W	g		w	
1000	8	Flash	Conceal Display[2]	(		8		H	X	h		x	
1001	9	Steady[2]	Contiguous Graphics[2]	)		9		I	Y	i		y	
1010	10	End Box[2]	Separated Graphics[2]	*		:		J	Z	j		z	
1011	11	Start Box	ESC[1]	+		;		K	←	k		¼	
1100	12	Normal Height[2]	Black Background[2]	,		<		L	½	l		‖	
1101	13	Double Height	New Background[2]	-		=		M	→	m		¾	
1110	14	SO[1]	Hold Graphics[2]	.		>		N	↑	n		÷	
1111	15	SI[1]	Release Graphics[2]	/		?		O	#	o		■	

THESE COLS ARE FOR CONTROL ONLY

[1] These control characters are reserved for compatability with other data codes

[2] These control characters are presumed before each row begins

Codes may be referred to by their column and row e.g. 2/5 refers to %

☐ Character rectangle

Black represents display colour

White represents background

Figure 9.19. Teletext character codes. Each character has its own unique seven-bit code which can be read from the above table

Teletext code

The displayed data can be presented in several forms (Figure 9.19) and control characters must be introduced into the digital code to provide for:

1. The selection of one of seven display colours (white, yellow, cyan, green, magenta, red, blue).
2. The selection of one of eight background colours (as above plus black).
3. The display of the selected characters with double height.
4. The selection of selected characters to flash.
5. The concealment of selected characters until the user wishes to reveal them.

The code used is a basic two level NRZ (non-return-to-zero) data waveform and is restricted to a 5.0 MHz bandwidth. The binary bit rate is 6.9375 Mbits/s and is timed by a clock pulse

MESSAGE BITS

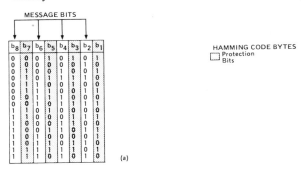

HAMMING CODE BYTES
☐ Protection Bits

(a)

DECODING ACTION

RESULTS OF PARITY TESTS A,B,C		INFERENCE	ACTION
A,B,C	D		
All Correct	Correct	No errors	Accept message bits
All Correct	Not Correct	Error in b_7	Accept message bits
Not all Correct	Correct	Multiple errors	Reject message bits
Not all Correct	Not Correct	Single error	Refer to Table to identify error. Correct error if in message bit

(c)

TESTS FOR ODD POLARITY

● Tested bits

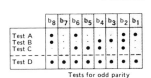

Tests for odd parity

(b)

Figure 9.20. In order to detect errors in the address hamming codes are used. Four bits are used to convey the message while the other four bits of the word are used for error checking. Four separate parity checks are performed and the bits tested are shown in (b). The results (c) show if any bit is wrong. It can then be inverted and corrected

whose synchronisation in the decoder is referenced to the peak of the penultimate '1' of a 'clock run-in sequence' transmitted after the colour burst.

The data is arranged in groups of eight bits known as a data 'byte'. Seven of the bits are used to define the character while the eighth is a parity bit and is used as an error check. The parity bit is chosen so that the total bits always add up to an odd number.

Each line contains 360 bits or 45 bytes. The first five bytes on each line are used to define the row being transmitted, while the remaining 40 bytes represent the characters in the line.

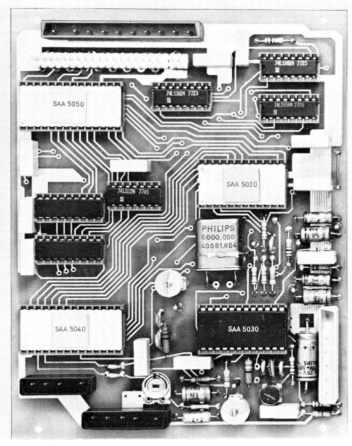

Figure 9.24. Mullard teletext/viewdata decoder module (courtesy Mullard)

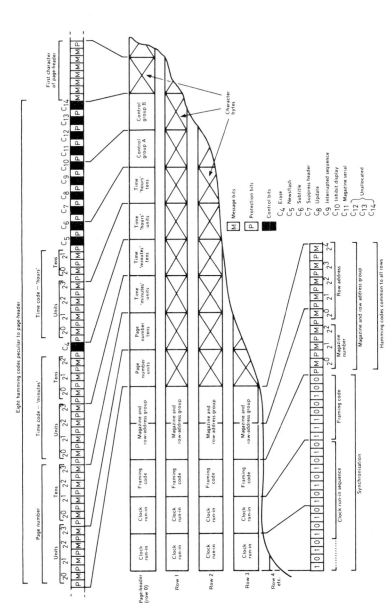

Figure 9.21 Synchronisation and hamming codes at start of page header and row transmission

With a seven bit binary code 128 different symbols can be represented. 96 of these permutations are used for different symbols and the remaining 32 codes are used for control characters.

In order to detect errors the fourth and fifth byte of every data line contains a special code consisting of four message bits and four alternate protection bits. The protection bits will depend upon the message bits. A combination of four parity checks can be made on this information and the data can be corrected for single errors or rejected if there are multiple errors. These are known as hamming codes and are used for sending address and control information (Figure 9.20).

The page header data lines have 8 bytes with hamming codes. The specifications for the teletext formats are shown in Figure 9.21.

Prestel

In order that a large part of the teletext decoder can be common to view data systems the same page format and coding methods have been made compatible. However, in the Prestel system (Figure 9.22) each character is preceded by a start bit and is followed by a stop bit. These are used to synchronise the decoder and separate the characters, unlike teletext which transmits a complete line at a time (Figure 9.23).

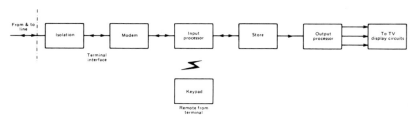

Figure 9.22. Block diagram of Prestel terminal

As normal telephone lines are used to send the requested information from the computer a modem has to be incorporated into the system. This is a modulator/demodulator and is used to convert the digital pulses to audio tones (2100 Hz for a '0' and 1300 Hz for a '1') when interrogating the computer and demodulating the audio tones to digital bits for displaying the information from the computer. Transmission speeds of 75 bits/second are used.

Bits $b_4 b_3 b_2 b_1$ / Row	Col $\to$	0	1	2	2a	3	3a	4	4b	5	5b	6	6a	7	7a
	$b_7 b_6 b_5$	0 0 0	0 0 1	0 1 0	0 1 0	0 1 1	0 1 1	1 0 0	1 0 0	1 0 1	1 0 1	1 1 0	1 1 0	1 1 1	1 1 1
0 0 0 0	0	NUL		(space)	[gfx]	0	[gfx]	@		P		—	[gfx]	p	[gfx]
0 0 0 1	1		Cursor on DC1	!	[gfx]	1	[gfx]	A	Alpha Red	Q	Graphics Red	a	[gfx]	q	[gfx]
0 0 1 0	2			"	[gfx]	2	[gfx]	B	Alpha Green	R	Graphics Green	b	[gfx]	r	[gfx]
0 0 1 1	3			£	[gfx]	3	[gfx]	C	Alpha Yellow	S	Graphics Yellow	c	[gfx]	s	[gfx]
0 1 0 0	4		Cursor on DC4	$	[gfx]	4	[gfx]	D	Alpha Blue	T	Graphics Blue	d	[gfx]	t	[gfx]
0 1 0 1	5	ENQ	CAN	%	[gfx]	5	[gfx]	E	Alpha Magenta	U	Graphics Magenta	e	[gfx]	u	[gfx]
0 1 1 0	6			&	[gfx]	6	[gfx]	F	Alpha Cyan	V	Graphics Cyan	f	[gfx]	v	[gfx]
0 1 1 1	7			'	[gfx]	7	[gfx]	G	Alpha White	W	Graphics White	g	[gfx]	w	[gfx]
1 0 0 0	8	Cursor ↑↓ BS		(	[gfx]	8	[gfx]	H	Flash	X	Conceal Display	h	[gfx]	x	[gfx]
1 0 0 1	9	Cursor ↑↓ HT		)	[gfx]	9	[gfx]	I	Steady	Y	Contig Graphics	i	[gfx]	y	[gfx]
1 0 1 0	10	Cursor ↑↓ LF		*	[gfx]	:	[gfx]	J		Z	Separated Graphics	j	[gfx]	z	[gfx]
1 0 1 1	11	Cursor ↑↓ VT	ESC	+	[gfx]	;	[gfx]	K		↓←		k	[gfx]	$\frac{1}{4}$	[gfx]
1 1 0 0	12	Cursor Home & Clear FF	S32 (Single Shift)	,	[gfx]	<	[gfx]	L	Normal Height	$\frac{1}{2}$	Black Background	l	[gfx]	‖	[gfx]
1 1 0 1	13	Cursor ↑↓ CR	S53 (Single Shift)	-	[gfx]	=	[gfx]	M	Double Height	↑	New Background	m	[gfx]	$\frac{3}{4}$	[gfx]
1 1 1 0	14	SO(Shift out)	Cursor RS Home	.	[gfx]	>	[gfx]	N		←	Hold Graphics	n	[gfx]	÷	[gfx]
1 1 1 1	15	SI (Shift in)		/	[gfx]	?	[gfx]	O		⫢	Release Graphics	o	[gfx]	■	[gfx]

NOTE:

Columns 0 and 1 form the C_0 control character set.

Columns 4b and 5b form the C_1 set of display attribute control codes. These codes are preceded by ESC when transmitted.

Columns 2,3,4,5,6 and 7 form the G_0 character set.

Columns 2a, 3a, 4, 5, 6a and 7a form the graphics character set.

TRANSMISSION AND CODING
Bit Transmission Rate
1200 bit/s receive, 75 bit/s transmit from the user terminal.
Coding
Start/Stop asynchronous.
Character envelope
10 bits.
1 start (binary 0); 7 data, 1 even parity, 1 stop (binary 1).
Data modulation
FSK in both directions
Standards to CCITT V23

THE TERMINAL
Frame format 24 lines x 40 characters, i.e. maximum 960 chs per frame.
Line 1 is reserved for frame number and price.
Line 24 reserved for system messages.
Character definition 7 x 5 dot matrix normally.
Colours: red, green, yellow, blue, cyan, magenta and white.
Full range of cursor facilities available.
Connection to telephone network: via jack plug and socket.
User interaction: by hand held numeric keypad or from a keyboard.

Figure 9.23. Prestel transmission codes

Figure 9.25. Examples of the uses of teletext

The information is supplied by many companies who update their own magazines directly into the computers. British Telecom is responsible only for the supply of the system hardware.

Due to the large amounts of information which will eventually be available the indexing can be complex, and the user has to be led through various stages to ensure arrival at the information required. At all times the user must be aware of the cost of requesting the information which will vary considerably.

British Telecom will develop a number of data centre locations where local callers can interrogate them. These computers will be updated from a 'National Update Centre' located in London. The data is loaded by an editor working from a terminal on to magnetic discs. When the information is requested by a customer it is taken from the store and buffered by the computer before being transmitted at line speed to the television set.

The potential development of such a system is considerable, especially as hard copiers are incorporated to print the information and international networks are established. The rate of development will depend on the use made of the system by the public and business and this will be determined by the cost to the user.

Television projection systems

As the uses for video increase the need to display the signal on a larger screen than that of a normal TV becomes more important. New devices to achieve this are constantly being introduced and it is important, therefore, when evaluating any system to realise the type of use for which the system was designed.

Amongst the current uses for such equipment are large screen projectors for the home, small video cinemas, training establishments, information displays of alphanumerics, flight and ship simulators, military commands, effects generators and concert hall displays.

Each type of system requires a different specification and consideration has to be given to such factors as:
1. Market price.
2. Size of screen.
3. Light output.
4. Definition.
5. Viewing angle.
6. Colour purity.
7. Operational flexibility.

Disappointment will obviously result if equipment is chosen solely on price without due regard to the use to be made of the system. Equipment ranges from a lens placed in front of a television screen to the Eidophor, capable of displays of colour signals on screens 12 × 16m (39 × 53ft).

Systems for monochrome are far simpler than for colour which, except where a single colour CRT is used, are usually the equivalent to three monochrome systems. As the light intensity increases the problems related to heat dissipation need considerable attention and can become a limiting factor when designing the equipment.

Some units have fixed focus between the projector and screen and, therefore, it is essential, when considering the equipment, to establish that this distance and the necessary limits in positioning the equipment are suitable for the customer's premises. Other equipment is completely contained in a single unit which not only protects the system but allows easier storage and operation. Focusing and alignment are adjusted at the factory (Figure 9.26).

Figure 9.26. Mitsubishi Electric VS500 large screen television

The design of the systems makes use of special screens which, by the use of special material and shaping of the surfaces, increase the reflected light at a cost of reducing the maximum viewing angle before distortion and colour changes becomes a problem. The material for such screens varies and can be easily damaged when transporting or continuously dismantling and storing.

Cathode ray tube projectors

Small systems whereby a Trinitron is focused onto a special screen via a mirror and lens are produced by Sony and other manufacturers and have been successfully marketed for the home and other small display areas. The aluminium screen material provides a gain of about eight over a normal reflective surface at the expense of reducing the viewing angle. The screen size allows a 1.27 m (50 in) diagonal picture to be projected.

Improvements in such systems produced equipment using three separate CRTs for separate projection of the red, green and blue images to produce the complete picture on the screen.

Commercial systems using CRTs commonly use high brightness CRTs of between 76 and 150 mm (3 and 6 in) in diameter. In order to provide a bright picture, high beam energy is required. Increasing beam current beyond a certain design factor causes the spot size to increase and results in a loss of definition. High screen voltages of between 30 and 50 kV are therefore used to increase the beam energy. These voltages are used in association with phosphors of high efficiency.

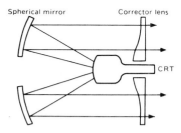

Figure 9.27. The Schmidt system

In order to project as much light as possible from the CRTs a Schmidt optical system is generally used (Figure 9.27). This is the same type of system used in astronomical telescopes but in this instance the principle is used in reverse. The CRT is placed at the focus of a parabolic mirror which produces parallel rays which are transmitted through a correction lens to compensate for any variations of the mirror from a true paraboloid. The economics of larger systems depends on increasing the size of the CRT which produces more light but increases the cost and results in a reduction in the efficiency of the optical system needed to transmit it. The cost of Schmidt lenses has been reduced by a system which consists of bonding onto a flat lead glass plate a thin preformed resin layer closely controlled in profile and thickness by a glass master mould. From the master a large number of replicas can be made which reduces the cost but matches the standard of a good hand-worked lens.

The calculations for the design of the lens are made to suit particular throws and are optimised for particular distances of usually between 4 and 10 m (12 and 32 ft). For such systems attempts are made to keep the optics small by controlling the viewing area in order to keep the cost of the equipment reasonable. Light output tends to be small due to the small assemblies and the heat conduction problem that arises.

Light guide projection tube (Advent)

A different approach to the same problems is made by Advent who produced a new tube in which the Schmidt optics are an integral part of the tube (Figure 9.28). In order to do this the picture size and projector to screen distance has to be standardised. Its advantages, however, are that the optics are sealed and cannot be damaged by handling or the atmosphere.

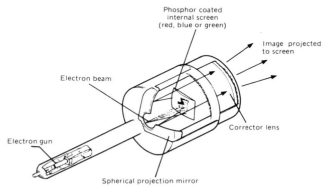

Figure 9.28. The Advent Videobeam

The electron gun scans a phosphor aluminium target which is diagonally 90 mm (3½ in) in size. A 150 mm (6 in) spherical mirror, precisely positioned in relation to the target by a stainless steel optical barrel, collects the light and projects it out of the front of the tube and through an acrylic aspherical corrector lens. The targets are coated with either a red, green or blue emitting phosphor and the three separate tubes are used to produce the complete picture. Focus is obtained by using permanent magnets with additional secondary electromagnetic windings for operational adjustment.

Three sets of yokes are provided for deflection, dynamic convergence and static positioning. Outputs of about 20 lumens are achieved.

Light valve (General Electric)

As the light available from CRTs is restricted by the phosphors, beam curent and screen voltage which can be used, it becomes necessary, in order to achieve displays several magnitudes brighter, to use a separate light source and modulate this with the television signal. In the system designed by General Electric the light source is a xenon arc lamp and the modulating light valve is a transparent viscous oil surface (Figure 9.29).

Much lower electron beam voltages and current can be used within the valve in comparison to a CRT and these are in the order of 6–12 kV and 5–10 µA beam current respectively.

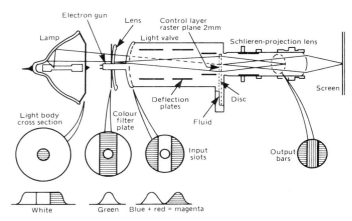

Figure 9.29. General Electric light valve

The electron beam produces a charge on the transparent viscous oil surface which, due to electrostatic attraction, makes grooves of varying depths and steepness depending upon the TV picture element. On the front of the tube a Schlieren lens images the light passing through the oil into a slit and passes this through the output bars. If the oil is smooth no light passes through the critically spaced output bars but when the surface is modulated the light is diffracted and passes the bars to the screen. The brightness on the screen depends upon the depth and steepness of the grooves.

In order to produce a colour picture each picture element is coded with a diffraction grating and the output bars are used to separate the light into its colours and to pass only the specific colour required. The red elements use a 16 MHz modulating signal and the blue a 12 MHz modulating signal. These are supplied to the horizontal plates and produce the diffraction lines at right angles to the TV raster lines. The green is controlled by modulating the vertical plates and passing the light initially through horizontal slits. The output bars on transmission only let through those part of the spectrum which are correctly modulated to suit the spacing of the bars. Using this method reduces the colour picture by approximately half the light and half the resolution of the monochrome picture. However, from the single light beam a perfectly converged picture is obtained at levels of 750 lumens or even higher.

Titus tubes, Philips (developed in France by LEP)

This tube (Figure 9.30) uses an external light source which is modulated by the ability of certain crystals to rotate the plane of polarisation of light. In the Titus tube a single crystal plate of deuterated dihydrogen potassium phosphate $(KD_2.PO_4)$ is used. Each point of the plate acts as an independent Pockels cell in which the plane of polarisation of the incident light striking the crystal is rotated proportionally to the modulating voltage on the plate. The plate is scanned by a constant current electron beam.

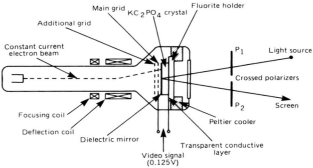

Figure 9.30. The Titus tube

The light from a xenon lamp is passed through a calcite polarising beam splitter and only one polarised component of the light is passed to the tube. The beam of light is modulated in its polarisation by the crystal and is reflected from the dielectric mirror, deposited on the crystal plate, and passes to the screen via the beam splitter again. Only the component of modulated light with the correct plane of polarisation passes to the screen.

The tube has a characteristic whereby no line structure is visible and the picture is free of flicker. This is due to the long discharge time constant of the plate, which at the operating temperature, remains charged between two scannings.

Colour is obtained by the use of dichroic mirrors which are used to split the colours to the tubes and recombine the reflected beams. The system requires a cooler to keep the operating temperature of the crystal at about $-50°C$.

In operation the tube is capable of outputs of 2500–3000 lumens but half the arc lamp light is lost due to the necessity to initially polarise the light. In this respect the efficiency is considerably less than the oil-film light valve.

Eidophor

The Eidophor uses a film of viscous liquid on the surface of a spherical mirror as the modulating source. The light from a xenon arc lamp is deflected to the spherical mirror by a system of lenses and mirror. Without disturbance the light would be reflected back but when a video signal distorts the surface of the control layer the light is deflected and bypasses the mirror bars proportional to the depth of deformation of the layer and illuminates the screen.

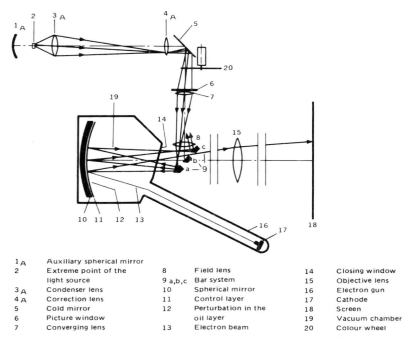

1 A	Auxiliary spherical mirror				
2	Extreme point of the	8	Field lens	14	Closing window
	light source	9 a,b,c	Bar system	15	Objective lens
3 A	Condenser lens	10	Spherical mirror	16	Electron gun
4 A	Correction lens	11	Control layer	17	Cathode
5	Cold mirror	12	Perturbation in the	18	Screen
6	Picture window		oil layer	19	Vacuum chamber
7	Converging lens	13	Electron beam	20	Colour wheel

Figure 9.31. Black and white or sequential colour Eidophor

In order to produce a colour system the Eidophor can operate in two alternative modes (Figures 9.31 and 9.32). In the field sequential mode the field rate and the bandwidth of the standard monochrome system are tripled and a motor driven colour disc is incorporated in the light path between the xenon lamp and the mirror bar system to produce each colour field in turn. This, of course, requires a special TV system. In the more conventional system three mechanically integrated light valves operate to produce the red, green and blue pictures and these are combined for display on the screen.

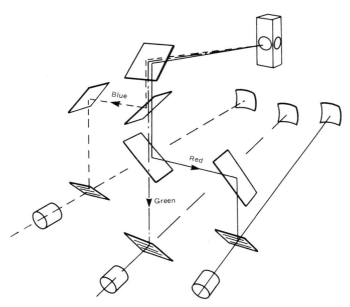

Figure 9.32. In the 'simultaneous colour' version there are three mechanically integrated light valve units with individual control layers, electron guns and mirror bar systems for the red, green and blue picture channels. The illumination optics system is modified to include a single 2.5 kW xenon arc lamp and a dichroic mirror system which selects the red, green and blue primaries for the individual channels. A built-in servo mechanism automatically controls and maintains picture registration

The system is capable of about 7000 lumens output and is widely used in simulators, CCTV in theatres and sporting arenas and other places where a large audience is involved.

Liquid crystals

Liquid crystal light valves (Figure 9.33) have been produced suitable for alphanumeric systems and these function by the liquid crystal being addressed by a CRT from one side while an arc lamp is reflected from the other. The reflected light is modulated by the polarisation of the liquid crystal layer in front of the mirror which changes as the internal signal voltage, produced by the input light signal, varies. This causes the light from the arc lamp to be either transmitted or scattered. Although different colours can be projected by altering the voltages across such a device, their luminance cannot be altered.

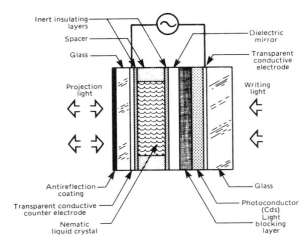

Figure 9.33. Sectional view of a liquid-crystal light valve

Conclusion

Large screen television is a relatively new industry compared to the rest of television. It is, therefore, very much in an experimental stage both in the development and marketing of products.

In the entertainment industry Sony has recently announced a new prototype projection system capable of cinemascope presentation. The screen can either be 4.3 or 2.35.1. The system has an output of about 20 foot candles compared with 10 for the normal film projection system. The system is aimed at the small cinemas and uses three 230 mm (9 in) CRTs and three 170 mm (6.7 in) lenses to project onto a screen 240 × 100 cm (95 × 40 in).

Large screen television is of considerable interest to the military and although much work has been attempted to replace the oil film to overcome contamination of the vacuum and oil bubbles for large output systems this has not met with success at present. Rubber compounds and other substances have been used but the high light output has not been achieved.

High output CRTs, using sapphire faceplates able to dissipate considerable heat, have allowed very high light outputs to be achieved. These are required for such work as military forward commands operating from helicopters. These systems are naturally very expensive and need to be robust.

Systems for the military must, as far as possible, eliminate the normal errors tolerated by entertainment systems. Registration, non-flat mirrors, colour fringing and optical misalignment cannot be as easily tolerated on high light output systems used with 1029 line TV systems for command posts showing maps and events and where the information can be at the edge or corner. Digital memories are therefore fitted to the separate CRTs to provide the necessary correction.

Lasers have not proven to be a success in any system to date although considerable work has been done in the USA and Japan.

A considerable amount of work by many major companies is being carried out using improvements to known techniques and new substances which can modulate light in various conditions. There is always a chance, therefore, of a major breakthrough in the foreseeable future which will revolutionise these products.

Chapter 10

Digital Television

The practical applications of digital video have already had a considerable impact on television breadcasting. Field stores have made possible many of today's visual effects, timebase correctors and synchronisers have improved signal timebase stability and synchronisation, digital standards converters have allowed the exchange of programmes without apparent technical deterioration and teletext services have opened up a complete new field for the provision of information into the home.

Eventually the complete studio complex will be fitted with digital equipment as digital recorders and cameras become standard equipment. Transmission lines will also benefit as the signal will be capable of being reproduced at each distribution centre to its original standard.

The studio complex designed for digital signals will be very different in technical layout and signal distribution to the analogue signal processing studios we have today. Such studios, however, may be many years in the future and until the advent of the complete digital studio we will continue to see the introduction of separate pieces of digital equipment each requiring an analogue to digital followed by a digital to analogue interface with the existing analogue equipment. Such conversions are termed a 'codec' and due to the need to quantise the signal, a resulting impairment of the signal occurs (Figure 10.1).

Four such units in cascade can cause perceptible impairment and in today's well equipped studio several of these can be found in a typical signal chain. It is becoming essential, therefore, that digital standards are quickly agreed so that the signals can be passed in a digital format between different equipments in order to avoid such conversions.

Why digital?

Once it is functioning, digital equipment produces predictable results. Unlike analogue, equipment, whose performance is subject to variation and alignment, digital equipment operates on a switch-on switch-off basis and the resulting pictures are stable and immune to level or phase variations. Since the signal can be regenerated as often as desired without degradation, long transmission lines and multiple tape generations will no longer be problems.

Once digitised, the signals can be stored in a digital memory for as long as desired where they can also be processed. The signals can be written and read at different speeds, time stretched, delayed, compressed and read out in a different order to that in which they were written. This has made possible all the new visual effects that have become common today in addition to the timebase correctors, synchronisers and standards converters.

Because of the repetition of digital processing circuits, many of the boards perform the same function and are common, making maintenance by substitution of boards a simple routine. Large scale production of the same board is also more economical.

Due to the large world-wide computer industry, broadcasting will obviously benefit from using the same techniques and components. Digital coding will also allow interfacing with computers for greater control and more sophisticated systems.

Digital circuitry is not without its problems and although immune to many distortions, the signal rapidly deteriorates and immediately disappears in unfavourable conditions. Problems associated with digital video are caused by quantisation noise, sampling of the analogue signal, error rates, clock jitter, noise spikes on mains and inter-symbol interference. This latter problem is caused by the bit in the binary coded word, which represents a symbol, interfering with other symbols in the data stream. Usually the interference is between adjacent bits.

The major disadvantage of digital video is the large bandwidth required to accommodate the high bit rates which are used.

Quantising the video signal

The basic signal used in digital coding is a data bit, which is a pulse having one of two possible states – it is either present or absent. Within certain limits the size and precise shape of the pulse is of no importance. A system using digital techniques, therefore, needs only to detect the pulses to reproduce the original signals. They are, therefore, not distorted by those factors that affect the analogue waveform, whose precise amplitude and phase relationships must be preserved in order that the signal is not distorted. The precision with which an analogue signal can be processed is determined by the quality of the system components while that of digital signal is limited by the number of bits and the operations used to perform the processing.

The digital pulses are represented by a 1 or 0, depending upon their presence or absence, and groups of pulses are combined to produce a 'word'. In the digital coding used for television each word consists of eight bits and the position of each bit within the word represents a specific value. As a binary system is used, in which each bit position increases in value by the power of 2, information relating to 2^8 different analogue levels can be defined. This allows the analogue video level to be sampled at 256 different levels and for each level to be given a distinct code within an eight bit word. To quantise (as the process is known) the analogue video waveform by 256 steps is sufficient to allow its reproduction with a level of detail which is undetectable from that of a continuously variable analogue signal.

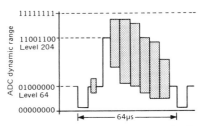

Figure 10.1. Proposed IBA quantising levels

In order to allow for overload signals the analogue signal is restricted to less than the dynamic range possible with such a digital code. In the proposed IBA composite coding standard (Figure 10.1) it is suggested that the 'black level' of the waveform should correspond to level 64 (code 01000000) and 'peak white' to level 204 (code 11001100).

Data transmission

The digital bits can be transmitted by either of two methods. Where distances are below 15 m (50 ft) the eight bits are normally transmitted simultaneously on eight parallel lines. A ninth line is used for the transmission of the clock information which is required in order to read the code. For longer distances the bits are made into a serial code where the first bit is the least significant. A ninth bit is also transmitted and is used for detecting errors and extracting the clock pulse. The bit rate in such a suggested system is $9 \times 2 \times f_{sc} = 79.8051375$ MHz for a PAL 625-line system (approximately 80 Mbits/s).

Composite or component coding?

There are two possibilities for encoding the signal – *composite coding*, whereby the standard colour encoded signal is digitised, and *component coding* whereby the luminance and colour difference signals are separately encoded. The latter method has the obvious attraction that it is independent of the colour standard and transcoding between PAL and SECAM is not required.

Secam cannot be digitally coded as a composite signal due to both colour different signals not being simultaneously available. It is therefore essential for SECAM users to convert the composite signal to components Y,U,V before digitally coding. PAL however can be satisfactorily coded by either method. There are advantages when using component coding, as frame stores, noise reduction circuits and special effects are easier to design. Video tape editing would benefit from component encoding as it eases the problems associated with the eight-field PAL sequence.

However, the introduction of digital equipment will be gradual and it is essential that digital equipment interfaces with existing analogue equipment.

A major problem arises if the Y,U,V sampling system is based on a line related instead of subcarrier frequency related structure for then digital conversion between composite and component signals becomes very complex. A subcarrier frequency system would be meaningless in SECAM where there is no reference burst on which to lock.

The composite PAL signal requires only two thirds of the data rate that is necessary for component coding. This produces considerable benefits when considering data storage and line transmission problems. The PAL system suffers from cross colour interference and low diagonal resolution and the component method of coding offers the advantage of eliminating these inherent problems. However, as long as the composite PAL signal is transmitted to the viewer then the advantages of component encoding cannot be realised.

It is, however, component coding which will be standardised at first. The decisions now have to be reached as to the sampling rate of the luminance and colour difference signals. The competing systems at present range from 12-4-4 to 14-7-7, where the numbers represent in MHz the proposed sampling frequencies of the luminance and colour difference signals.

As it is anticipated that the standard must be capable of meeting the broadcasting requirements for the next 20 years it is essential that the standard is sufficiently high but also economic to operate. The most favoured compromise which would be suitable for all systems is a sampling rate of 13.5-6.75-6.75 MHz for the luminance and colour difference signals respectively, and this may be accepted as the standard.

Nyquist frequency

The frequency of the words is controlled by a clock which synchronises the system. This has to be a multiple of the colour subcarrier frequency and the minimum sampling frequency which theoretically allows the original analogue waveform to be reconstructed without distortion is known as the 'Nyquist frequency'.

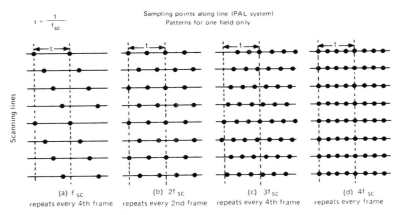

Figure 10.2. The required relationships exist for orthogonal structure at $2 \times f_{sc}$ and $4 \times f_{sc}$. The correct relationship does not exist for $3 \times f_{sc}$. For sampling at $2f_{sc}$ the sample points are interleaved. A comb filter can be used to remove the aliasing effects. $3 \times f_{sc}$ sampling does not produce a symmetrical pattern about any vertical line

Nyquist found in experiments that the sampling rate of an analogue signal must be at least twice the highest frequency contained in the signal if the samples are not to contain errors. If the sampling rate is less than the Nyquist frequency the original analogue signal cannot be reconstructed without errors. Products known as 'aliasing components' are generated by the high frequency components of the analogue signal and appear as Moiré patterns in areas of fine detail. The lowest Nyquist frequency for PAL and NTSC can be shown to be three times the subcarrier frequency (f_{sc}) but it was found this created difficulties, especially when converting between component Y,U,V and composite systems. This is due to the relationship between the subcarrier and frame frequency in the PAL system preventing the location of the sampling points from forming an orthogonal structure on the scanned raster (Figure 10.2). This causes difficulties in signal processing and the design of filters. The required relationship, however, exists for $2 \times f_{sc}$ and $4 \times f_{sc}$ sampling rates.

A sub-Nyquist frequency of $2 \times f_{sc}$ was suggested by the BBC in order to reduce the bit rate required by higher sampling frequencies. The picture impairments resulting from a $2 \times f_{sc}$ sampling rate were initially thought to add in a studio complex but experiments showed this was not the situation.

As bandwidth will be a universal problem the sub-Nyquist sampling frequency of $2 \times f_{sc}$ provides a major advantage for composite encoding systems.

Digital video recorder

The digital studio cannot start to make real progress until the development of the digital video recorder. Once developed and operational, multi-generation tapes will, theoretically, be capable of replaying signals equally as good as the original signals together with the addition of multi-track digital audio.

Present day digital tape recorders, shown as demonstration machines, are producing tapes equally as good as the best analogue recorders and substantially better when recording and playing multi-generation tapes.

The ability to store high density data bits on tape has increased enormously in the last few years and the possibility exists for even higher densities in the future as tape and head technology develops. The introduction of long playing home recorders, described in a previous chapter, show how these improvements have been applied to the analogue recorder. Using sub-Nyquist techniques for the digital recorder it will require a data rate of approximately 80 Mb/s and this can be achieved today with realistic and economic amounts of tape.

The requirements of the digital recorder are different to those of the analogue recorder. In the latter a normal video bandwidth with a high signal-to-noise ratio is required, whereas the digital signal is tolerant of noise but requires a much larger bandwidth. The signal can be detected with signal-to-noise ratios of the order of 20 dB, so that track widths can be considerably reduced and the packing density increased. Eventually the pre-amplifier noise becomes the limiting factor to reductions.

Head-to-tape speeds are increased to record the higher frequencies but it is essential to maintain the head-to-tape contact if multi-head systems are used. Success with wide bandwidth recorders will depend considerably upon the head and tape manufacturers.

Recording modulation

Recording of the low frequency component of the digital code is impracticable and the recorded bandwidth is limited from a few hundred kilohertz to several megahertz. Special codes are used to overcome the lack of the low frequencies which can cause threshold shifting and result in incorrect data being detected on replay.

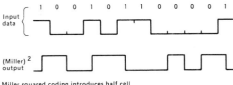

Miller squared coding introduces half cell transitions to reduce the LF component of the digital signal

Figure 10.3. Miller squared coding introduces half-cell transitions to reduce the l.f. component of the digital signal. This may prove a suitable code for VTR and overcome the problem of low frequency recording

'Miller squared code' is one such code (Figure 10.3). Normally a series of zeros would result in no transitions and require a low frequency response. The code is, therefore, restructured so that 'ones' are represented by a transition in the centre of a cell and zeros by a transition at the leading cell boundaries. With such a code exceptions to the rule are made where zeros follow ones.

Digital errors can be very objectionable and, therefore, it is essential to detect any wrong information. To assist in the detection a parity bit is inserted and checked on replay. This additional information obviously increases the recording requirements of the system. Detected errors can be concealed by inserting an interpolation of adjacent information into the space of the erroneous word.

Recording audio

The advantages of digital recording can be extended to audio, and demonstrations by Sony have shown one of three helical scans being used for the audio and the other two tracks being used for video. This has allows 16 separate audio channels to be recorded.

Other systems could record the signals linearly or the audio could be matrixed with the video.

Conclusion

The digital revolution is now firmly established in broadcasting and although it is only periphery equipment which is being used at present the major items are already being demonstrated if not actively exploited.

It is always difficult to decide the correct time to standardise a specification as premature standardisation can limit future development, but procrastination can limit progress and prevent the development of specific equipment. Few manufacturers will spend large amounts of money on new equipment which may become obsolete with standardisation and the tendency is to demonstrate the feasability of the technology on existing equipment. However, the new technology may need radical redesigns and new thinking to fully exploit the possibilities.

At present the European Broadcasting Union technical committee and the American SMPTE new technology committee are investigating the range of options and experimenting to discover the effects of different standards on recording, transmission, chroma-key, editing, picture expansion, video-to-film transfer and the performance of codecs in cascade. The technical quality must obviously be balanced by the economics of a system. Although there is a great desire to obtain a world-wide standard it is accepted that there are specific advantages to different systems and compromises will have to be made. The aim is to have a world-wide standard by 1982 for component coding.

Chapter 11

Postscript

In a little more than 50 years we have seen the development of television progress from Baird's mechanical experiments and Sir Isaac Shoenburg's development of the British 405-line system to the ability to send high definition colour pictures from almost anywhere in the world via satellite and portable earth stations.

Although many names are associated with specific breakthroughs which have suddenly advanced the technology, today's high standards are due to the skill and ingenuity of the many engineers, technicians and production staff working in laboratories and studios throughout the world. We should also not forget the component manufacturers who have advanced the technology of their own profession and in the process made many techniques and specific equipment possible.

Although with its increasing use more people are involved in video than ever before it is for the professional engineer and broadcaster a small industry but world wide in its relationships. It is this feature which makes the industry so attractive to many people as they personally can feel involved as the industry changes.

The older engineer in the UK has seen the industry develop from a 405-line system where all programmes, except films, were live through the development of VTR and the fundamental changes this made to broadcasting; a change of system to 625 lines and the transmission by UHF to finally transmitting in colour. In addition to these fundamental changes the engineer has had to re-educate himself from valves to transistors then ICs and finally microprocessors and computing. There has been no time in the history of television when the engineer was not having to adapt himself to new technology, equipment and systems.

In the near future the engineer will again have to readjust his way of working and re-educate himself as the studios change to digital electronics. Many of the older engineers will be pleased to have retired by this time. The younger engineer has, however, a complete new challenge before him as equipment and systems change and new possibilities and ideas evolve. Video can never be boring for the competent engineer and no matter how long one has been in the profession it is still very difficult to keep oneself fully informed of the new technology and possibilities.

We can only hope that all the effort is used to benefit the world and that its unmatched potential to influence people is not used wrongly by those in power.

Even with all the wonderful engineering the main purpose of television is still only for showing programmes and for these it has an insatiable appetite. While films, plays, books and concerts can be used for many years outside television they can become discarded material with only one showing on a national television network.

The engineers can agree their international specifications and produce ever better equipment and systems but the debate on what is good television and what should be shown will continue in every country, organisation and home.

Index